Praise from me
What OLD MEN Kn

"John Telford is the champion of the underdog." — **Dennis Archer**, Mayor of Detroit, 1994–2001, and a former associate justice of the Michigan Supreme Court

"A masterpiece! This *Almanac* for life and living is in turn hilarious, poignant, and profound. Dr. Telford's inspirational, informative, and *transformative* words cut like a laser through any attempts at deception by those hypocritical and self-serving 'leaders' who would mislead us." — **Professor Joshua Bassett**, Director of the Wayne County (Michigan) Community College District-sponsored Institute for Social Progress

"A seasoned leader in education and social activism." — **Bill Bowles**, Librarian, Detroit Western International High School

"John Telford has taught, guided, and inspired me and countless others like me for more than fifty years, and he is still doing it." — **Reginald "Reggie" Bradford**, educator and former quarter-mile star, Detroit Pershing High School and the University of Michigan

"John Telford first impacted my life in 1960 when I was only sixteen and he was my track coach at Detroit Southeastern High School. As a sixty-seven-year-old 'Aged Sage' who still dreams the 'impossible dream,' I continue to draw inspiration and encouragement from him." — **Rev. Arkles C. Brooks**, Pastor of Gospel Chapel of Detroit

"Telford is an *urban legend*." — **Hugh Burrell**, columnist, the *Michigan Chronicle*

"A legendary leader." — **Lloyd Carr**, head football coach, the University of Michigan, 1995–2007

"When the more *intelligent* (and less *affluent*) *Republicans* read this book, they are going to switch political parties in a hurry!" — **Robert Chiarini**, seventy-four-year-old Poet and Sage, and the Bard and Laureate of Shelby Township

"Old Man Telford's *OLD MEN* is funnier, more profound, and—in parts—even more savagely explosive that his spellbinding *memoirs*!" — **State Senator Hansen Clarke**, United States Congressman from Michigan

"Telford's burning fury at racism and classism is *epic*." — **Kenneth Cockrel, Jr.**, past interim Mayor and Detroit City Council President

"This satirical and memorably quotable new *Dictionary* will delight all democrats (both will a small 'd' *and* a capital 'D'). It may also infuriate some Republicans—but once they pick it up, neither Democrat nor Republican will put it down." — **United States Congressman John Conyers**, longtime Michigan Democrat

"In his youth, John *bullied* bullies and outran *Olympic champions*. Now, nearly sixty years later, they've rightfully named a track after him, and he's still sprinting full-speed on his righteous track." — **Dr. Wayne Dyer**, author of the national best-sellers *Your Erroneous Zones, Pulling Your Own Strings, The Sky's the Limit, Gifts from Eykis*, etc.

"Sensational!—John Telford is a *hero* to some, a *real pain* to others." — *Detroit Free Press* columnist and associate editor **Ron Dzwonkowski** (in an April 18, 2010 review of the author's autobiography, *A Life on the RUN—Seeking and Safeguarding Social Justice*).

"'*Rogue*' before '*going rogue*' became a roaring cliché, Dr. John Telford is a rebelesque Sage whose captivatingly anecdotal '*Dictionary*' has hilarity, philosophy, *chutzpah*, reams of rare advice, and *much more* in this panoramic look at life from the left and beyond. All men (and women) old and young need to know *What OLD MEN Know*. It's part words to *live by*, part words to *die laughing* by." — **Brad Edwards**, Metro Detroit FoxTV2 news reporter and alternate anchor, six-time Emmy-winning news writer

"Telford is a magnet for controversy." — **Jean Eggemeyer** in *Dome Magazine* (reviewing the author's 2010 autobiography, *A Life on the RUN—Seeking and Safeguarding Social Justice*)

"Telford is an inspiring crusader who in turn was inspired by my father." — **Geoffrey Fieger**, Dr. Jack Kevorkian's celebrated trial lawyer

"Dr. John Telford redefines the linguistics of the day humorously and bluntly, while advancing the imperiled cause of universal human rights. His unique perspective on life, passion, politics, psychology, parapsychology, education, ecology, sociology, and other elements within the human experience is courageous and full of wit. He is an inspirational spirit I respect as a man, a fellow writer, a refreshingly original and creative thinker, and a fearless fighter for all humanity. All members of *both* political parties (or *no* political party) who care about our earthly survival need to own, read, and refer to this spellbinding book." — **Alford G. Harris**, Detroit poet and philosopher

"Coach Telford is a legend." — **Spencer Haywood**, former Olympic and NBA star

"A visionary civil-rights crusader." — **Keith Johnson**, president, the Detroit Federation of Teachers

"John Telford makes me dare to *dream*." — **Dr. Kevin Johnson**, director of the philanthropic Phoenix Friendship House in Detroit

"Dr. Telford is an *Old Icon* rediscovered by the masses." — **Dr. Stuart Kirschenbaum**, Michigan state boxing commissioner, 1981–92

"Dr. Telford is our champion for truth and justice." — **Jeffrey May**, motivational speaker, Roanoke, Virginia

"One of America's top human-rights pioneers." — **Tom Nelson**, Sergeant (retired), West Bloomfield (Michigan) Police Department, MENSA member, and the author's former graduate student at Oakland University

"John Telford saved my life." — **Mike Oldham**, educator and former Super Bowl receiver with the Washington Redskins

"An educationally innovative genius." — **Greg Owens**, former middle school principal in three Michigan districts

"The best teacher Detroit has produced." — **Keith Owens**, Information Director for the Wayne County Treasurer's Office

"John Telford is a rebel and a Renaissance man." — **Huel Perkins**, Metro Detroit FoxTV2 anchor

"A mentor of *mentors*." — **David Points**, commander (retired), United States Navy

"*What OLD MEN Know* is a truly *great* book in the word's most magnificent sense. This insightful *Definitive Dictionary and Almanac of Advice* will delight Democrats and give Republicans *fits*. The Dems should circulate a million copies, and the Repubs might become angry (and curious) enough to circulate *two* million." — **Robert Plumpe**, defense attorney, Eastpointe, Michigan

"Dr. Telford's philosophy has inspirationally impacted my own." — **Professor john powell** of the Ohio State University, executive director of the Kirwan Institute for the Study of Race and Ethnicity

"A prodigious teacher with a wealth of knowledge and transformative insights." — **Dr. James Ray**, superintendent (retired), Flint (Michigan) Schools

"If one is able to disregard some of its scathingly hilarious and not always entirely 'tongue-in-cheek' vitriol (and scatology) aimed at Republicans, one will discern immediately that *What OLD MEN Know* is far more than a satirically '*Definitive*' *Dictionary*—it is a *cautionary* and *socially definitive masterpiece* that our nation's beleaguered leaders (Democrats *and* Republicans alike) need to heed and to read from *cover to cover*." — **Dr. Robert T. Samaras**, Professor of Education (retired), Wayne State University

"A selfless servant for all humanity (and that includes *Republicans!*)" — **Lamont Satchell**, former superintendent, Detroit Public Schools

"In turn, a celebration of life in the fare of encroaching death and a clarion call for progressive social revolution." — **Yusef Shakur**, community activist

"A phenomenal societal trailblazer. John lives by *love*, teaches with *heart*, speaks his *mind*, and does it all without fear of *anyone* or *anything*." — **Rev. Horace Sheffield III**, activist Detroit pastor

"While Telford dodges the label 'radical,' he is far more than a bedrock liberal." — **Caleb Southworth**, former editor, the *Metro Times*, Detroit and Ann Arbor

"John has never hesitated to attack the white *and* the black establishment— and both Republicans *and* Democrats, young and old—when they're *wrong*." — **Gina Telford**, young Native American, African-American, Irish-American wife of the author (and the one member of the fair sex quoted herein)

"Sagacious septuagenarian John Telford cites the Irish poet John Keats, whose timeless Ode pronounces truth *beauty* and beauty *truth* in a world wherein "*old age* shall this generation waste." These are sentiments whereupon the two Celtic Johns—one forever young and the other 'Old'—agree entirely. Throughout this incisive *Definitive Dictionary*, first-generation Scots-American and self-styled 'Auld Author' Telford's pithy definitions, advisements, and observations sparkle like rare diamonds. His *Almanac* absolutely *electrifies* the reader. His outrageously hilarious puns and rank political insults slash sardonically—and deeper than the cutting edge of a Highland claymore." — **Dr. Carl Wagner**, Principal, New Haven (Michigan) High School

"Some call Telford wild, a loose cannon, even *crazy*—but you can't help hanging on his every word. His linguistic style is hypnotic: He really makes you *think*." — **Tom Watkins**, Michigan's former superintendent of Public Instruction

"A legendary leader." — **Dr. William Waun**, General Director of Secondary Education (retired), Rochester (Michigan) Community Schools

"What John Telford *writes*, he *lives*." — **Willie Wooten**, Vice President (retired), Detroit Public Schools Organization of Administrators and Supervisors (OSAS)

"It took real nerve to dish us this raw *Dictionary of Democracy*. Trailblazing hero John Telford can teach even the practically *un*-teachable members of this anti-righteous, youth-raping, sellout society. He is an *archangel* who still believes that Almighty God can create miracles." — **Ray Wright**, Detroit and Pontiac (Michigan) community activist

"Have you comprehended the expanse of the Earth?
Where is the way to the dwelling of light,
And where is the place of darkness . . . ?"

—The Book of Job

In 1887, Aged Sage T. H. Huxley observed that the *known* is *finite*; the *unknown* *infinite*. "Intellectually," Huxley wrote, "we stand on an islet in the midst of an illimitable ocean of *inexplicability*. Our business in every generation is to *reclaim a little more land*." A century later the sagacious Carl Sagan in his master work *Cosmos* assured us that while alien civilizations may not share a spoken and written language, all *technical* civilizations—even *extraterrestrial* ones—do share a common "language": The absolute law of Science and Mathematics. Far-away galaxies spinning around one another follow the same laws of gravitational physics as govern the motion of an apple falling to earth or of *Voyager* on its way to the stars.

Sage for the Ages Blaise Pascal reminded us in his *Pensées* that we must seek our dignity from the government of our *thought*—that we should have no *greater* measure of dignity even were we to possess *worlds*—which can swallow us up like grains of sand. Thus, it is by *knowledge* and by *thought* that we contemporary Aged Sages *comprehend* our expansive and ever-*expanding* world.

What OLD MEN Know

A Definitive
Dictionary
and Almanac
of Advice

Dr. John Telford
Septuagenarian Sage

HARMONIE PARK PRESS
Sterling Heights, Michigan

© 2011 by Dr. John Telford
All rights reserved. Published in 2011

Printed and bound in the United States of America

Published by
Harmonie Park Press
Liberty Professional Center
35675 Mound Road
Sterling Heights, Michigan 48310–4727
www.harmonieparkpress.com

Cover design:
Peri Poloni-Gabriel, Knockout Design, www.knockoutbooks.com

ISBN 13: 978-0-89990-154-1 (alk. paper)
ISBN 10: 0-89990-154-9 (alk. paper)

Library of Congress Cataloging-in-Publication Data

Telford, John, 1936–
    What old men know : a definitive dictionary and almanac of advice / Dr. John Telford, septuagenarian sage.
        p. cm.
    Includes index.
    ISBN-13: 978-0-89990-154-1 (alk. paper)
    ISBN-10: 0-89990-154-9 (alk. paper)
    1. American wit and humor—Dictionaries. 2. Life—Humor. I. Title.
    PN6165.T45 2011
    818'.602—dc22
                                                                    2010041971

I dedicate this *Definitive Dictionary* to my own *personal* <u>Old Man</u>—my father, John "Scotty" Telford (born in Larkhall, Scotland, December 3, 1902; died in Detroit, May 21, 1987). That rough-hewn coalminer, prizefighter, and autoworker was *Jack Dempsey, Malcolm X, John Wayne*, and the Scottish freedom fighter *Sir William Wallace* all rolled into one wild, hot-tempered, hard-drinking daddy.

The mad vigilante of Detroit's tough Twelfth Street and McGraw neighborhood circa 1918–50, John "Scotty" Telford was a civil-rights crusader before there ever *was* such an appellation. My dad *bullied* bullies, *hunted* hunters, and raised his son to do the same—long before he ever joined the august ranks of the bona fide, certified *Aged Sages* as defined and celebrated in this torrid tome.

Contents

Foreword

Near the dawn of the twentieth century, my own personal *"OLD MAN,"* John "Scotty" Telford—an only *briefly* schooled coalminer and prizefighter but avid student of world affairs—was born in Scotland. He ultimately would become an octogenarian. During 1902, the year of his birth, the United States selected Panama as the site of a canal joining the world's two great oceans, the Texaco Oil Company was established in America, and there was a massive miners' strike—also in America. Britain's Boer War commander Lord Kitchener (for whom my late uncle Frank Kitchener Telford was named) came home to a hero's welcome after the Peace of Vereeniging ended that imperialist war. On Egypt's Nile River, the first Aswan Dam was completed. Rudyard Kipling's *Just So Stories* and Joseph Conrad's novella *Heart of Darkness* were published, and Auguste Rodin sculpted his *Romeo and Juliet*.

The next year, Scott in the Antarctic reached the planet's farthest southern point, scores of Jews were massacred in a pogrom in Bessarabia, and Bulgarians murdered Muslims in Macedonia. Pope Pius X was crowned before a crowd of 70,000 in Rome, Turks massacred 50,000 Bulgarians, and 10,000 Chinese troops moved into Manchuria. Pierre and Marie Curie were awarded the Nobel Prize for physics. In Mexico, Emiliano Zapata and Pancho Villa led a revolution. In *los Estados Unidos* (tr.: *the U.S.*—for the benefit of uni-lingual Republicans), the Wright brothers first flew, and the Boston Red Sox won baseball's first World Series. Jack London wrote *The Call of the Wild* and George Bernard Shaw wrote *Man and Superman*.

Four years after that (in 1907, the year of the birth of my mother Helen Telford, herself to become a sainted Sage ninety-one years later), the U.S. Army formed the first military air force, British troops killed four freedom fighters in Ireland, riots convulsed India, and the great Indian activist Mohandas Gandhi fomented yet a second civil-disobedience campaign —this time in South Africa. By the time I was born twenty-nine years later in the first month of 1936 on the legendary Scottish poet Robert Burns' 177th birthday, the magnificent Native American warrior chief Geronimo had slipped away to the Happy Hunting Ground, a 1916 race riot in St. Louis had killed hundreds, another large-scale race riot had broken out in Chicago in 1919, and lynchings of blacks by racist whites in the southern, southwestern, and midwestern United States during the first quarter-century had killed hundreds more. The Irish-American/Native American Jim Thorpe had won the 1912 Olympic Decathlon and Pentathlon. The *Titanic* had sunk and the *Hindenburg* had burned and crashed. Einstein had written his Theory of Relativity, the Russians had overthrown and executed the Czar, millions had died in World War I—the "war to end all wars"— and the ill-fated League of Nations had been founded.

The two Jacks—African-American Johnson and Scots-Irish-American Dempsey—had won and lost the world heavyweight championship. Jerry Siegel and Joe Shuster had created the "Superman" comic strip, the stock market had crashed, and the legal sale of alcoholic beverages in the United States had been banned and then re-legalized. Detroit's Eddie Tolan (later my gym teacher) had been proclaimed the "world's fastest human" for winning the 100- and 200-meter dashes at the 1932 Olympic Games in Los Angeles. The Nazis had ascended to power in Germany. That year of my birth also happened to be the nadir of the (Great Depression from which Democratic President Franklin D. Roosevelt's New Deal—with the essential but horrendous help of World War II—would presently extricate the country.

In that momentous summer of 1936, Jesse Owens won four gold medals in the Berlin Olympics to the dismay of Nazi dictator Adolf Hitler and became one of my (and America's) eventual all-time heroes. Jesse would also autograph a track meet program for me one thrilling day when I was officiating the 1967 NCAA in Detroit's Cobo Hall.

Also during 1936, the Fascists won the Spanish Civil War, Edward VIII abdicated the English throne, Rudyard Kipling died, and Margaret Mitchell penned *Gone with the Wind*.

By the time my father passed away in May 1987 after having drawn earthly breath for 85 percent of the century, his son had been presented a Papal Medal by Pius XII during an undefeated European tour with the U.S. track team and had earned three college degrees and become a public school administrator. World War II, the Korean War, and the Vietnam War had been fought, a deadly wartime race riot had raged throughout my hometown Detroit, the Nazis had exterminated six million Jews and others they deemed "undesirable," atomic bombs had decimated Hiroshima and Nagasaki, the hydrogen bomb had been developed by the United States and eventually acquired by several countries, and the United Nations had been founded.

Detroit's Joe Louis had won and lost the heavyweight title after a record twenty-five successful defenses, Detroit-raised Sugar Ray Robinson had been proclaimed the greatest pound-for-pound boxer of all time, and UCLA's All-American track and football star Jackie Robinson had integrated major league baseball. The United States Supreme Court had declared racially "separate-but-equal" K-12 public schools to be inherently *unequal*, the McCarthy Communist-witch-hunting trials had occurred, Jim Crow and anti-miscegenation laws had been struck down, Elvis Presley and the Beatles had burst onto the scene, the Cuban Revolution had been achieved, and the battles of the 1960s for American blacks' basic civil rights had been fought and partially won in the midst of fiery rebellions in Detroit and other cities across the country. During that explosive decade, the two Kennedys and Malcolm, Ché, and King had been assassinated, and an American astronaut had walked on the moon.

Also, Watergate had transpired, Israeli athletes had been killed by terrorists at the Munich Olympics in 1972, the Irish Republican Army had exploded deadly bombs on the English mainland, and there had been famines in Ethiopia, riots in South Africa, and a revolution in Iran. César Chavez had organized the grape-pickers on the West Coast. Muhammad Ali had established himself as the greatest heavyweight prizefighter of his era (and possibly *any* era) and was on his way toward becoming a world ambassador for freedom and egalitarianism. America had elected as president and vice president an aging ex-movie actor and an inveterate golfer who couldn't spell "potato" and thought that they speak Latin in Latin America. The nuclear accident in Chernobyl had happened, the deadly scourge called AIDS (Acquired Immune Deficiency Syndrome) had begun to proliferate throughout the planet, dissident Soviet scientist Andrei Sakharov had been released from four years of internal incarceration, and the Iran-Contra affair had rocked the Reagan administration to its core.

Since my father's 1987 death, the Berlin Wall has been torn down, South Africa has been liberated, the Soviets wisely withdrew from Afghanistan, Canadian Olympic sprinter Ben Johnson and other athletes in track and other sports were caught using anabolic steroids to enhance performance, the Persian Gulf War over oil has been fought, and thousands of

Australian aborigines have marched to protest their squalid living conditions. The Exxon Valdez oil disaster, the Oklahoma bombing, and the space shuttle Challenger tragedy occurred.

A father-son duo of Republican presidents have led the United States into wars and other travails—the *father* into that 1991 war over oil, the *son* into a falsely-premised similar war over oil and into a world-wide financial meltdown. Also during the son's administration, contracts were signed with British Petroleum (BP) that have resulted in unsafe drilling which caused a massive oil leak on the ocean floor of the Gulf of Mexico. A recent series of earthquakes has shaken the planet. Terrorism and nuclear proliferation have become dire threats. Sea piracy has resurged. The impacts of global warming and the depletion of the planet's ozone layer have encroached, caused by our over-use of fossil fuel. In the midst of all this, America's first mixed-race president—serendipitously, an intellectual and spiritual throwback to the brilliant and courageous JFK—has been elected to lend our nation and the free world some sorely-needed wisdom, hope, and plain *rationality*. Concurrently, China has emerged as a formidable economic and military power.

Much of this I set forth specifically and comment on in items in this publication and in my autobiography, *A Life on the RUN—Seeking and Safeguarding Social Justice*. Together, the lives of my late father and me have spanned nearly ninety-eight percent of the tumultuous twentieth century—and buoyed by his indomitable and enduring spirit, I have now survived unto the threshold of the second decade of the potentially even-more-tumultuous twenty-first.

Having been a *student* and *sycophant* who "sat at the knee" of that wise and well-read albeit unheralded Aged Sage also named *John Telford* who sired me does not alone qualify me to author this audacious volume which you discerning readers are about to digest. Still, my privileged status of *student/sycophant* to my valiant *OLD MAN* (literally) bears enormous weight nonetheless, as you will presently note. My father taught me histories both *ancient* and merely *old* that aren't to be found entirely in books—histories that can impact the future of our species through examples both positive and negative.

The twentieth century was a period of unprecedented change—a cataclysmic hundred years whereof my fighter father and I have been not only *products*, but in our own minute (my-NOOT) and microcosmic avenues, *catalysts*. *What OLD MEN Know* is a sensate product of the twentieth century experience and a "galvanizer of *good*" for the twenty-first. While

I do confess to having an inordinate amount of *Democratic* fun in it at the expense of some of my fellow Americans of the *Republican* persuasion, this for the greater part is a serious work that is yours to read and be therefore edified, uplifted, and morally motivated *regardless* of your political views (and for the information of you Repubs, the correct word here *is* indeed *"regardless"*—not *"irregardless"*). Thus, all of *you*, too, may thereby help to shape the *preferred future of human-kind* in the twenty-first century—as well as for the centuries to come.

JOHN TELFORD
Doctor of Education

Detroit, Michigan
4 July 2010

Introduction by Dr. Wayne Dyer
(one of this pulsating publication's duly anointed Aged Sages)

What _OLD MEN Know_ is indeed a daringly _definitive_ but also a very _different_ kind of _dictionary_—yet like a dictionary, one can read it from beginning to end or from any part in the middle. Its "Auld Author" has quirkily chosen to alphabetize prominent or timelessly famous (and infamous) people by their _first_ names rather than their _last_ in citing their deeds and misdeeds in this _Definitive Dictionary_. He differentiates "<u>Old Men</u>" (capitalized) from mere "old men" (not capitalized) in conferring upon the former the august title _Aged Sage_. A veritable _Aged Sage_ himself, he was my track coach in 1958 at Denby High School in Detroit, and I became his associate coach at Detroit Pershing High eight years later. So since he's proclaimed me one of his _Aged Sages_, at least I can _suggest_ that while over time I've hopefully acquired a modicum of _sagacity_, I 'm not quite as "Aged" as _he_ is yet! Seriously, John Telford prodded me to pursue my doctorate, and he edited my dissertation. Much of what I have accomplished I owe to his mentorship, as do countless others whose lives he touched in his half-century as an educator which he recounts in his incendiary autobiography, _A Life on the RUN—Seeking and Safeguarding Social Justice._

    You will enjoy Dr. Telford's references to a reformative process he calls "Creative Insubordination." You will also find that he loves to poke fun at the _distaff_ side of the human equation, as well as at _Republicans_ (hence, as he would say, "Republicans, check your _Webster's!_"). At times he gets rather graphically explicit about us oldsters' failing bodily functions and perhaps a tad too cute when he makes sly implications regarding the size (or rather, the implied _lack_ thereof) of the private parts of male members of the GOP. Also, his blunt use of slang synonyms for reproductive or excretory organs in characterizing individuals whose politics differ from his may discomfit some readers. Still, the pervasive wisdom in this edgily amusing, frankly politically _skewed_ yet brilliantly _philosophical_ treatise makes it a _must read_ for those Sages, semi-Sages, or Sages-in-training—young and old, male and female, Democrat and Republican—who hope for a _fairer_ future for all humankind.

Preface

At the publication time of this *Definitive Dictionary and Almanac of Advice*, its Raffish Old Writer had been absolutely *writhing* for a number of months in the pre-geriatric throes of his fifth year as a full-fledged, self-styled *Septuagenarian Sage Supreme*. He therefore finds himself increasingly disposed to succumb to mid-day naps from which he frequently awakens late in the afternoon just in time to sip a "wee dram" of Drambuie from the ancient Isle of Skye. The Old Bugger is nonetheless prepared to take full, alert responsibility for the contents of this palpitating publication. Given the fact that much of it is presented in a humorous and often sardonic vein, a large section of the public may regard it as having been written mostly "tongue-in-cheek" and thus might be inclined to sample it entirely in that same spirit.

However, that would be to let the political, poetic, and philosophical parts of this exegesis go unread or lightly considered, and many of those parts were written in what can best be described as a sometimes somber seriousness. While the timeless truths to follow aren't set forth as any form of personal revelation of quasi-mystical lore, this Old Writer does offer the reader many definitions, quotations, quips, and concepts to ponder deeply—some verging on the *surreal*—along with what he confidently believes is relevant counsel for coping with the daunting human challenges of the dawning millennium.

Not the least of these will be the nation's imperative to stand with our president as he strives to clean up after eight years of GOP misrule, as he strives to make America oil-independent with a homegrown green industry, as he strives to clean up the catastrophic mess created by British Petroleum, and as he strives to extricate our country from its two wars. These all *remain the circumstances* whether you're a member of the political party that has an *Ass* for its logo or whether you're a member of that other even less lucid party of the *Pachydermous* persuasion.

In either (or *neither*) case, the Old Writer wishes to assure *every* reader that every single *syllable* in this syllabus was written in the *selfless service of all Americans* (and indeed of all *humanity*). Thus, it is by *humanity* and *future generations* thereof that its worth will best be judged. Its *"Auld"* author recognizes no lesser court of appeal. *Abuse*, he has long grown personally accustomed to suffer as a crusading and unabashedly ultra-liberal school administrator; *calumny* has long been his daily *familiar* for the same reasons; and at ongoing *slander* he smiles in stoic contempt (but no longer with [much] *bitterness*).

All that having been said, your Modest Old Author invites (or dares) you now to turn the page and peruse the titillating *Telford's Table of Topics* in what you will discover to be a totally *transfixing* tome. . . .

Telford's Table of Topics

A

A–Bomb * Abomination * Abraham Lincoln * Absurdity * ACLU * Acute Angina * Addictive Relationships * Adultery * Adversity * Advice * Afghanistan * Agape * Aged Sages * Ageism * Agnostic * Ain't * Akasha * Al Gore * "The two Alberts" * Alcohol * Ali * Altruism * American Revolution II * Anal Sex * The Ancient Caledonian Code * The "Ancient Wisdoms" * Anger * Animal "Husbandry" * Anomie * Anonymous * Answer to *Both* of the Philosophical Questions Posed by the Old Man on the Mountaintop * Anthropology * Anti-Rebel * Anus * Apocalypse * Arrogance * Art, Music, Athletics, and Vocational Programs * Arthritis * A-- H--- * Assigned Seat * Athletics * Atlantis * Atman * Attica * "Auction Blocks and Jim Crow" * The "August Appellation" * *Auld* * *Auld* Celt, *Auld* Celt's *Pulse* * Author of the *Landmark—*and Incredibly *Brilliant—Definitive Dictionary and Almanac of Advice* Entitled *What OLD MEN Know* * Autocrat

B

"Baby Boomers" * Back * Bad Books * Bad Boy * Bad Marriage * Bagpipes * Balance * Balls * "BAMN" * Bank Bailout of 2008 * Barbarism * The Bard * Basketball * Beards * "Beast with Two Backs" * "Beaver Shot!" * Beavis * Bedtime for Bonzo * Beehive * Beer * Betrayal * Betty Grable * Bill Clinton * Bill of Rights * Bill of *Wrongs* * "Bird" * Birthday * The "Black Arts" * Black Panther Party * Black Republican * "Black" Witchcraft * The "Blame Game" * Blast-Off!! * "Bling," "Bling-Bling" * Blondes * *Bloody* Lowndes * Boink * Bonzo * Bore * Borrower * Boxers * Boys * Brain * Breaking Up with a Wife or Lover * Brotherhood * Brothers * Buggery * Bullfighting * Bully * Bureaucracies * Bureaucrat * Bush's Brain * Butthead * "By God, We'll Fight!"

C

Cage Fighting * Caledonians * Cancer * Capitalism and Its "Henny Penny" Corollary * The Capitol Building in Washington, D.C. * Castrate * Catheter * Cats * Cautionary Tale * Celibacy * "Cell Blocks and Death Row" * Cemetery *

Censorship • Certainty • The Champion's "<u>Succeed</u> Creed" • Change, *The Change* • Chaos • Character • Ché • "The Check's in the Mail" • Chest Hair • Children • Chimp • China • Chip Saltsman • Christ • Christmas • C.I. • Circling the Wagons and Then Shooting *In* • Civilization • Clarence Thomas • Classical Music • Classism • Clinical Depression • Clit • Clowns • Coal Mine • Codger • Coincidence • *Cojones* • Colin Powell • College Athletic Team • Colors, *Defined* • Come • Common Sense • Communism • Complex Problem • Compliment • Compromise • Computer • Conceit • Confidence • Conformity • Conscience • Consciousness • Conservation • Constitution of the United States • Consultant • Contrast • Coot • Cooties • "Corporate Cats" • Corporatocracy • Corrupt • The Cosmos • Counterfeit Rebel • Country • Coward • Cowardice • Creaky • Creating • Creative Insubordination • The "Creatively Maladjusted" • Creep, Creepy • Crocodile • Cronyism • Crow • "Crude and Lewd" • Cruelty • Crying at Weddings • Cultural • Relativist • Cultures • "Cum" • Curiosity • Curmudgeon • Cuties • Cynic, Cynicism • *Cyrano de Bergerac*

D

"Daddy" • David L. Holmes • Death • Deception • Decrepit • Dem • Demagogues • Democracy • Democrat • Democratic Party • Demonization • Demons • Depression • Desert • Desire • Destiny • Detroit • Detroit Public Schools • Detumescent • The Devil • DHEA • Dialect • Diapers • Dick Cheney • Dickhead • Dick's Head • Die • "Different Drum" • Diligence • A Dime and a Cup of Coffee • Dinosaur • Diplomacy • Discontentment • Divas • Dodderer, Doddering • Dodgers • Dog-Fighting • Doggy Diapers • Dogs • Don'ts (for <u>Old Men</u>) • Dork, Dorkhead • Do's (for <u>Old Men</u>) • Dragon • Drama Queens • Drambuie • "Drill, Baby, Drill!" • Drink • Drunkenness • The Dumbing-Down of America's Textbooks • Dunce, Dunderhead • (On) Dying • Dysentery

E

Ears • Ebonics • Education • Educators Who Haven't Figured Out Yet that the Worst Way to Teach Kids Is to Test Them to Death • Egalitization • Ego • Egoism, Egotism • Ejaculate • Elder • Elizabeth Taylor • Empathy • "Encore Anxiety" • Endangered Species • Envy • Erection • Erection-Inhibitors • Eschew • E.S.P. • The Eternal Presence • The Eternal Shepherd • Eternity • Ethnocentrism • Euclid • Evil • Evolution • Executive Ability • Expedience • Experience • Extremism • The "Eye of Osiris"

F

Fables • Faith • Faithful • Fame • Fanatic • Fascism • Fascist • Fate • Favor • Federal Regulator • Federated Regionalism • Feeling Important • Fellatio • Feminism •

Fibula * Fight * Fine Dining * Finney High School * The First Requisite for "Immortality" * The 500 * The "500" Club * Five Thousand Teenagers * Flaccid * Flat on Your Back in Incredible Pain * Flattery * Flatulence * Fly * The "Fold-Under" Cock * The "Fold-Under" Cocktail * Forbidden Nooky * Forget * Forgiving * Fortune * The 43rd President of the United States * Frank Sinatran * Franklin and Eleanor Roosevelt * Free Verse * Freedom * Freedom of the Press * "Friend" * Friends Who Ascend to Power and Wealth * Friendships * Fundament * Fundamentalists

G

Gall Bladder * Gambling * Gas * Gazing Outward Together * Geezer * Genius * Geoffrey Fieger * George Orwell * George W. Bush * George Washington * Geriatrics * German Shepherd * Getting in Trouble * Giants * Give, Giving * Global Warming * God * Going Wee-Wee * The "Golden Rule" * Goldman Sachs * Golf, Golf Course * Good Books * "Good-But-Not-Gaudy" * Good, Goodness * Good Listeners * Good Man * Good Name * "Good Night, Mrs. Calabash, Wherever You Are" * Good Old Days * Good Woman * G.O.P. * Grace Lee Boggs * Grammatical Rule Against Ending a Sentence with a Preposition * Grand-daddy * Grand-kids * Grand Marnier * Great * The "Great Beyond" * The Great "Recession" of 2008 * Grief * Grudge-Holding * Gynecologist

H

Hair * Haiti * Hallowed Ground * Hallucination * Happiness * Hard Man * Harder * Hard-On * Harpaxophiliac * Hatred * "Hattism" * "He Who Wandered by the Sea / Of Middle-Eastern Galilee . . ." * Head Hair * Health Care * Healthy Irreverence * A Healthy Mile * The Heart * "Heart" * Heart Attack * Heaven * Hell * Henry David Thoreau * Hero * Hibernians * "Hides in the Weeds" * The Highest-Stress Job * Hips * History * Home * Hoodoo * Hope * Hopelessness * Horizon * Horror * "Hose" * Hostage * Housekeeper * How (Not) to Fight a Woman * How Old Is "Old"? * How to Lose Weight * Hubris * Hugs * Humanism * Humanist * Humanitarian * Humility * Hump * Hunters * Hydrogen Bomb * Hypnotherapists

I

I * Idea * Ideals * Ideologue * Idiosyncratic * Idiot * Ignorance * "I'll Miss You" * Imagination * Imbibers * Immaturity * Imp * Impossible Things * Impotence * Incompetence * Incorporated States of America * Ineffectual * Infinity * Inflation * Influence * Injustice * The Injustice of the Faux-Just * The Inquiry Process * Insanity * Insipid * Instinct * "Instruction Manuals" * Integrity * The Internet * Interplanetary (and Ultimately Interstellar) Space * Intolerance * Intuition * Iraq War *

Irishmen • "Is You *Is*, or Is You *Ain't*??" • Isis • It Ain't No Fun Lying Sedated in a Hospital Bed . . .

J

Jackal • Jackie Robinson • "JC-ICBM" • Jealousy • Jekyll-and-Hyde Jester • Jogging • John Boehner • John Kerry • john powell • Jokes 1–9 • Jonah • *Joy!* • Justice

K

Karl Rove • Khartoum • Kid Rock's Four S's • Kidney Stones • Kilts and Tartans • Kismet • Knees • Knowledge • "Kum" • Kwame Kilpatrick

L

L. Brooks Patterson • Labor • "Ladies from Hades" • Language • Lapdog • Laughter • Law Enforcement • Leadership • Learn • Learned • Legacy • A "Legend in His Own Mind" • Leisure • Leprechaun • Liar • Libertarian • Liberty • Life • Life's Greatest Secret • Light • "Like to Fight" • Liquidity • Literature • "Little Girl in High Chair Guzzling from Beer Can" • "Live *Heroically!*" • Lobbyist • Logic • "Lolita" • Loneliness • Longevity • Loquacity • Lost Worlds • Love (*noun*) • Love (*verb*) • Love Affair with Life • Love and War • Love or Hate • Loved Ones • Lover • Luck • Lunacy • Lunatic • Luxury

M

Mackinac Island Fudge • Making the First Move • Malcolm • Male Chauvinist • The **Man Who Never Failed** • "Manassa Mauler" • Manners • The **Marijuana Law** • Marriage • Married Man • Martin Luther King, Jr. • Martyr • Marva Collins • Masochist • Mastodon Tusks • *Me* • The "Me" Generation • Medicine • "Mediocrity" • Mediumship • Medusa • Members of the Political Party that Uses an *Elephant* as its Symbol • (The Five Miscreant) **Members of the United States Supreme Court Who Voted in 2010 to Permit Corporations to Have Equal Status with Individual U.S. Citizens** • Memories • Mercy • Merit • M-F • The **Mickey Mouse Club** • Million-Dollar Legs • Mince Pie • Minister Mary Edwards • Minute • "Minute-Men" • *Miracles* Observed, Experienced, Imagined, Known, or Anticipated • Misanthrope • Mis-educated • Mispronunciation • Mission • Misspell • Mob • Moderation • Modesty • Mohandas Gandhi • Molars • Monetary Economic System • Money • Monogamy • Monsters • Monuments • "Moral Maggotry" • *Most* Dogs • Mother Teresa • Mothers of Soldiers Killed in Iraq • Mothers of Soldiers Killed in Vietnam • Multi-National Corporations • Murderous Missiles Named for Ancient Greek Gods • "Mustang" • Myth

N

Nags * Napoleon's Pickled Pecker * Native Americans * Nelson Mandela * Nepotism * Neutrality * Niagara Falls * Niccolò Machiavelli * *Nineteen Eighty-Four* * Non-Rebel * "Normal" * "Nucular" * Nuke

O

Obama * Old * The Old Crusader's Credo * Old Fool * Old Goat * The Old Man's All-Time Heroes * The Old Man's Best Teachers * The Old Man's First Axiom * The Old Man's Second Axiom * The Old Man's Third Axiom * The Old Man's Fourth Axiom * The Old Man's "Friends" * The Old Man's Greatest *Accomplishment* * The Old Man's Greatest *Fear* * The Old Man's Greatest *Masterpiece* * The Old Man's Liquid Viagra * The Old Man's Most Precious Possession * The Old Man's Secrets and Advice for Connubial Bliss * The Old Man's Secrets and Advice for Losing Weight Healthfully * The Old Man's Secrets and Advice for Staying Out of Debt * old men * Old Men * Old Men's Childhoods and Yesteryears of Youth * Old Men's Easy Technique for Losing Weight without Ever Getting Out of Bed * Old Men's Spirits * Old Poet * Old *Violins* * old women * Old Women * Older * Oldest * Oldster * Opinion * Opportunity * Optimism, Optimist * Orgasm * Outer Space and the Nearest Planets * Owl * Oxymoron * The Ozone Layer

P

Pacifism * Pagan * Pagandom * Pantheism * Parapsychology * Parasites * Passing * Passion * The Past * Pat Robertson * Patriotism * Peace * Peace Everlasting * Peace of Mind * Peace With *Justice* * Pedagogue * Pedant * Pederast * Pee * Pee-Pee * *Pee-Wee Wee-Wee* * Penis * Penis Anxiety * Penis Uneasiness * Penniless * People Old Men Have from Long Experience Learned to Avoid * People Whose Company Old Men Are Copacetic With * The "People's Republic" of China * Perception * Pessimist * Petty Tyrant * *Pezzonovante* * Philosophical Questions Posed by the Old Man on the Mountaintop * Philosophy * Pictures of Bullfighters Painted on Velvet * Pictures of Elvis Painted on Velvet * Pilgrims * "Pillar of the Community" * Pity * Places Old Men Have from Long Experience Learned to Avoid (or *Should* Avoid) * Places Old Men Have from Long Experience Learned to Frequent or Wished to Seek Out (or *Should* Frequent or Seek Out) * Plagiarism * Plague! * Poet * A (Non)-Poetic Parody * A Poetically Prescient Pre-Requiem *Requiem for Jamaal* * "Poet-*tential*" * Politicians, Politicos * Politics * Poop * Poorhouse * The Pope * Porpoises * Positivist * Praise * Prejudice * Prejudiced People * Pride * Progress * Prosperity * Prostate * Prostrate * Pseudo-Communism * Pseudo-Educator * Pseudo-Fascist * Pseudo-Rebel * Public-School Segregation * Punctuality * Purpose * "Pussy-Whipped" * Putting Cute Little Coats and Hats on Cute Little Dogs and Cats * Putz * Pygmy * The Pyramid

Q

"Quail" * Quaver * Quayle * Questions to Consider * Quiet * Quirky * *"Quod Sum Eris"*

R

Racism * Racist * Radical * Rap * Rapture * "Rat Pack" * Read * Real Estate * A Real *Mensch* * "Realio-trulio" * Rebel * Rebeldom, Under the "Rebel Dome," Rebelhood, Rebelness, Rebelry * Rebelesque Synergy * Rebelize * Reconciliation * Redundancy * Reform * Regal Rebel * Regretful * Regrettable * Relatives * Religionism * Remorse * *Renegado* * *Repub* * Republican * Republican Party * Republican *Private Part* * Re*puzzled*can * *Resource*-Driven and *Technology*-Driven Economic System * Responsibility * Revelrous "Rules" for Retirees * Revolution * The *Reward* for a *Good Deed Well Done* * *Rex Reborn* * Richard Cheney * Richard Nixon * A *Riddle To Ponder* * Ridicule * Righteous Indignation * Risk * Roadkill * "Robeism" * Robert Bobb * Robert F. Kennedy * Robert "The Bruce" * Rogue Rebel * Romance * The Royal "We" * "RRR" * Rush Limbaugh

S

A Sacred Duty of All *Educators* * Sad Shit-uation * A *Sagacious Secret* Shared by the Old Man on the Mountaintop * Sages for the Ages * Sanskrit * Sarah Palin * Savagery * Scheming * Schloin * Schmuck * "School of Hard Knocks" * Schools * Science * Scotch * Scots * Scrotum, Scrota * "Second Sight" * Secret * The Secret of *Strength* * Secret Sinners * Secrets of the Centenarians * Security * Seed * "Seeds" * Seer * Self-Confidence * Selfishness * Self-Knowledge * Self-Sacrifice * *Semi-Rebel* * "Sensus, non aetas, invenit sapientiam" * Separation of Church and State * Septuagenarian * Sex * Sex "Reformers" * Sexual Exploitation * Shaman * Shamanic Self-Transformation * Sheep * Sheep in *Sheep's* Clothing * Shit * Shriveled * Silence * A Silly (Non)-Syllogism * Silver and Gold * Sin * Situational Ethics * Skirts * Skull * Slavery * Sleep * Slow Learners * Slowing Down * Small-Membered * Smile * "So What?" * Social Activist * Socialism * Sociopath * Socrates * Soda Pop * "Softness of Head" * Solitude * Something That Happens to a Boy During Puberty * Something That Is *Borrowed* * Something That Is *Immortal* * Something That Is *Inevitable* * Something That Is Irrecoverable * *Sonnet for a Safer Sea* * Sons of Thor * "Soul" * Spartans * Sprinters * Statesman * *Status Quo* * Steal * Steve and Kathy Swigard * Stock Market * "Strangely Believe It" * String Theory * "Strongman" * Subordin*ate* * Subordinate * Success * Sugar Ray Robinson * Suicide * The Sun * Superordinate * Superstitions * "Swallow and Follow" * Sweat

T

Tact * "Take This Job and *Ship* It . . ." * Talent * Taxes * Taxidermy * Teach * Teacher * "Teapartyers" * Teeny Wee-Wee * Television * Ten Trillion Years * Tennis

* Termagant * Theology * Thesaurus * Theseus * Thieves Who Steal from Plain Private Citizens * Thieves Who Steal from Public Coffers * Things Old Men Have from Long Experience Learned to Avoid * Things Old Men Have from Long Experience Learned to Seek Out * Thinking * The "Third City" * This Old Man's Mantra (TOMM) * Thought * Thurgood Marshall * Time * Time Conquered * Time Wasted * Timeless Tale * "To Restrain the Worst Instincts of the Profit Sector" * "To Sleep Is to Dine" * To Teach * Tobacco * Tolerance * Tom Barry * Toupée * Traditional Grammar * Tragedy * A Tragic Truth(?) * Tranquility * Trifles * Truth * Trying Not to Think About It * Twenty Thousand Teenagers * The Twilight of the Aged Sage * Two Tales Out of (Sunday) School * Tyranny

U

UFO * "Ugly" * Ugly Fat * Unconsciousness * "Uncontrollable" * Uncreative Subordinate * Understanding * Unions * A Uniquely Human Enigma * The United States of America * The United States Senate * The Universe * The Universe of Ideas * Universities * Unjust * "Unreasonable" Men * Unsung Poets * Uranus * Urethra * Urine * Utopia

V

"Valley Girls" * The Vampire's Favorite Soup * Vanity * Varicose * Variety * The Veda * Venus * Vi-agg-ra!! * Vice * Vietnam War * Vigilance * Vigilantism * The Violin * Visionary * Voodoo * The Voting Rights Act

W

Waiting for the Deer * Waitresses * Waking Up Grumpy * War * "War of Whores" * Warlock * The "Warrior Within" * "Wasted" Affection * Wasteland * Waterboarding * Wayne State University * Wealth * "Weapons of Mass Destruction" * Wee * Wee-Wee * "Well-Rounded" * Wet Wipes * Whack * What Happens When an Old Man Dies * What Happens When an Old Man Tries to Play Full-Court Basketball * What Old Men Don't Know * What Old Men Know * What Only Old Men Know—and Have Learned to their Infinite Sorrow * Wheezy Geezer * "White" Witchcraft * "Who" * "Whom" * Whop * Whores * "Whumperer", "Whumping" * Wicca * "Will You Still Love Me in the Morning?" * A "Winged Race of Men" * Winston Churchill * Wisdom Teeth * Wise Old Women (W.O.W.) * Witch * Wizians * Wonder * Woody * Worms and Maggots * Wounds * "Wrath of God" * "Wrinkled White Ass" * Writers

X

Xerxes * "xyW" * "xyz"

Y

"Yes-man" * *You* * "You'll *See* It When You *Believe* It" * Young Men * young men * Young Women * young women * Your Auld, *Auld* Author * Your Auld Author's Grandma's Cookie Recipe * Your Destiny * Your Wife's Birthday

Z

Zack Robinson * Zipper * Zoos * *ZZZ . . . ZZZ . . . ZZZ . . .*

A

A-BOMB — The fearsome atomic explosive that vaporized countless innocent Japanese men, women and children in Hiroshima and Nagasaki in 1945 and opened our planet's nuclear Pandora's Box *irrevocably.*

("*Striptease,* Atomic Tina, dear, in Hydrogen Hotel. / We'll sleep in HEEroSHEEma here, 'til we awake in Hell!" —from the 1956 poem, *In Hydrogen Hotel.*)

See **HYDROGEN BOMB**

ABOMINATION — (No, Republicans, we're not exhorting anyone to "A-bomb a nation." Check your *Webster's.*) An *abomination* is something to be *abhorred.* (And again: No, *no,* Repubs!—"abhorred" doesn't mean that some horny, whore-addicted guy named Ab consorted with a "lady of the evening," either. Better check your *Webster's* again, you GOP dummies.) An abomination is an entity so *abominably abhorrent* and *fearsome* that it's almost *unthinkable.*

See **A-BOMB; AGEISM; CLASSISM; FASCISM; RACISM; SLAVERY; WAR**

See also **MURDEROUS MISSILES NAMED FOR ANCIENT GREEK GODS** (In all *conscience,* we certainly shouldn't have named these horrific weapons of mass destruction for the deities of an ancient and innocent Southern European people who are too long-*dead* to protest.)

ABRAHAM LINCOLN — An Aged Sage for all eternity.

Honest Abe's great, brooding statue seated within the Lincoln Memorial in our nation's capitol—gigantic though it be—is dwarfed by the monumental deeds of the man it memorializes. President Abraham Lincoln saved the Union we optimistically (if not always *accurately*) refer to as the _United_ States and kept it on its convoluted path toward the destination it some day hopefully, will reach—_real and true unity_ and _real and true_ democracy.

See **AGED SAGES; GIANTS; MONUMENTS; SAGES FOR THE AGES**

ABSURDITY — A _handicapping_ characteristic, should it be discovered to be present in any profession except _politics_ (or within the top administration of the Detroit Public Schools).

See **DETROIT PUBLIC SCHOOLS; POLITICIANS, POLITICOS**

ACLU — These famous (to some overt and covert fascists, _infamous_) four letters stand for your and my American Civil Liberties Union.

By all that's holy (and _un_holy), we all need to get down on our knees right now and _thank the_ good _Lord_ (and/or the Eternal Presence) for the ACLU. For _God's_ and _America's_ sake, and for every one of our _children's_ sakes, please become a card-carrying member today if you aren't one already. Send your ACLU money, money, _MUH-nee_— the ACLU is the only bulwark left _between us_ and fascism!

Think this is an exaggeration?

See **FASCISM; FASCIST**

ACUTE ANGINA — What Repubs think is a female's _prettyish pubic_ region.

See **REPUB (RE_PUBES_?)**

ADDICTIVE RELATIONSHIPS — Destructive interpersonal connections.

Aged Sages—at least, _most_ of them—usually don't fall victim (anymore) to addictive relationships. You're in an addictive relationship if these statements apply: "He (she) is _everything_ to me despite his (her) flaws"; "My difficult situation with him (her) isn't really _that_ bad"; "I can't _make_ it alone!" And yes—even Aged Sages, if they're romantically fixated on the wrong person, can be capable of erroneously believing _all_ of these things.

See **AGED SAGES; CLINICAL DEPRESSION**

ADULTERY — Perhaps the most painful betrayal of all betrayals, ultimately for *both* involved parties—the betrayer and the betrayed.

ADVERSITY — Often, the ultimate test of one's integrity.

Adversity is a condition marked by misfortune and calamity. It is in adversity that we discover who we really are. We also discover who our *friends* really are. <u>Old Men</u> who have suffered adversity in any form know that it's a circumstance which sorely tries the sufferer's friends. As *false* friends disappear during adverse times, *true* friends remain *regardless*—and they remain for the duration of their days on the planet. Adversity, as the Aged Sage Mark Twain once said, is also a condition that one can learn fairly easily to endure—as long as it is *someone <u>else's</u>*.

See **AGED SAGES; INTEGRITY; <u>Old Men</u>; <u>Old Women</u>; WISE OLD WOMEN (W.O.W.)**

ADVICE — Something that <u>Old Men</u> like Your Auld Author give liberally, as it is usually of no (immediate) monetary value.

We old dudes also recognize that our advice isn't always received in the spirit in which it is given, and those who need it the most generally welcome it the least. We further recognize that in the rare instance someone gives advice to *us* at our advanced age, it is ordinarily of little use to us, so we simply and sagaciously pass it on like a hot potato as quickly as we can.

AFGHANISTAN — At this writing, a bottomless sinkhole for U.S. troops.

See **IRAQ WAR**

AGAPE (*uh-GOPP-ay; noun*) — The love that is ready to go to *any length* to restore <u>community</u>.

(The word *agape* isn't used here in the *adjectival* sense of having one's *mouth wide open*, which even most *Republicans* know is pronounced *uh-GAYPE*.) To quote the Reverend Martin Luther King, Jr.: "We can learn the practical meaning of *agape* (*uh-GOPP-ay*) from the young folks who joined the civil rights movement, putting middle-class values of wealth and careers in second place and donning overalls to work in the isolated rural South because they felt the need for more direct ways of learning that would strengthen both society and themselves." Amen.

See **GIANTS**

AGED SAGES (AY-*jid* SAY-*Jiz*) — <u>Old Men</u> (and <u>Old Women</u>) *capitalized*— those righteous souls who by virtue of their hard-earned *learnings* and painfully-won wisdom merit the august appellation *Aged Sage*.

This is in contrast with mere "old men" (and "old women") *not capitalized*, as defined by this undauntedly <u>Denotative</u> *Dictionary*. If you, gentle reader, aren't an *Aged Sage* already, you hopefully may *become* one, should you live *long* enough, *intuitively* enough, and <u>*righteously*</u> enough—and I have to confess here that this is equally true even if you're (gasp!) a *Republican*.

Former national ACLU legal director john powell, who uses no capital letters in his name, is a man that this writer sees as the perfect proto-type of a contemporary Aged Sage. (No, on second thought, he's a <u>*non*</u>-prototypical Aged Sage—because he is too *rare and unique* to *proto-typify* <u>*anything*</u>.) The most purely brilliant student Your Old Author ever taught, this tall, gaunt, gray-bearded Sage founded the National Institute for the Study of Race and Poverty at the University of Minnesota Law School. At this writing, he directs the Kirwan Institute for the Study of Race and Ethnicity at the Ohio State University and consults worldwide.

In a perfect universe, the soft-spoken, ascetic, vegetarian powell—a former Harvard professor—would be or become a Justice of the United States Supreme Court. (Are you reading this, President Obama?)

See **FEDERATED REGIONALISM; john powell; OBAMA; <u>Old Men</u>; <u>Old Women</u>**

AGEISM — The practice of *age discrimination*.

This form of prejudice against us old fellows has blessedly become illegal in the United States, yet it nonetheless remains insidiously omni-present in too many corporate, municipal, and academic venues.

To employ the aged is often to obtain invaluable knowledge and even more priceless wisdom. Unfortunately in this regard, too many shortsighted, "modern," and still-wet-behind-the-ears employers can't see beyond the end of their *neoteric noses*. (Republicans, check your *Webster's*—and remember: "n" comes after "m" but before "o.". . .)

AGNOSTIC — Someone who honestly and sincerely doesn't profess to know what some charlatan "Christian" preachers *pretend* to know—and what some ignorant (or blindly faithful) folks are so <u>sure</u> of.

AIN'T — There *ain't no such word as <u>ain't</u>, so it ain't* going to be used (much) in this here rootin', tootin', high-fallutin' tome.

AKASHA — A Sanskrit word meaning *sky, space,* or *aether (ether, the ethereal)*.

A very few really *old* <u>Old Men</u> compellingly claim to have meta-physically divined that there exists a mysterious information source called the "Akashic Records" situated in an *astral realm* where all ancient information about our contemporary selves, our past lives, our immediate futures, our future lives, and even untold generations upon generations of our (current) corporeal genetic history is to be found.

As we struggle to survive the storm of life's continuing crises, these very few old, *old* Aged Sages indicate that they can teach some rare Chosen Ones how to access the Akashic Records and use them to help put the pieces of our past back together and thus *strengthen* ourselves immeasurably.

Note: Your Auld Author fears that these really old, *old* Aged Sages have conceivably become less *Sagacious* and in fact have instead become either senile, crazy, or addicted to loco weed and Captain Morgan's Spiced Rum. (Then again, could it somehow be fascinat-ingly conceivable that maybe they're actually <u>on</u> to something that truly *does* delve beyond the physical and the corporeal? What do <u>you</u> think?)

See **AGED SAGES; The "ANCIENT WISDOMS";** *AULD*

AL GORE — A man who actually was duly and truly elected and should have become President of the United States.

Al Gore is also a prescient male *Cassandra* for environmentalism. Repubs, you may (or may not) want to check out Cassandra under *Greek Mythology* in your encyclopedia (if you've got one).

See **CLARENCE THOMAS; JOHN KERRY;** The **OZONE LAYER; REPUB**

"The Two **ALBERTS**" — "The Two Alberts" are a couple of visionary (and long-gone-to-glory) Aged Sages named "Albert"—Einstein and life-saving doctor in-Africa Schweitzer. They came and come very close to epitomizing the Platonic ideals this too-terrestrial tome is (partially) about.

An incisive Schweitzer quote: "A heavy guilt rests upon us for what the whites of all nations have done to the colored peoples. When we do good to them, it is not benevolence—it is *atonement*."

A very *scary* Einstein quote: "I know not with what weapons World War III will be fought, but World War IV will be fought with sticks and stones."

Walter Isaacson noted in a landmark *Time* magazine article (July 17, 2006) that Nobel Laureate quantum mechanics pioneer Paul Dirac has proclaimed Einstein's Theory of Relativity to be *the greatest scientific discovery ever made*.

Schweitzer, Einstein's contemporary and one-time countryman, dedicated his life and his heart to the health and well-being of his blood-brothers and sisters who peopled the so-called "Dark Continent."

See **GIANTS; VISIONARY** (*noun*)

ALCOHOL — Something which Old Men (and Old Women) know that guzzling *too much of* can drown your life, via your *liver*.

Alcohol can also destroy your marriage, your pocketbook, and your peace of mind—not to mention your life and the lives of your family.

See **CLINICAL DEPRESSION**

ALI — A world-renowned Aged Sage (born Cassius Marcellus Clay in Louisville, Kentucky in 1942).

Most Old Men (save a fast-dwindling few still alive who saw the fearsome "Manassa Mauler" chop down the six-and-a-half-foot Texan Jess Willard) recognize Ali as the greatest of the heavyweight boxing champions and the second-best prizefighter, pound-for-pound, of all time.

In a memorably funny episode that nearly created an international incident, Ali warned reporters who picked George Foreman to win their 1974 Zaire title fight that the African nation's dictator Joseph Mobutu Sese Seko would "cook them in a pot and eat them." The government of Zaire (previously known as the Congo and now known as the Democratic Republic of Congo) sent an unhappy telegram to Ali's camp that went something like this: "Please ask Mr. Ali to desist from calling us cannibals. We are not cannibals—and Mr. Ali's remarks are hurting our image in our efforts to promote international trade."

Aged Sage Ali (Muhammad Ali) was far more than a champion boxer. He sacrificed his best years in the ring for opposing an immoral war. He was in his heyday and remains today a world ambassador for peace. It is ironic that he made war in the world's second-most violent and barbaric sport (cage fighting now being the first).

See **CAGE FIGHTING; "MANASSA MAULER"; SUGAR RAY ROBINSON**

ALTRUISM — The comparatively rare practice of putting the welfare of others before one's own.

See **GIVE, GIVING**

AMERICAN REVOLUTION II — An impending insurgency for which Old Men know there exists a clear and present need—but, this time (hopefully) without bloodshed.

This revolution should comprise a coalition of young and old Hispanics, blacks, Arabs, Asian-Americans, Native Americans, blue-collar whites, and long-term laid-off white-collar whites that must mobilize under the miraculously elected non-white President Barack Obama (who now has emerged as did George Washington, Abraham Lincoln, Martin Luther King, Jr., and Franklin Roosevelt when needed). It must take the country back from the banks and the multi-national, warmongering corporate czars—as Teddy Roosevelt once did and as Robert F. Kennedy would have done had he survived the assassin's bullet.

See **LIBERTARIAN; MALCOLM; OBAMA; ROBERT F. KENNEDY**

ANAL SEX — Sex that doesn't produce any *offspring* (except perhaps an occasional lawyer or lobbyist of the Republican persuasion).

The **ANCIENT CALEDONIAN CODE** — An explicitly honorable—and, in parts, *draconian*—dictum.

This Code has been passed down through the dark Celtic centuries by some descendants of Scotland's liberator Robert "The Bruce" and his followers to their infinite great-grandsons, to wit: "Never strike a female. Never cheat or steal. Keep your hands off another man's woman. Apologize when appropriate and admit when you're wrong. Defend your family and your clan, and apply the sword to avenge any slur (unless it be perpetrated by a woman). Protect women, children, animals, the elderly, the helpless, and the feeble of mind and body—and judge and value all men by their *deeds alone*."

See **ROBERT "THE BRUCE"**

The **"ANCIENT WISDOMS"** — Sagacious and cautionary dicta that are almost completely lost now beneath the dark shade of time, born and evolved of the sacred sciences of the distant past.

In every age, throughout every level of physical knowledge and of theosophy, an educated minority of all civilizations has endeavored faithfully to preserve the core remnants and echoes of *one identical system* and its fundamental traditions. Thus, many streams of the same water had a common course from which they emanated. Also, as the antediluvian ancestors of the elephant and the lizard were the mammoth and the plesiosaurus, so—according to the "ancient wisdoms"—were the progenitors of humankind the "giants" of The Veda and the Book of Genesis.

See The **"EYE OF OSIRIS"**; The **VEDA**

See also the three volumes of *The Secret Doctrine* written in England in 1888 by H. P. Blavatsky (a woman), and reprinted by Theosophical University Press, Pasadena, California, 1974.

ANGER — A *vengeful* and often *disorienting* passion.

One of President John F. Kennedy's least-quoted but perhaps most-applied advisements was, "Don't get *mad*—get *even*." (Or as Aged Sage Publilius Syrus said in his two-millennia-old *Maxims*, "Don't *wish* ill for your enemy—*plan* it.")

Old Men know to apply anger *prudently* and *selectively*. If a man wrongs you, it's sometimes best for the sake of your blood pressure (and perhaps the *retention* of much of your blood) to shrug it off rather than get mad *or* try to get even: If a man wrongs you in an *illegal* way, don't get mad, but do get even by relying on those who uphold the law to do their work.

However, a *caveat*: If someone, say, *molests your grandchild*, you're not just going to "get mad"—you're going to get *foaming-at-the-mouth enraged*. You will then want to get *even* via a practice-proven old Motown method that was perfected on Detroit's East and Near West Sides called "BAMN"—By Any Means Necessary. Just be prepared to sacrifice 'x' amount of *blood* (and/or of time in an *incarcerative environment*).

ANIMAL "HUSBANDRY" — A process practiced (in this definitive example, without a "husband's license") by one Rodell Vereen, age fifty, a southern gentleman in Longs, South Carolina in the year 2009.

Mr. Vereen was caught on a surveillance camera having sex with someone else's *horse*. A Longs homeowner bought the camera to prove someone was having sex with Sugar, her twenty-one-year-old mare. The video helped authorities charge Vereen—who already had been convicted of having sex *with the same horse* once before— with buggery. Perhaps he pathologically believed he was *married* to the horse, or he was just trying to find a new way to *ride*. (I *swear* I'm not making this up.)

See **BUGGERY; "STRANGELY BELIEVE IT"**

ANOMIE — A sociological term and psychological condition that means "a feeling of rootlessness, of *non-belonging*."

Old Men like Your Auld Author who have experienced this feeling with some frequency report that it is worse even than *loneliness*. Modern American society, with its proliferation of divorces, extreme geographic mobility, growing economic and political instability, and nuclear families fractured by time and space, foments an abject state of *anomie* in many increasingly isolated individuals to the extent that no other society has historically done.

A byproduct (or perhaps an *agent*) of this condition is the fact that since the 1970s, houses have been constructed with back "porches" (decks) but no *front* porches facing the street. Thus, the residents no longer can greet their neighbors and interface with passersby.

Anomie is a largely unrecognized cause of suicide.

See **AULD; CLINICAL DEPRESSION; LONELINESS**

ANONYMOUS (abbreviated Anon.; a.k.a. "A. Nonni Mouse") — An appellation and derivation that Old Authors like Yours Truly often affix to *purplish poetry* we hesitate to acknowledge publicly as ours.

The reason for our hesitation is our fear that it might be disdained by the same stripe of effete professorial pseudo-aesthete in some university English department who may (or may not) *also* deign to venture what could possibly be a *scornful* peek at, for example, these very same pyrogenic pages you seekers of truth and beauty are presently perusing with what Your Auld Author fondly hopes is utterly breathless attention.

See A (*NON*)-**POETIC PARODY**

ANSWER to *BOTH* of the PHILOSOPHICAL QUESTIONS POSED BY THE Old Man ON THE MOUNTAINTOP — Demonstrably, evidentially, historically, and *realistically*, the answer to *both* of these questions is, *ta-DA!*:

The three Kennedy brothers; presidents Jefferson, FDR, Eisenhower, and Clinton; Martin Luther King, Jr.; presidential hopefuls Gary Hart, Jesse Jackson, and Rudy Giuliani; governors Eliot Spitzer and Mark Sanford; Prince Charles; David Letterman; basketball stars Magic Johnson and Kobe Bryant (to name just two); boxers Muhammad Ali,

Joe Louis, Sugar Ray Robinson, Evander Holyfield, and Mike Tyson; former Detroit mayor Kwame Kilpatrick; and more actors, entertainers, and baseball and football players than you can name—plus billions of other men (and a growing number of women), young, old and Old—both undiscovered and _uncovered_!

The moral here _may_ be that _all_ (or most? Or many? Or some? Or a few?) _men_ are, in essense, _dogs_. Arf!

See The **PHILOSOPHICAL QUESTIONS POSED BY THE OLD MAN ON THE MOUNTAINTOP**

ANTHROPOLOGY — A brave and still nearly _new_ science that must _ever_ dodge the insidious trap of _ethnocentrism_.

See **HISTORY**

ANTI-REBEL — Someone—usually in a high position or of inordinate wealth —who protects a suppressive status-quo and his own socially exploitive self-interest.

Aged Sages have many a scar to show from battles with _anti-rebels_. Curiously, the anti-rebel sometimes starts out as a rebel or revolutionary before he attains power—as did Napoleon, Fidel Castro, and the early liberal Democrat version of Ronald Reagan. This is seldom true, how-ever, of a high-ranking anti-rebel within a bureaucracy such as a large local municipality or public school system. As often as not, he/she rose by making no waves and chortling fawningly at his/her super-ordinates' puerile jokes.

The motto of many an anti-rebel (and _non-rebel_) is, "The chief cause of problems is _solutions_." (Think about it.)

See **BUREAUCRAT; JACKAL; NON-REBEL**

ANUS (_descriptive noun_) — The opening at the lower end of the alimentary canal in humans and other animals.

Note: This noun is also often used in a pejoratively descriptive sense.

See **A--H---; GEORGE W. BUSH; URANUS**

APOCALYPSE — See **HYDROGEN BOMB; A *RIDDLE TO PONDER***

ARROGANCE (*noun*) — Overbearing, supercilious pride.

Actually, this <u>Old Man</u> here whut hev writ this tantalizing tome ain't really too *arrogant*—he know his big ol' butt get red just like Rush Limbaugh's and every other white man's when he sit on the commode too long. He's just simply aware that he's truly great—which is what God made him to be.

God—or, if you will, the Eternal Presence—created all of you to be great, too, whether you're black, white, or brown—but most of you are still in the slow, painful process of coming to understand that She/He/It endowed you with the potential to become great and undertake direct action to fulfill your greatness. The fine actress Natalie Wood, the great musical artist Wolfgang Amadeus Mozart, and the great pugilistic artist Muhammad Ali number among the rare souls who recognized their own greatness when they were virtually just children and they acted upon that rare self-recognition. It takes most of us far longer to recognize our greatness and then act on it. Tragically, some of us *never* do.

See **AUTHOR OF THE *LANDMARK*—AND INCREDIBLY *BRILLIANT*— DEFINITIVE DICTIONARY AND ALMANAC OF ADVICE** ENTITLED *WHAT* <u>*Old Men*</u> *KNOW!*

See also **GREAT; PRIDE; *YOU***

ART, MUSIC, ATHLETICS, AND VOCATIONAL PROGRAMS — Curricular and co-curricular offerings that are being cut or curtailed in urban high schools throughout the country.

This is unfortunate, because <u>Old Men</u> know that these are the very offerings that prevent kids from dropping out and give them a greater sense of accomplishment and self-esteem.

ARTHRITIS — Or in the rustic Old Redd Foxxian/Old Fred Sanfordian dialectical pronunciation: *Arthur Ritis*.

See **ATHLETICS**

A-- H--- — An obscene pejorative.

You puzzled Re*puzzled*can a-- h---s might wish to spend an hour or two playing the game of trying to unscramble the missing letters which I have *gamely* (pun intended) *scrambled* for you here: "s," "o," "s," "l," and "e."

See **ANUS; FUNDAMENT; GEORGE W. BUSH; RE*PUZZLED*CAN**

ASSIGNED SEAT — Something that no self-respecting rebel would ever *sit* in.

Does the *eagle in the sky* have an *assigned seat*? (This is a question that Detroit Pershing High School counselor David Clifford rhetorically asked me and my precocious colleague Wayne Dyer in 1966 when a student who had refused to sit in his assigned seat was sent to him for disciplining.)

See **REBEL** *(noun)*

ATHLETICS (sometimes ingenuously mispronounced with an additional syllable; *i.e.,* "ATH-uh-LET-ics" by some old jocks, coaches, sports announcers, Republican ex-presidents, and other assorted barbarians) — *Sports* such as running, boxing, bull-riding, rowing, etc.

Old Men know *viscerally* and to the bone that many forms of "ATH-uh-LET-ics" are endeavors which would in an arthur-ritic old ATH-uh-lete's younger years have been better avoided for the health and comfort of the old bugger's *back*—not to mention his knees, hips, ankles, shoulders, and other still-moveable parts. This is most particularly so with regard to boxing, wrestling, cage-fighting, bull-riding, hockey, pole vaulting, sprinting (particularly around tight turns), hurdling, dirt-bike racing, and/or any level of football above Little League.

See **FLAT ON YOUR BACK IN INCREDIBLE PAIN; PROSTRATE** *(adjective)*

ATLANTIS — According to legend, a now long-submerged island in the Atlantic Ocean so named by the ancient Aged Sage and philosopher Plato.

Atlantis may also have been the comparatively tiny tip of what some ancient historians claimed to have once been a vast continent. Atlantis could actually now be known to have been the first recorded human historical land, *had the traditions of the ancients received more inscribed attention than they have received heretofore.* Since the storied submerging of Atlantis, the face of the earth has radically transformed. There was a time when the delta of the Nile and the entire North African shore were part of Europe. This was before the formation of the Straits of Gibraltar and a further upheaval of the continent reconfigured the map of Europe. The most recent such upheaval occurred 12,000 years ago and was followed by the submersion of the peak of that continent, which may have remained for a few centuries longer in the form of Plato's storied island in the Atlantic.

ATMAN — What Hindus call the *Individual Soul.*

They also call it the "World Soul"—from which they say *all* Individual souls derive, and to which those souls are said to return, in congruence with the Eternal Presence's supreme goal for human existence.

ATTICA — A "correctional" facility in the eastern United States where a bloody prisoner revolt against unjust incarcerative conditions occurred nearly five decades ago.

Similar conditions still proliferate today in many prisons throughout America, which is building many more prisons. Since 1985, more than forty new prisons have been built in Michigan alone. The incarceration of *African-Americans* is a thriving industry. Most of the two *million* prisoners in this country are disproportionately black.

Attica is also the name of a region that was near ancient Athens, in southeastern Greece.

See **THESEUS**

"AUCTION BLOCKS AND JIM CROW" — These have metamorphosed into "cell blocks and death row," but the injustices remain.

The **"AUGUST APPELLATION"** — (no, Repubs—this isn't some form of appeal filed in the month of August—xyW [check your *Webster's*]. Good *try*, though)

The "August Appellation" is a distinguished title that this publication reverently (albeit in its Supremely Sagacious Septuagenarian Author's case, *immodestly*) confers upon Aged Sages.

See **AGED SAGES**

AULD — Dialect and Scottish for "old," as in the Scot poet Robbie Burns' classic song-poem "Auld Lang Syne" ("old long since"), which maudlin hordes of habitual over-imbibers are wont to caterwaul off-key every New Year's Eve.

See **CALEDONIANS; HIBERNIAN; IMBIBERS; IRISHMEN; "LIKE TO FIGHT"; SCOTS** (*noun*)

AULD CELT, AULD CELT'S PULSE — *See* **BAGPIPES**

AUTHOR OF THE *LANDMARK*—AND INCREDIBLY *BRILLIANT*—*DEFINITIVE DICTIONARY AND ALMANAC OF ADVICE* ENTITLED *WHAT Old Men KNOW* (a.k.a. "Your Auld Author") — *See* **ARROGANCE (*noun*); **AULD**; **GENIUS; YOUR AULD, *AULD AUTHOR***

AUTOCRAT — An overt or incipient fascist—and invariably, an *anti-rebel*.

See **ANTI-REBEL; FASCISM**

B

"BABY BOOMERS" — *See The* **"ME" GENERATION**

BACK (as in *spine*—or *spine* *supine*) — The part of the human physionomy that makes chiropractors wealthy. (<u>Old Men</u> know that a *good chiropractor* is worth double his weight in diamonds—and *triple* it if he takes midnight calls.)

> *See* **ATHLETICS; FLAT ON YOUR BACK IN INCREDIBLE PAIN; PROSTRATE** (*adjective*)

BAD BOOKS — Books that are widely read.

> *See* **SARAH PALIN**

BAD BOY — Someone *craved* by *good girls* (often even by *smart* good girls—go *figure*).

BAD MARRIAGE — An element or semblance of *pure hell on earth*. (Life is far, *far* too short to stay in a bad marriage for long.)

> *See* **HELL**

BAGPIPES — An ancient Celtic musical wind instrument whose shrill keening makes an *auld* Celt's pulse beat hard in his ears.

It also sets his eyes to darting wildly around seeking to snatch up a *sword*.

See The **ANCIENT CALEDONIAN CODE; *AULD*; *AULD* CELT, *AULD* CELT'S *PULSE*; IRISHMEN; "LADIES FROM HADES"; SCOTS** (*noun*)

BALANCE (*noun*) — A certain *psychic* perfection.

With *balance* comes *peace*; with peace comes power.

See **PEACE WITH *JUSTICE***

BALLS (*noun*) — *See* **COJONES**

"BAMN" — "By any means necessary."

See **NICCOLÒ MACHIAVELLI**

BANK BAILOUT OF 2008 — *See* **GEORGE W. BUSH**

BARBARISM — Brutal, cruel, or crude human conduct or conditions.

Example: Shooting a deer's jaw off and watching the terrified animal flee out of sight to die in agony 380 meters away in the brush.

See **BULLFIGHTING; CAGE FIGHTING; COCKFIGHTING; DOG FIGHTING; *REX REBORN*; WAR**

See also **PICTURES OF BULLFIGHTERS PAINTED ON VELVET; PICTURES OF ELVIS PAINTED ON VELVET**

The **BARD** — The one and only William Shakespeare, as immortal an Aged Sage as ever there was.

Shakespeare was the greatest playwright of all time. Enough said?

BASKETBALL — A game old men should never play (particularly *full court*).

Ditto tennis. Ditto flag football. Your Auld Author well-advisedly stopped playing flag football when he was a mere (but *maturing*) boy of fifty-eight.

See **HEART ATTACK; KNEES**

BEARDS — Tawny tufts of chin-whiskers that will inevitably go gray or white —unless <u>Old Men</u> dye them—or shave them.

We <u>Old Men</u> know this well, after having muddled through five or six gradual whisker-whitening decades on this unforgiving planet. If you're one of us old gents who—like Your Auld Author—are too lazy to shave and also choose to color your white whiskers, it's good to leave just a teeny little whitish patch for authenticity. Also, the wisp of white will make you look distinguished and even give you a (hopefully deserved) aura of wisdom.

Your Old Author's nubile young spouse says I shouldn't tell anyone I dye my beard, but it is indeed what I do and did so I can and could appear younger than my seventy-four-plus years on the cover of this enlightened and enlightening labor of love. (Still, since this book offers some three hundred pages' worth of pure pearls regarding what this particular <u>Old Man</u> knows, maybe this particular <u>Old Man</u> should let his beard go completely white to look even older?? I'll have to give it some thought. What do you think?)

"BEAST WITH TWO BACKS" — A medievalism.

See **SEX**

"BEAVER SHOT!" — No, Repubs—this isn't a newspaper headline about the rustic murder of an unfortunate beaver, or of someone <u>named</u> "Beaver." Actually, the teacher of a rambunctious teen named Denny Rooney sent him to me for exclaiming "Beaver Shot!" out loud when he was trying to look up girls' skirts. At the time (1969), I was an assistant high school principal in Walled Lake, Michigan.

See **"CRUDE AND LEWD"; IMMATURITY**

BEAVIS — See **BUTT-HEAD; RICHARD CHENEY**

BEDTIME FOR BONZO — Title of a film about the teaming of one of America's later-to-become top two elected office-holders with a <u>chimp</u>.

And *no*—the teamed official wasn't Republican Vice President Dick Cheney (although one could understandably—albeit mistakenly—*assume* so, since in many quarters his elected "teammate" has been *likened* to that specific anthropoid ape, intellectually). It actually was Republican President and ex-actor Ronald Reagan, toward the end of his career in Hollywood.

See **BONZO; CHIMP; DICK CHENEY; GEORGE W. BUSH; RICHARD CHENEY**

BEEHIVE — Something *never* to fall asleep beside.

BEER — A potent potable tragically presumed to be *absent* in the here-after.

As a popular polka lyric goes, "In heaven, there *is* no beer—that's why we drink it *here*." Or, as my buddy Wally has been heard to exclaim, in outraged tones: "What, no *beer*?" The late George Carlin—a white-bearded Irish American with a Scots name—opined that every *freeway* should have a "beer lane."

On or off the freeway, round-bellied old guys like Wally and me absolutely *revere* beer. We know a cold one in Detroit in July is refresh-ing. We also know a *lukewarm* one in London in August *ain't*—and too many six-packs at one sitting, cold or not, are bad for an old guy's waistline and other deeper-in parts of his aging anatomy.

See **ALCOHOL; PROSTATE** (*noun*) (also—again ingenuously—pronounced prostrate by the same incisive souls referenced in the "ATH-uh-LET-ics" item)

BETRAYAL — An act that—sooner or later—harms the *betrayer* as much or more than it does the *betrayed*.

Adultery is a prime example.

See **ADULTERY**

BETTY GRABLE — *See* **MILLION-DOLLAR LEGS**

BILL CLINTON — A man whom history will judge to be one of our better presidents, despite the Third Estate's still ongoing mewlings about Monica Lewinsky, *et al.*—*ad infinitum*.

BILL OF RIGHTS — Something President Barack Obama is going to need to restore and defend.

BILL OF WRONGS — Quasi-imaginary document with *not*-so-imaginary *results* fashioned by the Bush-*Minor* administration.

See **BILL OF RIGHTS**

"BIRD" — Something given in a gesture of derision (the hand brandished high with the middle finger extended).

Also, the shortened nickname of Charlie ("Yardbird") Parker, one of the greatest jazz musicians of the twentieth century.

Also, the *surname* (Repubs, xyW) of one of the greatest non-black basketball players who ever lived (hint for some dim-bulb Repubs: his first name is *Larry*).

See **"QUAIL"; "xyW"**

BIRTHDAY — Something the late, great comedian Jack Benny stopped having at thirty-nine.

If you can still count birthdays after owning up to having attained the Biblical three-score and ten *and then* some—as Ol' Jack did in private life—<u>Old Men</u> know that you'd better count your blessings, as well.

A birthday thankfully <u>*comes*</u> but once a year—except for those born on February 29. (So too do many Republicans <u>*come*</u> but once a year —particularly <u>*female*</u> Republicans (unless their men are *Democrats*). Aren't you glad you're not a birthday—or a female Republican?)

See **COME** (*verb*)

The **"BLACK ARTS"** — Evil magic, "black" magic.

It is intriguing from a psychologically subconscious *racial* perspective to note that "bad" things are designated as "black"; e.g., *black* magic, "the guy in the *black* hat," *Black* Bart, *black* witch, *black* heart, etc., and "good" things are designated as "white"; e.g., *white* magic, "the guy in the *white* hat," *white* witch, *White* Castle hamburgers (yum!), the *White* House, a "heart *as pure* white as the *driven snow*," etc.

(And of course *everyone* knows the *color* of the *Lone Ranger's* horse.)

See **"BLACK" WITCHCRAFT**

BLACK PANTHER PARTY — An organization of political and social revolutionaries.

Your audacious Auld Author brought the Panthers' representatives to the then-Macomb County Community College (now Macomb Community College) to speak in 1971 when I was the director of the Division of Basic Education there—and I did it against the wishes of the college's conservative president. (I brought in Jane Fonda, too.) Big trouble.

See **AULD**; **BLOODY LOWNDES**

BLACK REPUBLICAN — Simply, a *masochist*.

The black Republican is a growing—and genuinely *pathological*—anomaly.

The idea of any African-American—that is, any clear-thinking *middle-class* African-American—joining the twenty-first century Republican Party is nearly as enigmatically illogical as the oxymoronic concept of a *Jewish* Nazi. Ergo, *prominent* Black Republicans like Alan Keyes and Clarence Thomas in a certain sense almost appear to be a disturbingly throwback version of the collaborative Jewish *guards* in the German death camps of World War II.

See **JACKAL; LAPDOG; MASOCHIST; OXYMORON**

"BLACK" WITCHCRAFT — *See* **EVIL**

The **"BLAME GAME"** — Finding perpetual fault with one's family or friends rather than owning up (if pertinent) to one's causative role in their behavior.

Thosesadistic, insecure, self-hating, and unsympathetic souls who repeatedly play the "blame game," whether or not the blame is moderately *deserved*, find that to do so is far easier (and far *safer*) than offering understanding, empathy, and *forgiveness*—or better yet, offering thoughtful, genuine, and heartfelt praise.

BLAST-OFF!! — *See* **GRAND-DADDY** (alternative definition thereof)

"BLING," "BLING-BLING" — Urban slang terms for "expensive and flashy jewelry."

When "bling" is a gift to an initially *less*-than-ardent lady from a *much more*-than-ardent gentleman, it is also sometimes called "*female Viagra.*"

See **ELIZABETH TAYLOR**

BLONDES — Evolutionally, an endangered species, due to their recessive gene.

(*Natural* blondes are thus an endangered species.)

Also, the feminine version of the word consists of folks who don't necessarily *have more fun*, and who also aren't necessarily *dumb*.

BLOODY LOWNDES — A book by Hasan Kwame Jeffries that tells the remarkable story of the locals who transformed Lowndes County, Alabama from a citadel of white supremacy into the center of southern black militancy by creating an all-black, independent political party.

Google www.bloodylowndes.com

BOINK (*verb*) — Twenty-first century *hip-hop* slang for "copulate."

(*No*, Republicans, *copulate* doesn't mean that the policeman was advised that he arrived late. Check your *Webster's*, you dummies.)

The alert and involved elder born in this country before 1950 may or may not deem it worthwhile or necessary to learn what today has become nearly a new native tongue.

Twentieth century slang synonym: hump.

BONZO — *See* **CHIMP; GEORGE W. BUSH**

BORE (*noun*) — Someone who talks when you want him to listen.

BORROWER — Someone who sells his *freedom*. (You have to *reflect* on this one.)

BOXERS — Most *boxers* (the *men*, not the *shorts*) are *souls without artifice*.

Like the sprinters who physically resemble them, boxers' utterly self-dependent performance is on pitiless display in the arena, where they have no one to *team* with them or *throw a block* for them. They are men who are characteristically and utterly devoid of phoniness. Your Auld Author *reveres* boxers and *trusts* most of them, since my freedom-fighting, Scotland-born, coal-mining, Aged Sage father John "Scotty" Telford was one, God rest his fierce egalitarian soul.

BOYS — Male children: Young, wet-behind-the-ears not-yet-men.

A whole lot of *old men* are still *boys*, too, in the psychological sense. We've all heard this pejorative saying: "The only difference between men and boys is the price of their toys." Too many spoiled mama's boys never grow up; thus, their "boyhood" definitely does pay a second visit to some old men (uncapitalized) who never really matured emotionally (but their physical *youth* never pays them a second visit—at least, not in *this* life).

Also, Old Men (capitalized) may sometimes be boyish, and they still possess a sense of wonder that is *childlike*, but unlike some merely *old* men, they are never childish.

See **Old Men; old men**

BRAIN (*human*) — The most phenomenally miraculous product of evolution ever to grace (or _dis_grace or _deface_) the planet Earth.

Just as *lower animals'* brains have their limitations, so too does the *human* animal's brain. For example, our brains are unable to conceptualize *seven-dimensional space*, nor can we grasp intuitively why neural information-processing observed from the outside should give rise to *subjective* experience *on the inside* (nor indeed why we shouldn't keep trying to devise acceleratively ingenious ways to kill each other and also ravage our planet's ecology).

Alternate definition: A fairly common misspelling of "Brian" among some mis-educated high school students in urban America whose class sizes approached thirty-five when these sadly cheated little souls were inadequately taught to read and write in the first grade.

See **CONSCIOUSNESS**

BREAKING UP WITH A WIFE OR LOVER (*gerund phrase*) — A *hard* road.

Many old men have found the least difficult (and least *courageous*) way to do this is to let the *wives* or *lovers* do it. Still, perhaps it is the *kindest* way, as well.

BROTHERHOOD — The price, privilege, joy, and _condition_ of and _for_ mankind's ultimate survival.

BROTHERS — What all men—young and old—_are_ *under the skin*, although billions of us definitely haven't evolved sufficiently to _act_ like it yet (and *time is running out*).

BUGGERY — *See* **ANIMAL "HUSBANDRY"; "STRANGELY BELIEVE IT"**

BULLFIGHTING — *See* **BARBARISM**

BULLY (*noun*) — *See* **COWARD**

BUREAUCRACIES — Entities that are often amoral, *soulless*, and *virtually invisible*.

All Aged Sages whose creative initiatives have been historically thwarted by officious bureaucrats can agree unconditionally with this definition. Even governments and other large organizations that aren't expressly criminal can be basically *amoral*—essentially without a *soul*. Left unchecked, a bureaucracy will take on the characteristics of its leaders and become whatever they make it—and whatever its employees and others who interact with it allow it to become.

If, as often happens even in our still semi-democratic nation, a *governmental* bureaucracy that's supposed to be here to serve us and keep the "corporate cats" at bay becomes bloated, top-heavy, incompetent, and corrupt, and it demonstrates a lordly indifference to the lives of ordinary people—well, this country still purports to be a government by the *people*, right? So it's up to We the People to rebel and fix things, *first* via the ballot box—and, that *failing*—via a bloodless American Revolution II, and *that* failing, via a <u>bloody</u> American Revolution II, eighteenth-century-style.

(And *no*—this old first-generation Scottish-American here ain't really a radical revolutionary, unless our *Constitution* has become as radically revolutionary again now as it was perceived to be by the British Crown in 1776.)

Corporate bureaucracies often say they're here to "serve the people," so it *must ever be borne in mind* that of course this is <u>never</u> true. Corporate bureaucracies are basically here to <u>make money</u>, pure and simple.

So, too, have our *governmental* and *academic* bureaucracies and bureaucrats become *more about money, power, and perks* than they are about *serving the public*. In July 2010, United States Senator Bernie Sanders of Vermont correctly and courageously said, "While the middle class disappears and poverty increases, the wealthiest people in our country are not only doing extremely well—they are using their wealth and political power to protect and expand their privileged status at the expense of everyone else. They are hell-bent on destroying the democratic vision of a strong middle class which has made the United States the envy of the world." (Sounds like something Robert F. Kennedy would have said.) Senator Sanders also observed that the four hundred wealthiest American families are worth more than a *trillion* dollars and pay an effective tax rate of 16.6%—the lowest on record! Sanders wants to enact a graduated income tax (something Your Auld Author has long been calling for) on estates of more than $3.5 million. Normally, the plutocrats and perhaps some of the more myopic Teapartyers would cry "Socialism!" over the Senator's views, but in this case, they needn't, because indeed he already happens to be a professed Socialist—the *only* one in Congress. (If his views truly do represent *Socialism*, we'd better *capitalize* on them *quick!*)

When *We the People* do indeed ultimately rebel and fix things, we may still be able to exercise the options of doing it either from within or from outside the organization. A "Creative Insubordinate" who does manage to rise to a high position within a contemporary governmental or academic bureaucracy can indeed (oxymoronically!) become an *anti-bureaucracy* bureaucrat and fix things from *within*, as the intrepid Sen. Sanders endeavors to do.

See **AMERICAN REVOLUTION II; BUREAUCRAT; C.I.; CONSTITUTION OF THE UNITED STATES; "CORPORATE CATS";** The **OLD CRUSADER'S CREDO; OXYMORON**

BUREAUCRAT — Someone who puts mob *fealty* before the *common good*.

A bureaucrat also acts arbitrarily (and sometimes *vindictively*), is often grubbily engaged in doling out unearned pensions and collecting unjust taxes, lords his little corner of authority over anyone unfortunate enough to be in a subordinate or controlled position under him (or *her*), and would follow a *super*ordinate's typewritten directive to the letter even if its intent were distorted by a *typographical error*. Most bureaucrats would indeed make excellent Nazis, because they have fascistic hearts.

Old Men know that many governmental or academic bureaucrats aren't really there to govern or administrate. They're really there to a) loaf; b) issue asinine orders; c) *follow* asinine orders; or d) steal. And it goes without saying that no one enjoys being ripped off (unless he happens to be a harpaxophiliac).

The bureaucrat's motto is, "Never do *anything for the first time*."

See **FASCIST; HARPAXOPHILIAC; INCOMPETENCE; JACKAL; PETTY TYRANT; SCHMUCK; "YES-MAN"**

BUSH'S BRAIN — One of the few human brains in modern science that has been semi-miraculously discovered to be anatomically lodged in its owner's anal region.

Also, when in italics, a documentary about Karl Rove, G. W. Bush's erstwhile Svengali.

See **KARL ROVE**

BUTT-HEAD — *See* **BEAVIS; GEORGE W. BUSH**

"BY GOD, WE'LL FIGHT!" — Common table-pounding exclamation of balding, paunchy, old white wowzers in the United States Congress with under-the-table stock interests in armament-related or oil-related enterprises or who maintain cozy relationships with pertinent lobbyists— and who have no children or grandchildren likely to ever have to serve in the military in harm's way.

(This exclamation is also often uttered with regard to any Third World nation that demonstrates the incredible effrontery to aspire to anything approaching fair parity with us in the global marketplace.)

C

CAGE FIGHTING — A barbaric and disquieting throwback in contemporary Imperial *America* to the ancient gladiatorial arenas of ancient Imperial *Rome*.

Compared with and contrasted to the "Sweet Science" of *boxing*, the new professional "sport" of cage fighting is something more akin to a primitive form of *war* than to sport. (Incidentally, via this publication, I would like to tip off any cage fighter reading it that Rush Limbaugh and John Boehner [boner?] say they can lick any cage fighter who dares to accost them.)

See **BARBARISM**

See also **JOHN BOEHNER**

CALEDONIANS — *See* **SCOTS** (*noun*)

CANCER — The dreaded malady that almost every old man who lives long enough seems to *get*, or almost everyone he "came up" with—male or female—seems to *have*.

See **TOBACCO**

CAPITALISM AND ITS "HENNY PENNY" COROLLARY — The economic system that has a <u>basic precept</u> the "Henny Penny" Corollary.

The "Henny Penny" Corollary is, "If you *work*, you eat—if you <u>won't</u> work, you <u>don't</u> eat." (Henny Penny wanted to bake a cake, and she asked Turkey Lurky, Goosey Loosy, and Ducky Lucky to help her, but they all had things they would rather do, so Henny Penny famously baked the cake by herself. Then when Turkey Lurkey, Goosey Loosy, and Ducky Lucky sniffed the delectable aroma of baked cake, they all asked for a piece, believing it was their right to eat at least *some* of it, but Henny Penny didn't give them any.)

Despite its many instances of corruption and inequities, *capitalism*—with its mitigating *"Henny Penny" Corollary* still bravely functioning—did a good job of building modern America between the mid-nineteenth century and the mid-twentieth. By late in the twentieth century, however, the large multinational corporations' exploitative abuse of capitalism had contributed to the distribution of our country's wealth so profoundly *unequally* that now an inevitable second American Revolution indeed does loom on the immediate horizon if a means for reform isn't soon found and applied.

And it may be too late: Bush II's and the Halliburton Corporation's war with Iraq over oil that has cost obscene amounts of the taxpayers' treasure, coupled with Bush's bailout of the banks and sloppy monitorship of companies like British Petroleum, may prove to have been the "last straws."

The **CAPITOL BUILDING IN WASHINGTON, D.C.** — For the most part, an extraneous piece of real estate, many of whose parasitic familiars are non-contributive in any positive way to the commonweal.

In essence, they are non-functional except as the beneficiaries of lobbyists or as whores for corporations.

See **LOBBYIST**

CASTRATE — What certain female assistant superintendents in the Detroit Public Schools figuratively tried to do to strong male principals in the very recent past.

CATHETER — A medieval instrument of torture that is inserted with excruciating frequency into the minuscule private parts of some protesting old Republicans when they are hospitalized.

(Verily, that hellish implement felt as big as broomstick when it was also stuck inside the shrinking private part of a certain ornery old _Democrat_ who was suffering from kidney stones in the year 2007.)

See **KIDNEY STONES** (and pray you never get them)

CATS — Creative Insubordinates (C.I.s).

Did you ever get that supercilious "you can't be serious" look from a contemptuous cat that you tried to get to do tricks?

See **CREATIVE INSUBORDINATION; MOST** _DOGS; XERXES_

CAUTIONARY TALE — See **DRAGON**

CELIBACY — A state or condition that too often encroaches, persists, and prevails _immediately following marriage_.

In healthy adults, celibacy is an unwholesome, unhealthful, sadistic, masochistic, inhumane, and _inhuman_ state and circumstance. (Are you _hearing_ this across the big pond under that huge, pointy hat, Your Holiness?)

A crowning irony is that we call Catholic priests and mothers superior "father" and "mother" when they aren't legitimately allowed (biologically) to become _either_.

"CELL BLOCKS AND DEATH ROW" — See their causes and precursors, **"AUCTION BLOCKS AND JIM CROW"**

CEMETERY — An extraneous piece of real estate whose occupants are no longer contributive except as food for worms and maggots.

Some day all cemeteries except Arlington (and maybe Forest Lawn) may need to be converted to farmland. We could then, in actuality, end up eating what's left of our ancestors as the corn takes root. Remember the Charlton Heston film _Soylent Green_?

See The **CAPITOL BUILDING IN WASHINGTON, D.C.; DESERT** _(noun)_; **GOLF, GOLF COURSE; WORMS AND MAGGOTS**

CENSORSHIP — The *thief* of liberty.

The only truly dangerous word is the *suppressed* one, because then the only communicational door left open is for state-supported propaganda such as that written by Julius Streicher, the sole *non-military* Nazi hanged by the Allies after the Nuremberg Trials. Between 1923 and 1945, Streicher published *Der Stuermer* (*The Stormtrooper*) which implanted the spirit of anti-Semitism that did more than anything to pave the way for the Nazi death camps and led to the dehumanization and slaughter of millions.

See **DEMOCRACY; FASCISM; FREEDOM OF THE PRESS**

CERTAINTY — The only true certainty in <u>Old Men</u>'s (and <u>young</u> men's) lives is that sooner or later they will lose them.

See **"QUOD SUM ERIS"**

The **CHAMPION'S "<u>SUCCEED</u> CREED"** — "You aren't judged by the number of times you fail, but by the number of times you <u>succeed</u>."

<u>Old Men</u> who in their youth were champions know well this <u>Succeed</u> Creed. Muhammad Ali fought most of his first—and losing—fight with Ken Norton in excruciating pain after Norton broke his jaw early in the fight. Ali came back to beat Norton in a rematch, avenge a loss to Joe Frazier, and knock out George Foreman to regain the heavyweight championship. That's called following The Champion's "<u>Succeed</u> Creed". (It's also called a rare display of *cojones*.)

Please *memorize* this auxiliary <u>Succeed</u> Creed:

"The number of times you <u>succeed</u> is *directly proportionate* to the number of times you <u>fail</u> but <u>keep on trying</u>."

<u>Old Men</u> have come to learn that life is a *great grinding wheel*. Whether it wears you down or polishes you up depends on whether your *cojones* are made of *brass* or of *tinsel*.

See **COJONES**

CHANGE (*noun*), The **CHANGE** — *Change* is as certain as the coming of a comet. (*Shift* happens, right?)

Aged Sage john powell points out that even *mountains* *flow* (although they *flow* ever so *slowly*).

Actually, *you* can be *The* *Change*. It is *yours* to effect. As the rising young motivational speaker Jeff May exhorts, "If you *want* different, *do* different." Every day, recite this old saw to yourself: "If it is to *be*, it is up to *me*."

See **STATUS QUO**

CHAOS — The opposite of *order*, and the enemy of *thought*.

Also, *chaos* is the antithesis of *civilization*—which is *born* of *order*, *grows* and *thrives* with *liberty*, but with *chaos* perishes *utterly*. (According to the ancient Chinese commentator Kwoh P'oh, examining *primordial chaotic realms* in a work called *Shan-Hai-King, Wonders by Sea and Land*, transcribed by the historiographer Chung Ku from engravings on nine urns made by the Emperor Yyu [B.C. 2255], an interview is mentioned with men having *two distinct faces on the front and back of their heads* and with other monstrous creatures similarly formed and deformed "out of *chaos*."

P'oh reported that this work was compiled almost 3,000 years before his time [A.D. 276-325], at seven dynasties' distance from him, and fascinatingly, that these *chaotic* creatures had been imperfectly created to inhabit this primordial realm by an Eternal Presence *experimentally* and then *destroyed*—along with the realm—by the Presence shortly [in cosmic time] after having *created* the creatures, and created the *realm*.

(Actually, anything under the sun is *possible*—even *today*, we have *politicians* with *two distinct faces* on the *fronts* of their heads.)

CHARACTER — Contrary to common belief, *character* is a *character*istic that isn't *made* in a crisis—it is merely *demonstrated* in a crisis.

Phonies and the faint of heart may thrive in some endeavors; none win in the crucibles of (to cite *two* examples), a tough *prize fight*, or a wide-open *400-meter dash*—the race called the toughest in track, where the *tin* and the *chrome-plated* *melt*. (Paraphrased from the out-of-print *The Longest Dash—Track & Field News Press*, 1965 and

1971 [available on *Amazon* for $80], and quoted from again in *A Life on the RUN—Seeking and Safeguarding Social Justice*, Harmonie Park Press, 2010, pp. 108-9).

Those who possess *character* also by definition must possess *cojones*.

See **COJONES**

CHÉ — One of history's greatest revolutionaries (although he never lived long enough to become an Aged Sage).

Even the least insurrection-minded of contemporary Aged Sages generally respect Ché Guevara, ranking him right up there with the Scots' late thirteenth/early fourteenth century freedom fighter Sir William Wallace (who never lived to become one, either), the Thracian rebel slave Kirk Douglas—oops, I mean *Spartacus*—of the first century B.C.(he never got to become one either), the long-imprisoned and later-to-become South Africa president Nelson Mandela, the Revolutionary War general and later-to-become United States president George Washington, and India's martyr/liberator, the great Mahatma Gandhi.

Simón Bolívar (Bolivia is named for him), Mexico's Emiliano Zapata, and Haiti's Toussaint L'Ouverture and Jean Jacques Dessalines were four more rebels who didn't live to become Aged Sages. Revolutionaries often pay the ultimate price for their revolt early-on.

See **MALCOLM**

"The **CHECK'S IN THE MAIL**" — *Sure* it is. (Well, sometimes it really *is*, even if oftentimes it actually goes in the mailbox a day or two late—and a week after that, it *bounces*.)

See **DECEPTION**

CHEST HAIR — Something that some old men actually *dye*.

Most reasoning and reasonable Old Men know that to do this is *bad* form. It's even worse form to *shave* it (unless it's on your wife). Perming it isn't a good idea, either, or tying ribbons in it. (It's okay, though, ye merrie gentlemen, to shave your shoulder hair, back hair, and neck hair at *any* age—particularly if the neck hair is in the *front* of the neck. (If it's in the *back* of the neck, it's called a *mane*. Hi ho, Silver!)

We won't discuss *nose hair* here, except to say that a man grows *twelve feet* of nasal hair in his lifetime—eleven of it *seemingly* in his *eighth decade* on this earth, as is Your Auld Author. If the man happens to be a *Scot*, you can <u>double</u> that figure. (*See **AULD**)

CHILDREN — Grungy little gremlins who "should be seen and not heard."

(But <u>Old Men</u> know that sometimes it's good to listen to them anyway —and genuinely *hear* them.)

As <u>Old Men</u> drift ever closer toward that great divide of the ultimate *abyss*, we also find it somehow comforting to reflect that through our *children*, we gain a certain element of *immortality*.

CHIMP — *See* **BONZO; GEORGE W. BUSH**

CHINA — *See* The **"PEOPLE'S REPUBLIC" OF CHINA**

CHIP SALTSMAN — The 2009 candidate for the Republican National Committee Chairmanship who disgracefully distributed a dumb-ass CD to RNC members that featured the insulting tune, "Barack the Magic Negro."

See **A-- H---; IDIOT**

CHRIST — A hallowed word that means <u>teacher</u>.

Not only was Jesus Christ a Teacher, He was history's all-time greatest Social Activist, Revolutionary, and Fisher of Men. In *Romans 5:8*, we find that seminal precept wherein God proclaims that all of us miserable sinners are loved *unconditionally*, even at our *worst*.

This proclamation remains perhaps the most hope-filled Biblical passage ever penned, and seminal grist for the *greatest story ever told* (and I'm not talking about the *movie*).

See **SOCIAL ACTIVIST; TEACHER**

CHRISTMAS — A day when Christians and non-Christians alike buy cards and stuff for each other.

Also, a day when the relentless marketeers *particularly* ravish us. As ever in recorded (and undoubtedly _un_recorded) *history*, the money-men do indeed infest the temple.

C.I. — Abbreviation for Creative Insubordination, or for a Creative Insubordinate.

<u>Old Men</u>—those who are *"realio-trulio"* Aged Sages Supreme—learned early-on how to practice Creative Insubordination (C.I.) and be effective Creative Insubordinates (C.I.'s) when necessary.

A Creative Insubordinate is a *practitioner* of the noble art of Creative Insubordination—a "Real Righteous Rebel" ("RRR"). In addition to being history's greatest Social Activist and Revolutionary, the Biblical and historic Jesus was also of course the *ultimate* Creative Insubordinate. "He who offends the *least* of us offends also *me*" is a preachment which represents C.I. in its most admirable and timeless form. Mohandas Gandhi (the Mahatma) and the Rev. Martin Luther King, Jr. were other extremely effective practitioners of C.I.

In addition to practicing *righteous* Creatively Insubordinate *self-defense*, a Creative Insubordinate defends the <u>defenseless</u> (except when the defenseless ones in question have done evil deeds and have thus rendered themselves *indefensible* by the *righteous*).

See **CREATIVE INSUBORDINATION**

CIRCLING THE WAGONS AND THEN SHOOTING *IN* — What too many *Detroiters* have done *for too long*. (We Detroiters are often our own worst enemies.)

CIVILIZATION — An *advanced state and condition* of human society.

This *Dictionary* defines *"advanced state and condition"* as one in which a broad international level of methodological science, fine art and literature, peaceful and just governments, and general *civility* has been reached. Thus, a *true* *civilization* will be achieved only when *each citizen of the world* grants every single one of his fellow citizens *every single right* that he claims for himself, *bar none*, when *war* exists *no longer*, and when disputes are settled *civilly* and via *win-win compromise*.

See **RESOURCE-DRIVEN AND *TECHNOLOGY*-DRIVEN ECONOMIC SYSTEM; UTOPIA**

CLARENCE THOMAS — A man who holds the dubious distinction of having cast one of the deciding votes halting the Florida recount—and thus put George W. Bush in the White House.

Supreme Court "Justice" Thomas allegedly compared his private parts to those of Long Dong Silver for the clumsily attempted impressing of a law clerk he allegedly was harrassingly trying to boink. (If he was allegedly telling her the alleged truth regarding his alleged extended *endowment*, he possibly holds another alleged distinction—that of being the only *Republican* with that much alleged penile size.)

See **BOINK**

CLASSICAL MUSIC — The Aged Sage's liberating catharsis, and the *sublime* (if sometimes *subliminal*) *inspiration* of many young Sages-to-be.

CLASSISM — One of an interactive quartet of repressive "isms" that in the dawn of this third millennium has become as malevolent as *racism*.

(The others are *ageism* and sexism.)

Regardless of *culture* or *color*, Old Men know that all of the grass-roots workers of the world must awaken to the direly undemocratic threat of *classism* and unite to overturn it—*bloodlessly*, if possible, but *bloodily*, if not.

As that genius of *geniuses* Albert Einstein, one of the rarest of *all* Sages for the Ages, ultra-Sagaciously said, "The distinctions separating the *social* classes are entirely *false*; in the final analysis, they rest on *force*."

See **AGEISM; AMERICAN REVOLUTION II; FASCISM**

CLINICAL DEPRESSION — A state wherein the sufferer remains depressed and angry because the depression *itself* is the problem, or *psychosis*.

Left untreated (and unfortunately sometimes even *if* treated), the individual suffering from *clinical depression* will <u>create</u> a reason to be depressed despite friends' and loved ones' attempts to help. If *one* "depressing" element is removed, the individual will be all right (or even manically cheerful, often under the influence of drugs or alcohol) for a short time before seeking out and finding another *lesser* "issue" or "concern" to become depressed and angry about—no matter how trivial (to a normal person) that concern may appear to be.

Often the sufferers of *clinical depression* compulsively seek new adventures apart from family and loved ones in a fruitless attempt to "fulfill" themselves and escape feelings of psychic emptiness. Those suffering from this emotional disorder harbor a self-hatred or feeling of inadequacy that frequently was ingrained in childhood through parental abandonment or other severe trauma. Most tragically, in adulthood it manifests itself via a subconscious desire to *self-destruct* by alienating or destroying those they love and who love them and support them.

Ultimately, the sufferers of clinical depression *drive their closest* loved ones *away by punishing them with physical and/or verbal abuse, the "silent treatment," withholding sex (if the loved one is their mate— or conversely, sometimes their insecurities cause them to reverse their field and demand overwhelming <u>amounts</u> of sex), etc.* If the loved ones choose to stay and try to endure the abuse, they *destroy them physically and spiritually*—because by punishing their loved ones they *punish themselves,* which is their true but *subconscious* goal. Spouses who hang in and remain often sicken and die.

Unless the sufferer seeks treatment, and the treatment (often with medication) is successful, there are no winners here. Even the most resourceful of Aged Sages are powerless to help—particularly if the Sage in question happens unfortunately to be the *spouse* of the sufferer. (Sound familiar to anyone out there?)

Note: "*Situational*" depression—the normal and most common form of depression—can be eliminated by the *depressed person* by either <u>changing</u> or <u>leaving</u> the "situation."

See **ALCOHOL; "NORMAL"**

CLIT — Short for "clitoris," the tiny, nerve-rich female organ whose exact anatomical locus and precise physiological function are a *total mystery* to most male Republicans.

CLOWNS — Too many legislators whose locus of employment is our nation's capitol.

America's Aged Sages (we few *remaining*) recognize that the reason *circuses* are struggling to *survive* is because most of the clowns are working in *Washington, D.C.* And they're working for *lobbyists*— certainly not for *you*, dear readers. (But *you're* paying them.)

See **LOBBYIST**

COAL MINE — A death trap.

Many coal executives have been notorious for putting profits ahead of safety, thus causing countless mine disasters in the United States and United Kingdom within the past century. However, the miners themselves sometimes took risks they shouldn't have. My dad had to leave school at thirteen to go down with his father into the mines. He told the story of having discovered a shortcut he then frequently took from one tunnel to another through a narrow natural aperture which—had the surrounding rocks shifted only slightly—would have trapped him forever, and there would have been no Auld Author today to pen this transfixing tome and bug Republicans and other baboonish barbarians.

On his noontime break, Dad would eat the sandwich my grandmother had made for him and then doze for a few minutes on an empty potato sack he had laid across a thin board he had found. When a miner twice his weight and triple his age came off his shift, he would snatch my dad off his board and lie down on it himself. One day my dad drove a nail up through the board, covered it with the potato sack, and lay down on the board without touching the nail. The big miner came and snatched him off the board, flung himself down on it, yelped in pain, and shot instantly up and after my dad, who raced to an electrified wire that powered the coal carts and put his hand within inches of it. Knowing my dad would grab *it* if he grabbed *him*, and fearing the nasty shock, the big fellow left him alone after that.

CODGER — *See* **COOT** (as in "old coot")

COINCIDENCE — Something that is seldom truly *coincidental*.

A gorgeous little lady of the author's close acquaintance who had lost contact with her *mucho*-older (and at-the-time-*forbidden*) lover for nearly twenty years *just happened* to see his blackish old beard on a billboard, called the number listed on it, and resumed a fateful relationship that led to a bittersweet May-December marriage.

That's a true (and personal) story.

See **DESTINY; FATE**

COJONES (*Span.*) — *See* **BALLS** (*noun*); **CHARACTER;** The **Champion's** "**Succeed Creed**" —and (note to Repubs) decipher the definition of *cojones* from *context*

COLIN POWELL — The former general and Aged (Republican) Sage (an oxymoron?) who, like Saul of Tarsus, became "Paul" after experiencing an *epiphany*—a "vision on the road to Damascus," as it were—and switched his support to Democratic presidential candidate Barack Obama.

Powell's was the only voice of reason in the G. W. Bush Cabinet (wherefrom he ultimately, Sagaciously, and inevitably *resigned*).

COLLEGE ATHLETIC TEAM — The most exclusive fraternity (or sorority) of all.

COLORS, *DEFINED* — Black—The merciful (non)-color of the Shakespearean "*death's dateless night.*"

Blue – The rich, unclouded color of a *Michigan sky in autumn*. (And please keep in mind that blue is indeed a *color*—not a <u>condition</u>.) However, since the University of Michigan didn't offer Your Auld Author a track scholarship and he therefore spent his collegiate and post-collegiate track career taking revenge at a pace approaching ten yards per second (and sometimes exceeding it) on every Wolverine quarter-miler unfortunate enough to face him, he has seldom uttered

the words "Go Blue!" (except when his high school *athletes matric-
ulated there, or when a certain national championship **football
coach—his protégé—was *coaching* there).

Brown – The *warmest* color.

Green – The color for a *preferred future* (flush in the face of British
Petroleum and Standard Oil).

Orange – The color for which there is *no rhyming word*.

Purple – The color of *poetry* and *flowery prose*.

Red – The color of *rrrevolution*!

White – The (*non*)-color of corporeally unattainable *purity* gone mor-
dantly _gray_—absolute _white_ being nonexistent in the physical world
(and absolute *purity* being *non*existent in the *corporate* world).

Yellow – The color of the sweet sunlight that kisses this <u>Old Man</u>'s grandchildren and grows them. (Yellow is too pretty a color to call it the
color of *urine*—or of *cowards*.)

A bit of *trivia*: The *athletes were sprinter *Glenn Doughty* (later a
Baltimore Colts All-Pro receiver), quarter-mile star *Reggie Bradford*,
and star high jumper and basketball forward *Jon Lockard*; the **coach
was National and Rose Bowl championship coach *Lloyd Carr*.

COME (*verb*) — To arrive at a place thought of as "there" and "then" to
a place thought of as "here" and "now."

Alternate definition: A physical *cataclysm* called _orgasm_ ("OR-gazzum")
that most older male affiliates of the superbly sexy Democratic party
can generally generate in a female partner far better than can younger
men, whatever their party affiliation. (Practice makes perfect: experience is indeed good for many things!)

See **GRAND-DADDY**

COMMON SENSE — An <u>un</u>common trait in too many of us two-legged,
talkety-talking, tool-making, taser-wielding, *bomb*-exploding, sophis-
ticatedly *mass-murderous* species sometimes notoriously known as
Homo Sapiens.

(Note to Repubs and other assorted barbarians: No homosexual or homo-erotic jokes here, please.)

See **BARBARISM; REPUB**

COMMUNISM — A political system that sought to have all men benefit equally from the world's wealth and bounty.

Communism was corrupted by the Soviets and the Red Chinese into a form of fascism.

See **FASCISM; PSEUDO-COMMUNISM;** *RESOURCE*-**DRIVEN AND** *TECHNOLOGY*-**DRIVEN ECONOMIC SYSTEM; SOCIALISM**

COMPLEX PROBLEM — A problem that has a *simple solution* that is *wrong*.

COMPLIMENT — If a man tactfully tells his woman there's no other woman *like* her, he won't be lying (even if she's ugly)—and she'll undoubtedly be pleased to have been so "complimented."

Everyone loves to get *compliments*, of course—*especially* including your 'umble Auld Author—except that he always gets *embarrassed*, being of the (*usually* unvoiced) opinion that those who complimented him should have said *much more*.

See **ARROGANT;** *AULD*; **CONCEIT; EGOISM, EGOTISM**

COMPROMISE (*noun* and *verb*) — In national and international politics, a wishy-washy "peace-in-our-time" enactment wherein human rights historically have too often been abandoned.

Still, in some less vital enterprises, *compromise* is logically (albeit grudgingly) *unavoidable*, and it often can be *best* for each and all of the concerned parties.

COMPUTER — The impending master of our world(??!)

Your author submits for your edification this defiant but *cautionary* poem entitled "The Pushbutton Prayer":

O Great God Computer,
Compute me some *stars*.
Construct me a *meadow* from green isobars.
Present me a *poem*.
Produce me a *brother*.
Research me a methodological *lover*.
Compute me a *silver, moon-shimmering sea*—
But Great God Computer,
Pray *don't* compute <u>me</u>.

—A. Nonni Mouse (?)

Thank God there are still some things computers can't do—*yet*.

CONCEIT (as in *arrogance*) — *See* **YOUR AULD, AULD AUTHOR** (got to admit it)

CONFIDENCE — Belief in the trustworthiness, reliability, and *capability* of a person or thing. ("They can conquer who *believe* they can." – the ancient Roman poet Virgil.)

Virgil's right-on observation is why it is so important for teachers and coaches to *expect* nothing but <u>success</u> from their young charges. When Your Auld Author told his soon-to-be state high school track champions that he expected them to win those titles, their chances for victory truthfully were *uncertainties* in my mind. But they *believed* that *I* believed that they would win them, so *incredibly*, they <u>did</u>.

CONFORMITY — A characteristic component of *dullness* which can sometimes turn *malevolent*.

There are *two distinct kinds of men*: Those who sometimes won't conform or do as they're told, and those who always blindly *will* and *do*. In the aggregate, the latter have often proved to be far more dangerous than the former. The hard lesson that Nazi Germany taught us must never be forgotten.

See **MOB**

CONSCIENCE — The mirror of our souls—the ability to differentiate plainly between right and wrong.

"Hath not a Jew _eyes_?" the Jew Shylock asks in _The Merchant of Venice,_ the 400-year-old but timeless Shakespearean play. Old Men know that Shylock's plaintive question bears far broader implications even than perhaps The Bard fully intended; i.e.: "Hath not a Jew—or an _Arab,_ or an _African,_ or an _Irishman,_ or a _baby,_ or a _dog_—a cerebral cortex and a _thalamus_?" (Republicans, xyW.) Ergo—"Doth not a Jew have _feelings_? Doth he not _bleed_ as any man?"

As Steven Pinker opined in "The Mystery of Consciousness" (_Time,_ January 29, 2007), the undeniable fact that we are all made of the "same neural flesh" makes it impossible for us to deny any longer our _common capacity to suffer_—both physically and mentally—and thus we cannot in clear conscience tread roughshod on the bodies or the rights of either man or beast, American or non-American, black or white or anyone in-between. (Also, _apes_ can learn to _sign_!)

Too bad someone didn't read that _Time_ magazine article to "W" ("Dubya") just before he attacked Iraq. And as of this writing, our valiant soldiers have been fighting and suffering and dying in Afghanistan for eight years now, making this the longest and economically costliest war in U.S. history.

See **CONSCIOUSNESS**

CONSCIOUSNESS — An awareness of one's own existence.

(Quoth Aged Sage Jean-Paul Sartre: "I _think_; therefore I _am._")

Old Men know that every single remaining, waning moment of their _consciousness_ is a precious, finite, and fragile gift.

Also, the _biology_ of consciousness presents a sounder basis for _morality_ than the _scientifically unproven_ dogma of the ephemeral existence of the immortal soul. The physiology of consciousness therefore obliges us to _recognize and respect the elemental rights_ of other sentient beings.

See **BRAIN; CONSCIENCE; UNCONSCIOUSNESS**

CONSERVATION — Something that is both _ethically_ and _ecologically_ _sound._ (Hopefully this doesn't _sound_ conservative!)

CONSTITUTION OF THE UNITED STATES — Something President Obama will need to repair after the damage that was done to it by the previous administration.

(Named for this sacred and historic document, the U.S.S. *Constitution* is the celebrated late-eighteenth-century American sailing vessel that saw action in the War of 1812 and is still grandly commissioned for duty in the United States Navy. "O Ship of State," the allegorical and metaphorical poem by the Aged Sage Henry Wadsworth Longfellow, was written in tribute to the U.S.S. *Constitution* as a patriotic symbol of the United States itself. The poem warns of "false lights on the shore"—a warning we'd do well to heed today.)

CONSULTANT — Usually an *uncreative subordinate* (or a retired Creative *Insubordinate*).

A consultant—paid or unpaid—is by definition a *non-participant*. As such, he's often as useless as Judge Judy probably would have been at the Alamo.

The classic definition of *consultant* is someone who borrows your watch to tell you the time and then bills you for "services rendered."

CONTRAST — A striking exhibition of *unlikeness,* or of *opposites.*

Paradoxically, love and *hate*—and *joy* and *sorrow*—are never really far apart. (Neither, of course, are *male* and *female*.)

COOT — An old codger.

COOTIES — Something some old unwashed coots and codgers often have in their smelly, scraggly old beards and other hairy areas.

(Take a *bath* once in a while and wash out those *bugs,* you old buggers.)

"CORPORATE CATS" — Fat-cat executives of large corporations that have fled America's urban centers and now exploit the men, women, and children left behind, abandoned in those teeming ghettos to fall prey to the street's many ills, as listed in this poignant poem:

"Mama, please tell us why we had to die."
"Children, that's easy—I can tell you why:
You died so the junkies can smoke their *crack,*
And the dopehouse dealers can make their *'jack,'*
And the *politicians* can *sell* their *votes,*
And the *pimps* can preen in their long fur coats,
And the *crooked cops* can collect their pay,
And the *'corporate cats'* can run away,
And the *school officials* can *promote* their *friends*
While the *kids* don't get any books or pens,
And the drive-by *shooters* can perfect their *aim*
As the *filthiest* rappers get in *halls* of *fame,*
And the teenage *truants* can *watch TV*
Or lie in the bed and *catch HIV,*
And the high-school *dropouts* can *'act the fool,'*
And your *sisters* can be scared to *walk* to *school*—
And so the *Lord* can grant your *mama* the *indomitable soul*
To somehow *staunch* this tragic trauma—
Like a bleeding <u>bullet hole.</u>"

(The tragic state of contemporary Detroit and its failed schools and victimized children inspired this poem, but it also applies to any other dangerous, decomposing urban center in our country. Google <u>www.AlifeontheRUN.com</u>.)

CORPORATOCRACY — An inhumane, corrupt *political, governmental,* and *economic* system toward which the United States is moving at warp speed.

(Actually, "corrupt corporatocracy" is of course a *redundancy.*)

See **CORRUPT** (adjective); **REDUNDANCY;** and for an idyllic alternative, ***RESOURCE*-DRIVEN AND *TECHNOLOGY*-DRIVEN ECONOMIC SYSTEM**

CORRUPT (adjective) — <u>Thieving</u>—particularly (as it concerns and deeply *troubles* this writer) when *academic* or *governmental* <u>bureaucrats</u> are the <u>thieves</u>, and the *corrupt* parties are stealing from *kids.*

See **"CORPORATE CATS"**

The **COSMOS** — The Universe.

Even the greatest Sages for the Ages have been able to divine only that the Cosmos is an enigmatically endless entity with neither beginning nor end. ("The Cosmos bides its un-beginning end. / If *Bear* could see, or *Crab* could comprehend, / This microcosmic *rebel* might be seen / Upon *one shining pebble*, gleaming green.")

(Incidentally, as it circles our sun, our little blue-white-green-brown pebble whereupon we live and breathe grows ever *browner* in photos snapped from high in the sky. We'd best harken to *Al Gore*—and *soon*.)

See **AL GORE; INFINITY; STRING THEORY**

COUNTERFEIT REBEL — A counter-*rebel*.

Old Men define a *counterfeit rebel* as "an infiltrator in the rebel camp." A counterfeit rebel is a *contra*—an *anti-rebel* in disguise. The Nazi spy Price, powerfully portrayed by Peter Graves as the infiltrator of the rebellious American POWs in the classic film *Stalag 17*, is a dramatic prototype.

Extremely dangerous and devious, a *counterfeit* rebel must in no way be confused with a *pseudo*-rebel.

See **PSEUDO-REBEL**

COUNTRY — Old Men know that our finite planet—and finally, the *infinite* universe—must become mankind's *ultimate* country.

COWARD — *See* **BULLY** (*noun*)

COWARDICE — "To know what is right and not *do* it."

See **EVIL**

CREAKY — *See* **BACK; HIPS; KNEES**

CREATING — A uniquely *human*, as well as *divine*, act.

Creating is life's true essence and purpose—and to *create* is also a singularly fulfilling *reward* in *itself*.

CREATIVE INSUBORDINATION — A strategically effective process this Old Man learned long ago to practice when dealing with an incompetent and/or corrupt bureaucrat, whether from *outside* or *within* the bureaucracy, and whether the bureaucrat in question be a superordinate or a subordinate.

Creative insubordination becomes a particularly necessary practice when the bureaucrat is in a position of superiority or authority with regard to the *practitioner*, or with regard to a *persecuted third party* whom the practitioner intends to *defend*. (It is also important to bear in mind that one's *superordinate* isn't necessarily one's superior.)

What Creative Insubordination *ain't* is rebellion for rebellion's *sake*, rebellion to be *chic*, or rebellion to be *lazy* or *hostile* or *cute*.

Who can be a successful practitioner of C.I.? You can. Even you *Republicans* can (though most of you seem to be far less inclined to it). Anyone who needs to and wants to can do it. All it takes is courage and a willingness to strategize imaginatively (but *cautiously*).

Creative insubordination can be practiced upon an abusive *boss*, *spouse*, or lover, upon a counter-democratic institution or law or illegal practice such as ageism or *sexism* (or classism, or racism), turned inward upon *oneself* to pluck out a "superordinate" personal flaw such as *narcissism* or *alcoholism*, or even practiced upon an uncooperatively superordinate *object*—such as a perversely malfunctioning *machine*.

See **BUREAUCRAT; C.I.; DRAGON; STEVE AND NANCY SWIGARD—C.I.'s EXTRAORDINAIRE!**

See also **YOU**

The **"CREATIVELY MALADJUSTED"** — Those righteous rebels whose hard, unharnessed hands hold the ultimate fate of humankind.

"Creatively maladjusted" is a term coined by the Reverend Doctor Martin Luther King, Jr., who asserted that the "creatively maladjusted" are those rare folk who are "maladjusted" enough to risk their jobs and often their necks to do what's right in the face of Satan himself.

Martyred abolitionist John Brown, for example, was *definitely* "creatively maladjusted."

CREEP, CREEPY — *See* **DICK CHENEY; DICKHEAD; PAT ROBERTSON; RICHARD CHENEY; WORMS AND MAGGOTS**

CROCODILE — *See* **DICK CHENEY; EVOLUTION; RICHARD CHENEY**

CRONYISM — *See* **DETROIT PUBLIC SCHOOLS**

CROW (as in *eating . . .*) — Something to eat, if necessary, while it's still warm.

When *crow* is *cold*, it's much tougher to eat. If ex-Detroit Mayor Kwame Kilpatrick had immediately come clean with his sexual improprieties when they surfaced and "eaten some *warm crow*" regarding them and his other trangressions, he might just possibly still be mayor today.

Instead, he ended up being forced to "eat *cold* crow," resign and do lots of jail time.

"CRUDE AND LEWD" — What Denny Rooney's English teacher at Walled Lake (Michigan) Western High School called this *limerick* that Denny recited in class as his favorite poem, for which she sent him to me for discipline concerning it.

I clean the limerick up a little bit here by changing "f--k" to "coupling" and then "duck" to "duckling" to retain some semblance of rhyme):

> There was a young fellow named *Weaver*
> Who had intercourse with a _beaver_.
> The results of this coupling
> Were a three-legged duckling,
> Two squirrels, and a short-haired *retriever*.

As the stern assistant principal, I tried manfully to keep a straight face when Denny gave me the specific information regarding why he had been sent to me.

The kid apparently must have had some kind of fixation on *beavers*. Denny also generously shared his other favorite limerick with me. It was about a grinning young man from Nantucket who was so improbably well-endowed that he was actually able to service himself *orally*. (You may have heard it. If you haven't, I can assure you that it was *considerably* "cruder" and lewder" than was the one featuring the *beaver*.)

See **"BEAVER SHOT!"; IMMATURITY**

CRUELTY — In too many humans, this is a motiveless vice that requires only *opportunity*.

This particular <u>Old Man</u> confessedly finds himself hard put not to *apply cruelty in kind* when he sees it visited upon children and animals, and he admittedly has at certain pivotal moments in his life actively applied it thus in total cold fury. (So, incidentally, has his *father*.)

See **BARBARISM**

CRYING AT WEDDINGS — Something *many* men actually do (or <u>should</u> do), whether old or young (particularly if the wedding is their <u>own</u>).

Even more *women* do this *too*, of course—and <u>*often*</u> at their <u>own</u> (but usually for entirely different reasons than when the *men* do it). <u>Old Men</u> frequently cry <u>*copiously*</u> (Repubs, xyW) at fancy, *expensive* weddings— particularly if they're in the $30,000 range and it's their <u>daughters</u> who are getting married.

CULTURAL RELATIVIST — Someone who cares more for his *culture* than for the <u>truth</u>.

If pressed, a *cultural relativist* will support his *culture* while knowing that aspects of it aren't *true*. Aged Sages are by nature and by definition proponents of and seekers after (the) *truth*; thus they eschew cultural relativism. (No, Repubs—*eschew* doesn't mean they "chew it.")

CULTURES — Traditional lifestyles or ideologies whose heirs often wage war with one another when they can find no common ground.

Dissonant "cultures"—such as liberalism vs. fundamentalism, or capitalism vs. communism—are frequently forced into war because *values* can't be _imposed_ *without* war. (Unfortunately, values sometimes can't be prescribed through *reason*, either.)

Human beings—especially fiercely democratic, Creatively Insubordinate human beings, regardless of age—don't just blindly accept what their culture gives them, because they know they can't continue to do that if they hope to become truly *civilized* and *democratized*. It's no coincidence that a sinister abbreviation for culture could well be *cult*.

See **DEMOCRACY**

"CUM" (*noun* and *verb*) — An acronym for "Central United Methodist" (a church in Detroit where Your Auld Author managed the PEACE-for-Youth programs in the 1990s).

Also, a cutesy-poo variant spelling of *come*—as in *orgasm*.

See **COME** (*verb*); **EJACULATE** (*verb*); **GRAND-DADDY; "KUM"; ORGASM**

CURIOSITY — Something that historically has been said to have "killed the cat" —but it absolutely _made_ (albeit also conversely _consumed_) many an Aged Sage, including *this* one.

See **SCIENCE; WONDER** (*noun*)

CURMUDGEON — A particularly *irascible* old man or Old Man.

A *curmudgeon* is something that the best of Aged Sages strive (not always *successfully*) *never* to become.

CUTIES — Pretty people of the feminine persuasion whom some old unwashed coots and codgers would *rather* have *nibbling* on their ears than the cooties they do have that are nibbling on them.

Also, speedy, adept boxers who are very hard to catch and hit; e.g., Muhammad Ali (before 1967), Gene Tunney, James J. Corbett, Willie (the "Wisp") Pep, Benny Leonard, Billy Conn, Sugar Ray Leonard, Winky Wright, Floyd ("Money") Mayweather, and the nonpareil original Sugar Ray—the Detroit-born Sugar Ray Robinson.

See **CODGER; COOT; SKIRTS; SUGAR RAY ROBINSON**

CYNIC, CYNICISM — Someone who seldom sees a good quality in anyone (but never fails to spot a *bad* one).

The old lady who is escorted across a busy street by a Boy Scout while hoping he won't snatch her purse is a *cynic*. (If she <u>expects</u> it to be snatched, she is also a *pessimist*.)

See **PESSIMIST**

CYRANO de BERGERAC — The greatest play ever translated from French into English.

Playwright Edmond Rostand's Cyrano, the superlative poet/swordsman with the grotesquely long *nose*, mocked himself thus: "Was this the *nose* that launched a thousand ships . . .?" . . . and "When it bleeds: The Red Sea!" <u>*Magnifique!*</u>

D

"DADDY" — Something many children call a man—old or young—who practiced the *rhythm* method of birth control nine months before they were conceived.

"Daddy" is also something a young woman calls an <u>Old Man</u> with unbridled enthusiasm when he's making her feel good—and <u>Old Men</u> know how to make young women feel *very* good.

See **Young Women**

DAVID L. HOLMES (1888–1960) — An august and deserving member of the *Michigan Sports Hall of Fame*.

Had it not been for this great Aged Sage who coached track at Detroit Wayne State University between 1917 and 1958, this tempered tome ye be reading rat noo mought ne'er ha' been writ. (You'll note that every now and then I slip into Celtic accent and idiom for no good reason. Can't help it; it's "uncontrollable"—me grrrandfather's oop theer soomwheer *making* me do it.)

I also shift into *Ebonic* idiom sometimes. Can't help *that*, either—I've undoubtedly hung with the *brothers* in the 'hood and the locker room too long.

DEATH — The greatest of all mysteries.

While— as many believe— death may be the final and eternal sleep, conversely it could instead be the final *awakening*. Also, death is the (usually) less-preferred alternative to becoming a Salty Septuagenarian like your bashed, battered, and beleaguered yet *still-loving-to-be-alive* Auld Author is. Also, the message codgers' bumpy old bodies ultimately send the old eager beavers if they're having difficulty slowing down, intimating with an infinite air of finality that it's indeed time now for the tottering dodderers to decelerate to a final and *infinite* halt.

Remember, too, though, that death could simply be *just another horizon.*

Indeed, death may also be the *temporary limit* of our *mere momentary sight.* When as a grubby little second-grader Your Author was taken on a tour of the magnificent Detroit Institute of Arts on Woodward Avenue, he was powerfully and permanently affected by a painting by the Renaissance master Hans Holbein the Younger. It featured a skull painted in an anamorphic, distended distortion into the lower foreground. After the viewer has passed the painting, the elongated skull assumes normal proportions and the *live human figures* it sits before become misshapen—they appear to no longer be real or to even *exist.* Death, after the painting has been viewed and passed by, *appears* to become the true reality.

But *if*—as that same little knickers-clad schoolboy did in Anno Domini 1942—the viewer breaks away from his group and runs back *to view it again,* the figures *reappear* in life's proportions and the skull *re-elongates* to become unrecognizable once more. When I had to run past the death's head once again to rejoin my class and my irritated teacher, Mrs. McGinity, that time I deliberately didn't look at it at all.

Thus was I subconsciously, metaphysically, and defiantly telling death, "Death, you don't *exist,*" and "death, you *die!*"

Not even the most Sagacious of Aged Sages have ever been able to prove or disprove that even death is an absolute condition, like the condition of absolute *black* or absolute *white*—the latter being a Platonic ideal that doesn't exist in our earthly realm (except in a *big* blizzard). As the great contemporary Aged Sage john powell has suggested to me, there could well be *post*-death, *conditional,* infinitely-*multi-dimensional* shades of *gray* which in this life we cannot begin to fathom. Even *absolute* zero isn't truly *absolute cold* but only *approaches* it. And there's no absolute *heat*—unless there's a real physical place called Hell (the "*fire* place," as opposed to Heaven, which some rhymingly punnish old wags flippantly refer to conversely as the "*choir* place").

My own experiences with Hell—at least, *so far*—have been right here on our real, all-too-solid earth. So does, conversely but similarly, the

Kingdom of *Heaven* dwell—as the Great Nazarene said—within *our-selves*. We can often create our own Hells—or our own Heavens.

While life itself is the greatest of all puzzles, death is *indeed* the greatest of all mysteries.

See **COLORS, *DEFINED*;** (On) **DYING; SLOWING DOWN**

DECEPTION — *See* **IRAQ WAR;** "The **CHECK'S IN THE MAIL";** **"WEAPONS OF MASS DESTRUCTION";** **"WILL YOU STILL LOVE ME IN THE MORNING?"**

DECREPIT — Broken down and worn out.

Old men may become decrepit, but *Old Men*—never! (unless their ultimate *decrepitness* overtakes them as a result of their having sublimely committed themselves body and soul to the lifetime pursuit of a truly altruistic cause, such as the fight against racism, classism, and other barbarisms).

See **CLASSISM; DINOSAUR; RACISM**

DEM — A Democrat.

See **DEMOCRAT**

DEMAGOGUES — Fascistic individuals who practice methods and processes to which the American public was becoming increasingly vulnerable during the Bush II presidency.

See **IDEOLOGUES**

DEMOCRACY — (*Ostensibly* in the contemporary United States), *government* by the *people*. Democracy, as Winston Churchill once said, is "the worst possible system *except for all the others*."

American-style democracy is the only instituted governmental system which has the potential to transcend any singular culture. The reason genuine democracies don't fight each other is because they recognize that the same inalienable rights are applicable *everywhere* and to *everyone*, regardless of *culture*.

Also, any *conflict* which occurs *within* a democracy *over democratic issues* is engendered by those who don't understand that cherishing the contributions and contributors from *all* cultures is essential to the *survival* of the democracy. And, as the saying goes, freedom ain't *free*—nor, any more, is our democracy, which is phenomenally in danger of devolving into a different, non-democratic form of government.

This phenomenal danger was starkly demonstrated by the folks who physically threatened legislators who voted for President Obama's democratic health reform bill in March 2010, and by the elected members of the "(*dis*)-loyal opposition" who *condoned* those threats.

It was the great Lutheran theologian and Aged Sage Reinhold Niebuhr (who incidentally confirmed my mother Helen Telford in Detroit's Bethel Evangelical & Reformed Church in 1920) who said, "Man's capacity for justice makes democracy *possible*, but man's inclination to *in*justice makes democracy *necessary*."

See **CORPORATOCRACY; CULTURE(S)**

DEMOCRAT (with a capital "D") — A member of the Democratic Party.

As Will Rogers famously said, "I don't belong to any *organized party*— I'm a Democrat." Democrat-born, Democrat-bred; when I die, I'll be Democrat-dead! Forewarned is forearmed: Your Old Author's political and ideological leanings are mightily manifest, *non*? We Kennedy-era Democrats die *hard*, like the Energizer Bunny—we aren't anything like the fellow-traveling Dems whose deeds (or absence thereof) throughout the late, unlamented Bush/Cheney administration rendered them nearly unrecognizable as true Democrats.

For example, I'm all for continuing stem-cell research for myriad reasons —one particular reason being that perhaps a way could have been found to miraculously regenerate some of those Dems' *spinal* tissue to give them some sorely-needed backbone regarding the stem-cell issue and other contentious issues during that most recent eight-year era of a rogue Republican administration that eroded (re-*rogued*?) civil liberties and initiated a "pre-emptive" war of aggression based on a treasonous lie.

Also, died-in-the-wool Democrats may have the *ass* as their symbol, but they're *sexy*, too—no one ever heard of a "good piece of *pachyderm!*"

DEMOCRATIC PARTY — An American political party that is fast being taken over by "Demopublicans." Your Auld Author never dreamed he would *write* this one day—but sadly, the Democratic Party is now fast becoming one of two major parties *in an increasingly obsolete* political system embracing a monetary economic apparatus that perpetuates wars and global inequality, rather than egalitarianism, humanism, and peace with *justice*.

See **RESOURCE-DRIVEN AND *TECHNOLOGY*-DRIVEN ECONOMIC SYSTEM** (for an ideal [and *idealistic*] remedy)

DEMONIZATION — An insidious practice of bigots and corporate fat cats who propagandistically *demonize* reformers whom they fear.

These feared reformers include American school integrationists, universal health-care proponents, and national leaders like, for example, Venezuelan president Hugo Chavez. Chavez' actions have proved that he is genuinely for the people, not for the corporate fat cats. He was elected *democratically twelve* times, and he has put the wealth in the hands of *eighty percent* of the Venezuelan people, rather than the *twenty* percent (or less) that one finds in countries led by corporate-collusive honchos whose yoke, it grieves me to have to say repeatedly, our beloved America *particularly* suffered under throughout the entire eight venal years of the infamous administration of our 43rd president.

DEMONS — Old Men know that real ones do exist.

Psychiatrists have other names for *demons, e.g.,* "addiction", "hallucination," "clinical depression," etc. Many Old Men (and Old Women) have learned to their belated sorrow that if their spouse or significant other suffered from one of these demons and wouldn't or couldn't get help, having stayed with that person after years of trying fruitlessly to cope was tantamount to "going down with the ship."

See **ADDICTIVE RELATIONSHIPS; CLINICAL DEPRESSION;** The **DEVIL; HALLUCINATION**

DEPRESSION (with a capital "D") — The era in United States and world history wherein many still-living Aged Sages, including *this* one, came bawling and crying into a cruel yet wonder-filled world.

DESERT (*noun*) — *See* **DETROIT PUBLIC SCHOOLS;** The **CAPITOL BUILDING IN WASHINGTON, D.C.**

See also **WASTELAND**

DESIRE (*noun*) — That which prompts *all human activity.*

Also, a fabled cable-car in New Orleans celebrated in a play and film of that name. If you close your eyes, can't you just hear Brando shouting "*Stella!*"? (I liked him better in *Viva Zapata*, though.)

DESTINY — Ordinarily a matter of <u>choice</u> rather than *chance.*

Karma, which in Hindu philosophy represents the universal law of cause and effect, presents itself something like this: What one <u>is</u>, is a result of what one <u>was</u>; what one <u>will be</u> depends on what one <u>is</u>. There is no place for *luck* here. Our individual and collective *destiny* is up to <u>us</u>.

See **COINCIDENCE; FATE**

DETROIT — A once-mighty metropolis that still *lives* in *this citizen's* hopeful blood and in my prayerful soul.

Detroit is a tough town that must arise yet *again* from the ashes. My wife Gina and I used to recite the following poem, titled "Blue Salt," at the start of my weekly radio shows on WCHB Detroit, NewsTalk 1200:

> My name is Detroit.
> I'm a *blue-collar* town.
> *Blue salt* melts my mid-march snow.
> Speedy cars and sprinters spring from me.
> In a Motown moment, I can *spit the blues*
> Right back in a bureaucrat's eye.
> Have you never seen *blue salt*?
> No complex chemistry here—
> Only the *old* color
> Of a *new* sky.

One day the sky over the "D" will be blue again and I'll get back the radio show I lost when my sponsors lost their shirts in the Bush Administration-induced economic collapse.

DETROIT PUBLIC SCHOOLS — Throughout most of the first decade of the twenty-first century, an *employment agency* for female central office administrators to be able to make six-figure salaries and give their unqualified sorority sisters and friends principalships and directorships.

This sad situation resulted in the school district's test scores declining to become the worst in the nation by the close of the year 2009. Michigan Governor Jennifer Granholm was forced to send in an emergency financial manager, Robert Bobb, to clean up the extensive mess with a *machete* instead of a *mop*.

See **CRONYISM; NEPOTISM; ROBERT BOBB; WASTELAND**

DETUMESCENT — The alleged semi-permanent state of the private parts of many old men and most young Republicans. (Repubs, check your *Webster's—xyW*. Also, try getting a shot of testosterone.)

See **FLACCID**

The **DEVIL** — For too many of us, the *man* (or woman) in the *mirror*.

The devil is an evil entity which often attempts to *become* us via a smooth disguise against which many thrice-deceived Old Men have belatedly and ruefully learned to arm themselves. The last four letters in the word "Devil" reveal the *infinitely unforgiving nature* of the demonic spirit also known as Satan, Beelzebub, the Evil One, etc.). And don't be deceived into thinking that this malevolent spirit doesn't have the power to overtake you—so remain ever on guard.

See **DEMONS**

DHEA (DeHydroEpiaAndrosterone) — (We even scooped *Webster's* on this one!) DHEA is a molecular hormone that researchers have isolated from testosterone and estrogen. It will improve the quality of life over a long period of time and postpone some of the worst effects of aging.

See **SECRETS OF THE CENTENARIANS**

DIALECT — *See* **EBONICS**

DIAPERS — What we geezers begin to need again for the second time in our seventy- or eighty-odd years.

Initially, we just slip a piece of toilet tissue in the front of our pants when we leave the toilet stall after lingering there for ten minutes trying vainly to shake off the last, last, *final* drop—while in the meantime, other much younger pissers pee and come and go while we're still standing there draining forlornly, one drop at a time.

When we reach the point of having to put the tissue in the *back* of our shorts, we're well on our way toward proceeding (*receding*?) to the full-fledged diaper, then the cane, from thence the walker, and finally the *wheelchair*. Sorry, my buckling-kneed, bent-over, Septuagenarian brethren—I'm just telling the truth here.

(After this morbid bit on diapers, you-all could probably use a *joke*, though, and this reminds me of one—see Joke 1.)

DICK CHENEY — The vice president (president of *vice*?) whom the Bush II administration, with Cheney in the lead, did not so much <u>fight</u> the very real danger of terrorism as <u>exaggerate</u> it and then <u>exploit</u> it for partisan political purpose.

An incredible but unsurprising Cheney quote in the *New York Times*: "I don't believe that *waterboarding* is *torture*" (!!!).

See **CROCODILE; DICKHEAD; DICK'S HEAD; FASCIST;** *PEZZONOVANTE;* **RICHARD CHENEY; WATERBOARDING**

DICKHEAD — *See* **DICK CHENEY**

DICK'S HEAD — The head of Dick Cheney.

DIE (*verb*) — To pass out of existence.

Many <u>Old Men</u>'s fondest and most final hope is to die *heroically*. This is particularly and traditionally true—both today and in the past—of <u>Old</u> *Celtic* <u>Men</u>. The ancient *Vikings* also lived and hoped to die in this tradition, sword in hand. You better believe that there are far *worse* ways to die. On the day my fighter father died, I wrote this poem:

For Scotty

My Daddy didn't die where he was born—
Larkhall, whence ancient kin rode forth on raids
Or got well-bled at Culloden, or torn
At bloody Bannockburn by English blades,
A-gasping, *gang a-glie*:
"Dear Mother, I die free!"
No.
He croaked one drab, inconsequential day
On some gray bed in distant Michigan—
A billion heartbeats and a world away
From Highlands where the sons of warriors run
By bright burns blue and clear,
Chasing dew-dappled deer.

See **"LIVE HEROICALLY!"**

"DIFFERENT DRUM" — A hypothetical instrument of *irregular cadence* to which many *irregular* <u>Old Men</u> march.

Rochester Education Association president Dave Berube proclaimed to the 500 folks who attended Your Auld Author's 1991 retirement party that I march even when there <u>is</u> no drum. (Well, if I waited for somebody to beat a drum for me to march to, I'd never get any *exercise*— and being an <u>Old Man</u> now, I need it more than ever.)

DILIGENCE — "The mother of good luck," according to Aged Sage Benjamin Franklin in his *Almanac*.

If diligence is the *mother* of good luck, <u>tenacity</u> is the *father*.

A DIME AND A CUP OF COFFEE — What one *specific* <u>Old Man</u> got for being the first sprinter from a Michigan university ever to run 440 yards under 47 seconds way back in the 1950s (and what he gets now in the 2010s for bragging *incessantly* about it wherever he can).

The next time you see an old man sitting in a diner sipping a cup of coffee on a Saturday morning, check to see if there's a dime next to him—and if there isn't and you think he's got a story to tell, sit down beside him, give him a dime, buy him another cup of coffee, and sit back and listen to his story. After you have heard it, give him another dime and solicit another story. You might be surprised to learn something of real import from the old geezer.

DINOSAUR — What Dan Quayle and George W. Bush probably think a *thesaurus* is.

Also, what many of us hippety-hopping old humpers semi-miraculously still *aren't*.

Even though some frenetic young *minute*-men may mistakenly think we're extinct, we-all ain't mostly *dead* yet. All these Young-Joan-and-Josephine-jumping young jackrabbits need do is *check with Young Joan and Josephine!* (Ain't that right, Young Joan and Josephine?)

See "MINUTE-MEN"; **THESAURUS; VI-<u>AGG</u>-RA!!**

DIPLOMACY — The art of letting someone *have your way.* (Read that again.)

Also, <u>Old Men</u> who were employed as ambassadors or in some other capacity in the foreign service know that if you want to deceive a professional international diplomat, tell him the <u>*truth*</u>. Being a lying lizard himself, he will never *believe* you.

DISCONTENTMENT — A necessary catalyst for progress.

DIVAS — Prima donnas.

See **DRAMA QUEENS**

DODDERER, DODDERING — *See* **CODGER; COOT**

DODGERS (as in Brooklyn) — *See* **GREAT; JACKIE ROBINSON**

DOG-FIGHTING — *See* **BARBARISM**

DOGGY DIAPERS — *See* **INSIPID**

DOGS — Uncreative Subordinates.

See **XERXES**

DON'TS (for Old Men) — Don't play full-court basketball. Don't shovel wet snow. Don't climb on ladders to clean gutters. Don't eat highly-seasoned chitterlings ("chitlins"). Don't eat highly-seasoned *anything* at all. Don't eat *chitlins* at all. Don't get a dog (unless you want to pick up lots of poop and get a dog-sitter when you're out of town).

And don't *retire*—ever! If *you do* retire, don't *stay* retired—take it from Your Auld Author, who retired in 1991 after having served in ten jobs in the field of education and has served in *fourteen* full-time jobs *since* 1991, some of them *simultaneously* (never *could* keep a job for long!).

DORK, DORKHEAD — *See* **REPUB, REPUBLICAN**

DO'S (for Old Men) — Do get a cat (or *two*—but not *twenty*-*two*). Do wear slippers (around the *house*—but not to the *supermarket*). Do keep your ponytail combed (if you have one). Do get a paddleboat. Do open pistachio nuts for your grandchildren.

Also, if you can, do marry a gorgeous, soft-hearted young (or old) woman (unless you're *already* married—then don't, because bigamy is illegal).

Make sure that the gorgeous lady can cook good beef ribs, writes poetry, fixes your breakfast before noon, doesn't talk too much, doesn't talk too *little*, doesn't drink, isn't moody, isn't oversexed, isn't *undersexed*, is a good chauffeur, shops in thrift stores, goes to sleep when you go to sleep, wakes up when *you* wake up, likes to play Scrabble, likes to fish, is at least *semi*-sane, loves your grandchildren, and truly loves *you*—i.e., is really *for real*.

DRAGON — A frequent *winner* (sorry, folks).

Popularized allegorical fairy tales notwithstanding, it is good for any of you dewy-eyed young gals and guys out there who are reading this to be made aware that *the fact is*, often the *dragon wins*.

Then it eats St. George, burps, picks its teeth with the deceased would-be dragon-slayer's lance, and the fair damsel doesn't get to have her happily-ever-after storybook ending. Instead, she has to languish alluringly forever, dwelling with the dragon in his drafty old castle at Jurassic Park.

DRAMA QUEENS — *See* **ERECTION-INHIBITORS**

DRAMBUIE — Taken in moderation, a *guid* (good) *auld* (old) Scots drink for a Sage of *any* age. (A bottle that boasts a picturre of Bonny Prrince Chairlie on th' label needs nae furrther endorrsement!)

The Bonny Prince could have used several hearty swigs either before or after the disastrous Battle of Culloden Moor in 1745.

See **DRINK** *(verb)*

"DRILL, BABY, DRILL!" — So quoth Sarah Palin.

The potential contamination of the entire Gulf of Mexico has polluted hundreds of miles of coastline, and it has threatened to expand to more coastlines—and to the Atlantic Ocean. At this writing, the oil spill is the size of Delaware and Maryland combined. Much of the earlier $100 billion damage from Hurricane Katrina was not from the wind and the rain but from the failure of the Bush II administration to provide the needed $14 million for adequate protection. The protective barrier islands that were destroyed when Katrina hit would have significantly slowed or stopped the worst environmental disaster in U.S. history, but Bush had a "preemptive" war to wage in Iraq based on a deceptive premise—and $14 million was "too much" to spend on domestic protection. Bush, being an oilman himself, permitted contracts to be signed with British Petroleum during his administration with little attention to safety regulations.

DRINK *(verb)* — 'Tis *guid* (good) to drink lots of water (and a daily glass of red wine).

It's even better to sip a wee dram of Drambuie —or Grand Marnier!

DRUNKENNESS — Voluntary insanity.

The **DUMBING-DOWN OF AMERICA'S TEXTBOOKS** — A perennial practice of textbook publishers.

This counter-educative practice is not only basely insipid but also endangers our democracy by whitewashing some of this country's historic transgressions, including the importation and subjugation of African slaves, subsequent post-Civil War Jim Crow laws, and still-extant racial discrimination.

See **INSIPID**

DUNCE, DUNDERHEAD — *See* The **43rd President of the United States**

(On) **DYING** — As he lay dying of cancer, Mel L. Barclay, M.D., an Aged Sage Extraordinaire and a lifelong friend of Your Auld Author, wrote this touching and brilliantly metaphysical poem to his son and nephews on his "passing" for them to read after his death:

> Beautiful boys, I am gone from your places and times
> And instead live in a different part of things—
> Somewhere between *was* and *is* and *could be*.
> I am *far and near* and *here and there*.
> *Time* is only one of the places I have learned to dance.
> I take my breath in the midst of stars.
> I am the row or the column vector,
> And the *eigenvalue* as I *wish*.
> *Orthogonal in eleven dimensions and more* is play.
> (If only I could understand who I am.)
> I can see in as many directions as I please
> And know the *meaning* of what it is I see.
> I can fly.
> And I would trade all my powers
> To simply touch your face one more time.

Dying is a purely physical process that we all *undertake* (no pun intended) the *second we're born*. But it's not when and how we die that's most important—how we *live* is what counts the most.

Also, it's sometimes good for Old Men—and *all* men—simply to consider what the ancient Romans said: "*Bibamus, moriendum est!*" ("Death's inevitable; let's have a drink!") So, if you can't decipher the brilliant Mel Barclay's *eigenvalue* or comprehend even foggily his reference to or the concept of *orthogonal in eleven dimensions* (or even if you *can*), let's have us a drink or two, you and I, and toast Mel and the other many stalwart spirits gone into death's (and Shakespeare's) "dateless night." I would give anything if only they could all join us once more in that drink, and then again in one more, and in yet one *more....*

Dr. Mel L. Barclay (1942–2010) is pre-eminent among those kindred friends. He was a real *mensch,* and as I said at his memorial, "Few celebrated men are *great,* and few great men are *celebrated.* Mel Barclay was both celebrated *and* great." His wonderful family mourns him bitterly, as do I.

See The **COSMOS; DEATH; A REAL** *MENSCH*

DYSENTERY — A condition that almost caused Your Auld Author to lose a "good-but-not-gaudy" 47.7-second 400-meter race in Milan, Italy in July 1957.

That clocking was more than a full second shy of my then-personal best.

The moral? Don't drink Aranciata (the local orange soda) unless you drink it without domestic ice—which, after all, is merely the local protozoa-infested *water,* frozen.

See **ERECTION-INHIBITORS; "GOOD-BUT-NOT-GAUDY"**

E

EARS — Auditory organs which recompense old men for their hearing loss by becoming acutely *hairier—much hairier*.

This is particularly the case if the auld coots happen to be of Celtic heritage. Just check out Sir Sean Connery's (I'll bet you could probably practically *comb* them).

See **HAIR**

EBONICS — African-American dialectical speech and writing.

Old *educators* know that *Ebonics'* marked difference from standard "marketplace" English hampers its speakers' success in the local and global marketplace. Dialect can cause severe comprehension problems for many *black* students—especially many *younger* black students— as with the child who, when asked to used the word "so" in a sentence, comes up with, "I got a so' on my laig."

African-Americans who are to become adept at coping and excelling in America's still-white-dominated society can and should retain their dialectical speech for appropriate moments, but they must become "bilingual." This means they have to be given systematized traditional grammatical instruction in-depth in "standard" English—as a "second language," if need be.

(For more on Ebonics, see pp. 54, 62–64, 77, 82, 103, 126, 360, and 370 of *A Life on the RUN—Seeking and Safeguarding Social Justice*, Harmonie Park Press, 2010, www.AlifeontheRUN.com.)

EDUCATION — Is *liberation*!

Also, if *you have* no *education*, you've got to use your *brain*!

EDUCATORS WHO HAVEN'T FIGURED OUT YET THAT THE WORST WAY TO TEACH KIDS IS TO TEST THEM TO DEATH — *See* **SLOW LEARNERS**

EGALITIZATION — A process and procedure that America and ultimately the entire *world* must undertake and undergo in order to become *egalitized,* and thus become true *democrats* (with a small "d").

Please make it happen, O Multi-Racial President of the United States and Potential Rescuer of the Free World! I pessimistically presume that very few Republicans and only a few more of their fellow-traveling faux-Democrat Demopublicans are reading this—and if they are, many of them secretly or *openly* disagree with much that's in it.

EGO — Too often, *ego* is a monstrous veil that can engender a dark night of the soul and forever prevent its true awakening into the dawn.

Conversely, the *ego* can be a benign engine that drives an indomitable ambition which can produce worthy achievement.

EGOISM, EGOTISM — <u>Old Men</u>'s greatest stumbling block—or greatest *attribute.*

See **ALTRUISM**

See also **ARROGANCE**

EJACULATE *(verb)* — Something that old, *old* men can still do about twice a month, if they're lucky—and a few of them can do it even if they're old *doctors of education*!

Also, to (orally) *exclaim*, denoting *any* sort of excitement.

Noun usage: Semen.

See **COME** *(verb);* **"CUM"** *(noun and verb);* **GRAND-DADDY; ORGASM**

ELDER *(noun)* — An Aged Sage.

An Elder *(capitalized)* is someone, male or female, whose wisdom is to be revered and whose counsel is to be sought.

An "elder" (not capitalized) is someone much older than you who lived and relived the very same year over and over and over again until he was an old, old coot—but learned little or nothing from the experience of living it.

See **OLDSTER**

ELIZABETH TAYLOR — A voluptuous, multi-bejeweled and magnificently seasoned *grande dame* that half the world's male population has been hot to boink for over half a century.

To you, Liz, we Old Men kiss our fingertips. Keep on *keepin'* on, milady.

See **"BLING," "BLING-BLING"; BOINK**

EMPATHY — A rare characteristic of rare folk, whether old or young, who can truly intuit the feelings and spirit of another, and "walk a mile in his shoes," as it were.

See **UNDERSTANDING**

"ENCORE ANXIETY" — An emotion we feel long after our audience has left the theater and we're still on the stage, bowing to empty seats.

Old Men's need to revisit or remain involved in old causes, or perform jobs and activities from which they've "retired" or have technically *been forcibly* retired has been dubbed "encore anxiety" by sociology professors compelled to justify their jobs and credentials by giving new names to old phenomena.

Comebacking boxers and many old rebels like Your Auld Author who remain stuck in their respective arenas like barnacles clinging to the hull of an old schooner are motivated (or plagued) by "encore anxiety." As Simon & Garfunkel sang about a battered old pug's lamentative but fruitless cry to quit the ring, " 'I am *leaving*, I am *leaving*'—but the fighter still *remains*."

Some Aged Sages are compelled to stick with the same cause on the same battleground until it *kills* them or they just plain *expire*. For them, both psychically and *physically* there's no escape.

But for others, there are *new* ways, too, to remain what my brilliant friend and one-time protégé Wayne Dyer (who did the Introduction to this toothsome tome) calls a "relevant elephant." And all of us have an ongoing need to be *relevant* at *any* age.

ENDANGERED SPECIES — The magnificent Siberian tiger, the American eagle, the mountain gorilla—and presently the so-called "civilized" gorilla (*Homo Sapiens*), if we don't get our act together pretty soon. (To cite just one example, we must stop polluting our seas and coasts with mammoth oil spills!)

ENVY — The *penultimate* self-*punishment*.

See **HATRED; JEALOUSY**

ERECTION — A firm, lengthy penile protuberance engendered easily in an old non-Republican husband by a younger wife—particularly if she bears any resemblance to Halle Berry.

For want of a Halle Berry lookalike, a Kim Basinger or Beyoncé one wouldn't be bad.

Alternative definition: In Japanese pronunciation, an "*eRection*" is an *eLection*—something that in many countries is either non-existent or a mockery, but which in America had by 2000 and 2004 become too-easily rigged or stolen.

See **CLARENCE THOMAS**

See also **ROMANCE** (*noun*); **VI-AGG-RA!!**

ERECTION-INHIBITORS — Arthritis (even with Viagra) and nags (the non-equine kind).

Also, the Six D's: *diverticulitis, dysentery, divas, drunks, drama queens,* and *death*.

(Medusa was an erection-inhibitor, too. Remember her? The mythic Greco-Roman charmer with snakes for hair.)

ESCHEW — To shake off, renounce.

The more *Sagacious* of Aged Sages endeavor to eschew any lust for fame—not always too successfully. (Now, lust for a *good woman* can be quite another matter . . .!)

E.S.P. (Extra-sensory perception) — *See* **PARAPSYCHOLOGY**

The **ETERNAL PRESENCE** — The Infinite Intellect Whose <u>Existence</u> all <u>Old Men</u> and some mere <u>old</u> men <u>sense</u>—and long to *know*.

See **GOD**

The **ETERNAL SHEPHERD** — The Christ.

ETERNITY — The *sum* of all sums.

Many <u>Old Men</u> theorize that our eternal existence, if we are to have it, could perhaps transpire somewhere out there in the Fourth Dimension. (Or, as the oft-quoted, non-prototypical Aged Sage john powell has non-prototypically speculated, maybe it's in the *Fifth* Dimension—or the *Fifty*-fifth Dimension.

See **INFINITY; MINUTE** (*noun*)**; STRING THEORY; TIME**

ETHNOCENTRISM — The benighted belief in the inherent superiority of one's *own* group and culture, accompanied by a condescending attitude of casual contempt toward *other* groups and cultures.

See **ANTHROPOLOGY; HISTORY**

EUCLID — One of the most *sagacious* of Aged Sages.

Euclid was a mathematical wizard not only of *ancient* times but for *all* time. As Aged Sage Robert James Waller wrote in *The Bridges of Madison County*, "Euclid assumed [absolute] parallelness [as *law*] . . ., but a non-Euclidian way of being is also possible, where the lines come together, far out there . . . a spilling of _one_ reality into _another_."

See **HORIZON; SAGES FOR THE AGES**

EVIL — A force that often triumphs if—as saith the Quintessential Sage—good men stand idly by and do nothing.

See **"BLACK" WITCHCRAFT; DEMONS;** The **DEVIL; FASCISM; SAVAGERY; SELFISHNESS**

EVOLUTION — The ongoing adaptation of species to the environment via the integrating agencies of natural selection, hybridization, and mutation.

Every modern member of the species scientifically classified as _Homo Sapiens_ has a _reptilian_ core in its brain, but that crocodilian core shows up more in some men's behavior than in others'.

See **CROCODILE; DICK CHENEY**

EXECUTIVE ABILITY — The ability to decide quickly and then get _somebody else_ to do the work.

Old Men know that the ablest _executive_ is the one who has the _ability_ to _recognize_ ability in a subordinate and give him the opportunity to _lead_. Then both he and his subordinate are happy, because _ability_ is worth _naught_ without _opportunity_.

EXPEDIENCE — Something _Old Men_ know to be wary of in any man whose deeds have shown that his sense of responsibility or fairness doesn't extend beyond it.

An _honest_ used-car salesman (too often an _oxymoron_) once told Your Auld Author the true story of his showroom colleague who, upon catching sight of a fellow salesman's customers—an elderly couple who had come to close a deal—took them into his office and told them, "_Terrible_ news—your salesman _died_ yesterday. But don't worry; I'll take care of you if you'll just sign _here._ . . ."

At the very moment the shocked old couple sadly signed, their "deceased" salesman was out having lunch while his colleague stole his customers. (Remind you of anyone you know?)

EXPERIENCE (*noun*) — A tough teacher.

<u>Old Men</u> learned long ago that experience gives the test *first*, the lesson *second*.

Experience is also that which often *practicably* contradicts and trumps ivory-towered <u>theory</u> (particularly in inner-city high school English and social studies classrooms).

EXTREMISM — "No *vice*," according to 1964 Republican presidential candidate Barry Goldwater, "in the defense of *liberty*."

Seldom has this donkey-tailed old Democrat who be scribbling this here *Dickshunary* (*Republican* spelling) ever *agreed* with (much less <u>quoted</u>) a <u>Republican</u>, but the great Goldwater is an exception (although I *did* vote for his opponent, Lyndon Johnson).

See **RADICAL** (*noun*)

The **"EYE OF OSIRIS"** — The sun.

Osiris, one of the principal gods of historical Egypt, was the husband (and the *brother*) of the goddess Isis. He was often depicted in the representative pictograph renderings of The "Ancient Wisdoms" as a mummy wearing the crown of Upper Egypt.)

See The **"ANCIENT WISDOMS"**; The **PYRAMID**; The **VEDA**

F

FABLES — *See* **HISTORY**

FAITH – In the religious sense, something that can sometimes make a *virtue* out of *not thinking*.

See **FUNDAMENTALISTS**

FAITHFUL (*adjective*) — *Filled* with or demonstrating *loyalty* and *fidelity*.

"It is better to be *faithful* than *famous*." This is true *invariably*, whether the fidelity be for a *cause*, an *ideal*, a *friend*, or a *spouse* (but not necessarily for a *religion*). The quote is Theodore Roosevelt's, and Teddy was both famous <u>and</u> faithful in every way—including with respect to his spouse (even though his subsequent younger presidential cousin Franklin incidentally wasn't).

See **FAITH**

FAME — That which comes too *early* to the young and too *late* to the dead.

(Consider *Vincent van Gogh* and *Emily Dickinson*.)

FANATIC — Someone who takes "unreasonableness" right over the edge of *rationality*.

A fanatic does what he thinks God would do if only He knew the <u>true facts</u> regarding the issue.

See **"UNREASONABLE" MEN**

FASCISM — The unscrupulous political, economic, and physical subjugation, suppression and repression of the powerless *disadvantaged* by the *powerful advantaged*.

See **CLASSISM; INJUSTICE; RACISM**

FASCIST — Someone who hates and fears democracy as *Dracula* hated and feared the Cross.

Perhaps the all-time fascist prototype was the creepy, goose-stepping Austrian with the funny little square mustache whom Charlie Chaplin made inspired sport of in The *Great Dictator*, in which he pushed around a big balloon in the air with the map of the world on it. The *real* dictator Chaplin was funnily mimicking was the monster whose minions *notso*-funnily murdered six million Jews, Gypsies, and Poles in the 1930s and '40s and made lampshades from their skin.

And don't ever think that a fascist political leader—the figurative "Man on Horseback"—could never emerge and ascend in *America*. Let us not forget that the Weimer Republic was a democracy until its monetary system collapsed and Adolf Hitler came to power in a *free election*.

See **MONSTERS; "STRONGMAN";** *RESOURCE*-**DRIVEN AND** *TECHNOLOGY-* **DRIVEN ECONOMIC SYSTEM**

FATE — *See* **COINCIDENCE; DESTINY**

FAVOR (*noun*) — An act of *benevolence*. (Republicans, xyW.)

Old Men have learned that when one requests a significant *favor*, it obligates him—and when one *confers* one, it's best to confer it upon someone with a good *memory*!

Also, know that when someone reminds you that he *did* you a favor, he's about to *ask* for one.

FEDERAL REGULATOR — A *parasite*.

There are nearly half a million of these chaps in Washington being paid with our tax dollars. You've heard the joke about how many bureaucrats it takes to change a light bulb—they need one bureaucrat to administrate, one to direct the *administrator*, one to supervise the *director*, one to oversee the *supervisor*, one to monitor the *overseer*, one to consult with all of the administrators and supervisors and overseers and order-givers and whatnot, and *three more* to screw the light bulb into the water faucet.

Then they need an *additional* bureaucrat to ensure that all *light-bulb-screwing regulations* have been followed and then to determine why things went wrong. (Sounds like the Detroit Public Schools.)

However, it isn't the *water faucet* that is getting screwed—it's *you*, the American taxpayer. Little wonder that John F. Kennedy described Washington as a city with *Southern efficiency* and *Northern charm*.

See **PARASITE**

FEDERATED REGIONALISM — A metropolitan model wherein the large regional authority controls access to *opportunities* while the smaller municipal authority controls issues of *local identity* and *governmental responsiveness*.

The visionary version of federated regionalism as propounded by Aged Sage john powell is an effective way to promote *racial justice*. It is representative of people of color in municipalities where they are the majority, and it adds provisions for their full *regional* participation.

In powell's version, federated regionalism's prime target-projects become the majority-white suburban communities that are usually basically driven by majoritarian motives and whose residents and local leaders therefore often behave with abject self-interest. *Self-interested* local control too frequently becomes exclusionary local control. In powell's version, more attention and funding are applied to improve *urban infrastructure* rather than to provide new capacity for *suburban growth*. Powell's is a landmark prototype that demands adoption or adaptation by every far-seeing suburban, statewide, or nationwide legislative leader.

See **john powell**

FEELING IMPORTANT — Closely following the need for food, drink, shelter, and love, every man, woman, and child in this world needs to *feel important* and *relevant* and *significant*.

Old Men know that the man who can make all those needful folks *feel* they're *important* and *know* they're important will "own the *world*." Old Men make others around them feel important by becoming *sincerely interested* in them, remembering their *names*, listening (and *really* listening) to them, and encouraging them to converse about their lives and interests and joys and sorrows.

There! In only ten seconds, I've just laid on you a full course from Aged Sage Dale Carnegie, the late, great Scot himself.

See The **OLD MAN'S GREATEST** *FEAR*

FELLATIO — No, some of you *less* uncultured Repubs—*fellatio* isn't a character in Shakespeare's *Midsummer Night's Dream*.

In actuality, fellatio is an act Your Auld Author's Hollywood producer-director uncle Frank Telford drunkenly invited the president of Universal Studios to perform on him at a big studio banquet (after having first invited him to kiss a lower posterior part of him—and, for good measure, having also urged the gentleman to go to a certain very hot and fiery place of Biblical infamy). Uncle Frank was promptly fired and never directed again. He wound up his career writing scripts for *Gentle Ben*, a TV sitcom about a bear.

See The **BARD; REPUB**

FEMINISM — A political movement that has become a feminine form of reverse sexism that some imply has at times bordered on fascism.

Can you imagine the distaff outcry if some poor old man (or *young* man, or Old Man) initiated a movement called *Masculinism*?

Feminists need to *lighten up*—at least, *sexually*. There's almost nothing that a rebel woman (or man)—even a rebel *Feminist* woman—can do sexually that's *bad*. If the woman needs to lie under the man in order to climax, that's not going to render her any less a Feminist or make sexism worse in the world. And it's okay for her rampant rebel partner to let her get on top of *him*, if that's what she needs.

It's also okay for her to *talk*. Favorite words are *yes!*—because it's good to be a positive person, and *Omigod!*—because it's appropriately pious to *pray* during the act. That way, you don't have to feel guilty if you don't always go to church on Sunday.

It's even okay for her to be *tied up* (if she's a *gay* Feminist—if she's *straight*, it might pose a few *political* problems).

FIBULA — A little lie. (Definition reserved for gullible Republicans only.)

FIGHT (*noun*) — Something one particular old galoot from Detroit learned he never should have *picked* with any large individual known by the contradictory nickname "Tiny," having found this out the hard way in a biker bar on the outskirts of Muskegon five decades ago.

That same cautionary bit of useful knowledge that this old (at the time, *young*) galoot gained in that saloon would of course obtain even more *cautionally* regarding anyone nicknamed "Moose."

Also, Old Men have indeed learned that if one makes every fight a fight to the *death*—whether *fistic* or *politic*—one is going to *die* a whole lot of times. Old Men with the *capital* "O" and the *capital* "M" take on a fight only when they're prepared to *win* it. Over time, Old Men have learned to *choose* their battles (unless they're *Scots*, of course).

See **SCOTS** (*noun*)

FINE DINING — Eating gourmet meals and food; e.g., lobster, caviar, prime rib, filet mignon, (and also in somewhat more proletarian Detroit-area environs, delectable White Castle hamburgers called "sliders"), and drinking expensive sparkling water and wine.

Fine dining is something Detroit Public Schools' self-aggrandizing, inept female central administrators did a *lot* of on the taxpayers' dime (minus the "sliders"), while the kids couldn't get books, pens, or toilet paper.

"Eat, drink, and be *merry*—for tomorrow we *diet*." I *love* that pun— and *diet* was definitely what some of those fat, *faux*-educator females needed to do—*forcibly* (with my apologies to Jenny Craig and her commendably devoted patrons for my *bluntness* here).

FINNEY HIGH SCHOOL (Detroit) — Between 2003 and 2008, the high school reputed to be the toughest school in the toughest city in the country.

Be assured that this reputation was fully deserved. Your Auld Author taught and administrated at Finney High School throughout those specified years as the only retired school superintendent *in America* who had dared to return and teach in an inner-city classroom, and I was still doing it in my seventies. I was also the oldest regular non-substitute employee in the Detroit Public Schools in front of classes. I taught and fought and chased and caught and counseled and disciplined and loved some very troubled kids—and some very *wonderful* ones—with whom I remain in close touch.

Finney High School is 100 percent black (whatever happened to 1954's *Brown vs. Board of Education*?). Also, its swimming pool hasn't functioned for *nine years*. If a pool in Rochester hadn't functioned for nine *days* when I was the deputy superintendent there, the parents would have called out the Marines, the National Guard, and the Royal Canadian Mounted Police, and I'd have been fired *fast*.

See **CLASSISM**

See also **PUBLIC SCHOOL SEGREGATION**

The **FIRST REQUISITE FOR "IMMORTALITY"** — *To be dead.*

This is why Yourr Auld Author is *joost* a wee bit neerrvous t' hae been an *inhobbitant* of the Wayne State Univeerrsity Athletic Hall of Fame for lo these past theerty-thrree years.

Halls of Fame are rather like marble mausoleums festooned with overgrown vines and old ivy. Most folk who *inhabit* Halls of Fame are either fading *ghosts* of themselves, or else are *genuine ghosts, themselves!*

See **DEATH**

The **500** — The doomed British Light Brigade of the Crimean War, the subject of Tennyson's famed poem about the general officer far from the front line who issued an order that sent the brigade galloping forward on its charge toward certain death.

There is an analogical lesson for _today_ to be learned here, even if it _is_ a bit of a _stretch_: Don't issue broad mandates regarding student _testing_ and teacher _requirements_ far from the _trenches_. Are you _listening_, Education Secretary Arne Duncan?

The **"500" CLUB** — See **FUNDAMENTALISTS**

FIVE THOUSAND TEENAGERS — The approximate number of disruptive teens in Detroit's public high schools who are preventing their teachers from being able to _teach_ and their much more _numerous_ better-behaved classmates from being able to _learn_.

These disrupters need to be placed in small learning settings (e.g., some closed elementary buildings) and surrounded with support—remedial reading teachers, social workers, security and truant officers, counselors adept in anger management and conflict resolution techniques, and tough male principals—and then returned to the regular setting when their _grades_ and _behavior improve_.

This model should also be adopted in New York, Chicago, Philadelphia, East Los Angeles, etc.—as well as in some _suburban_ districts. Your Auld Author did it in Rochester, Michigan, when I was the deputy super-intendent there. I named the program ACE—Alternative Center for Education. When I first proposed ACE, a board member protested that we didn't have any kids in the district who needed such a program. "You're right, Mrs. Board Member," I responded. "Most of them have _dropped out_."

See **TWENTY THOUSAND TEENAGERS**

FLACCID — Deflated.

See **DETUMESCENT; REPUBLICAN**

FLAT ON YOUR BACK IN INCREDIBLE PAIN — An old man's location, position, and situation after testing his golf swing too soon after hip or knee-replacement surgery.

See **ATHLETICS**

FLATTERY — The dubious and deceptive art of telling the other person *precisely what he thinks about himself.*

Old Men know that they are well advised to be less fearful of the enemies who attack them than they are of the "friends" who *flatter* them.

FLATULENCE — An embarrassing auditory (and *olfactory*) condition that often *inopportunely* manifests itself in old men (and Old Men) just before, during, or immediately following an opportune *bedroom* moment.

FLY (*noun*) — A strip sewn along the edge of a man's trousers, to conceal the zipper, which in old men (and Old Men), is often forgetfully left unzipped.

Also, the pesky picnic insect that defecates in your potato salad and then buzzes onto your nose and flies off a tenth of a second before you try to swat it and smack yourself on the schnozz instead.

See **ZIPPER**

The **"FOLD-UNDER" COCK** — *See* **REPUBLICAN**

The **"FOLD-UNDER" COCKTAIL** — One-part Drambuie, two parts Scotch. Drink three of them inside an hour and your legs will fold under you (unless you're a *Scot*—or a particularly *hardy* Irishman).

FORBIDDEN NOOKY — The boss's wife, etc. (fill in the blank).

Warning: *You* are now entering a *danger zone* . . . (beep) . . . a *danger zone* . . . (beep, *beep*) a *danger zone* . . . (beep, beep, beep). . . .

FORGET — I forget what I was going to write here.

Hey, what do you expect? Your Auld Septuagenarian Scribe (ASS) is an incipient *geriatric* case, remember?

Oh, *now* I remember—I was going to say that even though I know that we Old Men are sometimes *forgetful* now, there are things in life we should *try* to forget, such as *heartbreaks*, for example. A young beauty who professed to love her old husband or lover may have turned out not to have been for *real*, or not to have been entirely *sane* or *sober*. Also, along Old Men's lifetime pathways, we have had friends and wives and lovers and fathers and mothers and sons and daughters who deserted us or whom we *deserted*—or with whom we had misunderstandings and from whom we thus became tragically and sometimes permanently estranged. Inevitably, too, we lost an *inexorably increasing* number of others to the stark finality of the poetic "foreverlasting darkness, undesigned."

Still, a broken heart is part of what gives us Aged Sages our strength and understanding and compassion. Hearts never broken are aloof and sterile; thus those *within whom they beat so pristinely* can never feel the real joys and sorrows of mortal imperfection.

See **DEATH; DINOSAUR; MASTODON**

FORGIVING — Most Old Men know all too well that to forgive a *trespass* is sometimes incredibly difficult.

They also recognize that to become *able* to forgive—and to do it fully and *genuinely*—is one of mortal man's (and mortal *woman's*) truest and most marvelously *altruistic* gifts.

See **GRUDGE-HOLDING**

FORTUNE — Mere *glass*—just when it gleams brightest, it *shatters*. ("Fortuna vitrea est—*tum cum splendet frangitur*." – Syrus, *Maxims*.)

Fortune is also far easier to *find* than to *keep*—and when it *leaves* you, so do many of your "friends."

See **"FRIEND"**

The **43rd PRESIDENT OF THE UNITED STATES** — *See* **DUNCE, DUNDERHEAD; IRAQ WAR**

FRANK SINATRAN (*derivative two-word adjective*) — *See* **"QUAIL"; "RAT PACK"**

FRANKLIN AND ELEANOR ROOSEVELT — *Giants.*

See **GIANTS**

FREE *VERSE* — Something that isn't so *free* when you have to pay twenty bucks for a *book* of it!

Also, as Aged Sage Robert Frost said, writing *free verse* is like playing tennis with the *net* down. Old Men prefer *rhymed* verse with their Starbucks coffee—especially if it's in *iambic pentameter*. (Republicans, check your *Webster's* dictionary [xyW] or your book of Shakespearean plays, in the unlikely event you *have* one. Example of iambic pentameter: ". . . And grievously hath Caesar answered it. . . ." Further helpful hint to you *more cultured* Repubs who may even be tentatively able to grasp the concept: Five two-syllable beats to a line [pentameter], with the accent on the second syllable [iambic] . . .).

When in 1960 I taught the play *Julius Caesar* to inner-city tenth-graders with its difficult late-sixteen-century idiom, I made them *memorize* that speech, which was Mark Antony's "Friends, Romans, Country-men" funeral oration, and I showed them the film in which Marlon Brando recited it so powerfully. They took turns lying supine on my desk with a coat over their faces while a classmate stood over them reciting. (My department head's only comments regarding this vibrant lesson were that my classroom was too noisy and my window shades weren't straight—but my classroom was only noisy when I *permitted* it to be noisy.)

See **TRADITIONAL GRAMMAR**

FREEDOM — A state of "having no *restraint*."

When that "restraint" is in the context of having a tyrant's chain around your neck or his boot upon it, we use the word "freedom" here in its purest political sense. In that context, the loss of *complete* freedom is the price that civilized people must pay for *liberty* protected by *law*.

And *freedom*, of course, is far from *free*. It comes and has come at a price often and historically paid for in *arterial blood*.

See **LIBERTARIAN; LIBERTY**

FREEDOM OF THE PRESS — The mother of all our other freedoms.

Never forget that the pen is *powerful*. This goes analogically for the electronic and print media, too, and now for the *internet*—which is becoming the freest and most powerful "press" of all. Remember the old saying about the pen being mightier than the sword? The pen has brought down *presidents*—and *words* have toppled *kings*.

See **CENSORSHIP**

"FRIEND" — The word is *common*; the person, *rare*.

See The **OLD MAN'S "FRIENDS"**

FRIENDS WHO ASCEND TO POWER AND WEALTH — These are true friends indeed *if they remain in your life*.

If they *don't*, Old Men have learned not to fret over them. Instead, Old Men bask inwardly and *genuinely* in their friends' good fortune. If and when the friends lose much of their wealth and fame, they'll be back when they need you again and when they're no longer so "busy." Wealth is far more easily *lost* than gained—and to re-coin a phrase, the truth of which Old Men are all too well aware: "Fame is *fleeting*."

FRIENDSHIPS — Something wonderful to rekindle (*old*) and cultivate (*new*).

And if there are some "friends" you'd rather not see, just *lend them money* (but not too *much*).

FUNDAMENT — Literally, the *buttocks* or the *anus*.

See **ANUS** (*descriptive noun*); **DOGMA; FUNDAMENTALISTS; GEORGE W. BUSH; PAT ROBERTSON; REPUBLICAN, REPUBLICAN, AND *REPUBLICAN***

FUNDAMENTALISTS — *See* **FAITH**; The **"500" CLUB; FUNDAMENT**; The **MICKEY MOUSE CLUB**

G

GALL BLADDER — A vesicle attached to the liver which receives bile from the hepatic ducts, concentrates it, and discharges it after meals.

Many old men (and *women*) have discovered to their sorrow that they *definitely have* a gall bladder—immediately before they have to *lose* it.

GAMBLING — A way of getting *nothing* for *something*.

(Yes, you read that right.)

See **STOCK MARKET**

GAS — *See* **PASSING**

GAZING OUTWARD TOGETHER — Something *real* lovers do.

True lovers don't just gaze perpetually and soulfully into each other's eyes. (This timeless piece of wisdom comes to us courtesy of the World War I French aviator Antoine de Saint-Exupery in his marvelous book *The Little Prince*—and he wasn't talking about the *rear-entry position*.)

Old Men have lived long enough to discover that all worthwhile things that extend beyond the mere *carnal* become even more beautiful when we can *share* them.

GEEZER — An old man.

See **WHEEZY GEEZER**

GENIUS — Supposedly, anyone with an I.Q. over 147.

Also, anyone who may *not* have an I.Q. over 147 but can take a *car* or an *airplane* or a *kitchen sink* apart, fix it, and reassemble it *correctly*.

See **AUTHOR OF THE** *LANDMARK—***AND INCREDIBLY** *BRILLIANT—DEFINITIVE DICTIONARY AND ALMANAC OF ADVICE* **ENTITLED** *WHAT <u>Old Men</u> KNOW* (who despite his so-called "genius"-level I.Q. is not only abjectly unable to take a kitchen sink apart and put it back together—he is also chronically unable to find either one of his slippers without his impatient *spouse*'s help.)

GEOFFREY FIEGER — A gifted activist defense attorney who could and should have been Governor of Michigan.

GEORGE ORWELL — A prescient Aged Sage whose nightmarish book *1984* was <u>*right on*</u>.

Orwell had everything right but the year: He could have entitled it *2000* or *2004*—or maybe <u>*2012*</u> if, God forbid, Barack Obama isn't re-elected.

See **GIANTS;** *NINETEEN EIGHTY-FOUR;* **SAGES FOR THE** <u>**AGES**</u>

GEORGE W. BUSH — The *puppet* president.

The deeds of (thankfully) ex-President Bush and his handlers; e.g., attacking a non-aggressor nation, corrupting five members of the United States Supreme Court and resorting to insidious measures to skew the outcome of two national elections, as well as condoning torture and indiscriminate wiretapping and incarceration without legal representation are not only fascistic—they are *treasonous*. Bush—himself a veritable *fundament*—proved to be nearly incapable of expressing any coherent idea, even when propped up by speechwriters and electronic prompters. His presidency has done more damage to the United States and to the entire world than any of the other worst ones *combined*.

It was the great crusading attorney and Aged Sage Clarence Darrow who said, "When I was a little shaver my papa told me that *anybody* can become President; I am beginning to *believe* it." Darrow's cynical words of nine decades ago as applied to presidents of his era have an eerily futurist tone: He could easily have been prophesizing the eight-year nightmare of the Bush II administration.

See **ANUS** (*descriptive noun*); **BANK BAILOUT OF 2008; DUNCE, DUNDERHEAD; FASCISM; FASCIST; FELLOW-TRAVELLING PSEUDO-DEMOCRATS; FUNDAMENT**

GEORGE WASHINGTON — An Aged Sage who had a *golden* opportunity to wear a golden *crown*, but democratically refused it.

George Washington was one of the most courageous and resource-ful revolutionaries of all time. His military genius and fateful lack of emperial ambition altered the course of history (with a bit of help from the French).

A little-known fact is that as a young man, the Father of our Country long-jumped a then-American record twenty-two feet, two inches two centuries before American long-jump record-holders Jesse Owens, Bob Beamon, or Carl Lewis were born.

Long-jumpers are also necessarily swift sprinters, but how fast big George could have negotiated 100 yards or 100 meters we'll never know, because—Ben Franklin notwithstanding—the stopwatch hadn't been invented yet.

See **GIANTS**

GERIATRICS — A significant part—but *only* a part—of what this dazzling dissertation is about. (Repubs, xyW.)

GERMAN SHEPHERD — A breed of canine it's wise to *befriend*.

Fifty-six years ago, my late, lamented college buddy and track team-mate Cliff Hatcher was attempting to make his move on a very willing young co-ed on a couch in her living room, but her very *large* German Shepherd crouched close beside them during Cliff's entire visit and continuously growled—causing the damsel to giggle so much she never got totally in the mood.

GETTING IN TROUBLE (and we're not talking about _pregnancy_ sans _wedlock_ here) — The _situational responsibility_ (and thus oftentimes the _fate_) of any _educational leader_ worthy of the name.

In 2000, Your Auld Author shared this concept with a Wayne State University class I was teaching on education reform; in 2001, I shared it again with the Detroit public-school principals I was supervising. Neither most of my class nor many of my principals completely grasped what I was telling them: That with leadership comes the obligatory but often dangerous duty to "get in trouble" for pointing out that "the Emperor has no clothes," when indeed he _has_ none.

Wise Old Educators realize that the institution we call "school" being an "agent of society" doesn't absolve it from the responsibility to serve as an agent for _progressive reconstruction_. American democracy's world-wide power and prestige are not defined by our economic status, nor by how many nuclear weapons we've stockpiled. They're defined by our moral force. The viability of this force is being threatened from within our own nation. We must find a way to reverse our current devolution from democracy to bureaucracy and corporatorcracy.

See **STATUS QUO**

GIANTS (a limited list—many also referenced elsewhere) — Thurgood Marshall, Marva Collins, Robert F. Kennedy, Grace Lee Boggs, Franklin and Eleanor Roosevelt, Winston Churchill, Nelson Mandela, Mother Teresa, W. E. B. DuBois, Golda Meir, Abraham Lincoln, George Washington, "The Two Alberts," Malcolm, Martin Luther King, Jr., John Brown (the abolitionist—not Queen Victoria's stable-hand companion), Paul Robeson, Emiliano Zapata, Jesse Owens, Muhammad Ali, and Jackie Robinson. (_Okay—Willie Mays_, too: particularly when he still played in New York!)

See **SAGES FOR THE AGES**

GIVE, GIVING — We make a living by what we _get_, but we make a _life_ by what we give. Old Sir Winston (Churchill) said that. It brings to mind the poem "Salvaging My Soul":

I shook the tallest tree,
Pierced every secret door;
Then searched the deepest sea
For what I'd sought on shore.

My task was unachieved—
I searched and sought in vain,
Nor *gathered why I gave*.

But now my soul is free;
No more need I explore—
At last it's clear to me:
I *gave* to be *restored*.

To give is to *receive*;
To give is to *regain*;
To give ...is *to be saved*.

Paradoxically, what we genuinely give, remains forever *ours*. Indeed, to give is to *get*. It took an otherwise fairly smart Oldster who peers out at Your Auld Author from his mirror every morning a veritable lifetime to learn this more fully, and he's still *learning* it. Others die without ever learning it or even *beginning* to learn it.

See **ALTRUISM; HAPPINESS; SOCIAL ACTIVISM**

GLOBAL WARMING — It's *real*, folks.

GOD — *Alpha* and *Omega*—the *Beginning* and the *End* (Book of Revelation).

Anyone who doubts God's existence need only listen to a few bars of Beethoven or Lizst. Without divine inspiration, could their mortal minds ever have created those divine sounds?

God is the Concept Sublime. God is Perfection. God is the Eternal Presence.

Incidentally, God is also a *Libertarian* (or at least a *Democrat*). He probably hasn't been a *Republican* since the days of Lincoln (if He *ever* was.)

GOING WEE-WEE — What an old *boinker* will likely do when the husband of the lady he's *boinking* catches them in the act and nudges the old boy's anal region purposefully with the cold-steel barrel of a .45.

The experienced old *boinker* carefully and cautiously *boinks* in guaranteed secured areas only, in order to avoid going wee-wee under the circumstances described. Better yet, he arrives upon the realization that such dangerously illicit *boinkings* are better left *unboinked*.

Also, going wee-wee is something old men take *forever* to do, but it only takes them a few quick minutes to *boink* (if they still can *boink* at *all* without *Viagra*).

See **BOINK; WEE-WEE** (*verb*)

The **"GOLDEN RULE"** — "*Do unto others* that which you would have others *do unto you*."

Sounds pretty simple, doesn't it? Here's a *variation*: "Do **not** do unto others that which *you would definitely not want* them to do unto you."

The "Golden Rule" was taught by *Zoroaster* in Persia, *Confucius* in China, and Lao-Tze (founder of Taoism) in the Valley of the Han. It was taught by *Jesus Christ* on the shores of the Sea of Galilee and by the *Buddha* on the banks of the sacred River Ganges five hundred years before Jesus transfigured the Western World in the few final years of His three short decades on this earth prior to His *own* storied *Transfiguration*. (Jesus never got to become an Aged Sage, but He's a Sage for the Ages.)

Wouldn't *you* agree that these five eternal icons form a rather impressive multi-millennial theophilosophical aggregate?

The Native American Lakota inform us that we are not separate from all others—nor from the forces, events, and entities that surround us. We are all *interconnected*.

Once *you* have read the ancient and timeless "Golden Rule," digested it, and begun to believe in its power and righteousness and started to *practice* it, you don't really need to ingest and digest too many other advisements and definitions herein. This is because then *the whole world will become yours* regardless of whether or not you ever read the rest of *this* singular Old Man's theological and philosophical meanderings and political rants.

In the paraphrased words of my talented sculptor friend Robert Landry, who had an exhibit at *Ground Zero* in New York City, "The direction of our *human* evolution hinges on how we will choose to *define* our humanity. The thoughts and creativity that drive our actions foster and further either *the refinement of a disciplined humanist mind* or the *untamed urges of an ego-driven, barbaric array of neural reflexes.* Thus, inevitably we will become either *nurturers* or *conquerors.* It's not possible to be both. Ultimately what we do unto *others* we do unto *ourselves.*"

See **BARBARISM; EGO; EGOISM, EGOTISM; HUMANISM**

GOLDMAN SACHS — *Criminals.*

President Obama needs to call out the Marines, have them surround the GS Building, and force GS to return the bailout money to the American people. Otherwise, some well-bled and numerous remnants of a ragtag, righteous, millions-strong army of multi-racial American Neo-Revolutionaries toting AK-47s, Glocks, .357 magnums, .45's, hunting rifles, machetes, and butcher knives—or (hopefully) alternatively, toting word-processing laptops with internet access—may well do it *for* him very soon.

GOLF, GOLF COURSE — Even though the venerable sport of golf originated in Scotland, this venerable *auld* Scottish-American *non*-golfer sometimes *thinks the unthinkable* thought that maybe we should close all golf courses and grow turnips on them to feed the children in Haiti, in Bangladesh, in East Los Angeles, in Silver City, Mississippi, and in Detroit—particularly in the Sixteenth Street and McGraw and Mack/Connor neighborhoods. (Sorry, Tiger—but we're sure you'd do almost as well in some *other* sport—in or *out* of bed.)

See **BACK; CEMETERY; QUAYLE** (as in former Vice President Dan)**; HIPS; KNEES**

GOOD BOOKS — Books widely *praised* but seldom *read.*

In this regard, the Bible—also incidentally called "The Good Book"—undoubtedly is the uncontested champion prototype of *unreadedness* even though it is copiously *quoted* by saints and sinners alike (most often by *sinners*, Your Auld Author sometimes suspects).

See **BAD BOOKS; SARAH PALIN**

"GOOD-BUT-NOT-*GAUDY*" — What an overly critical Detroit sportswriter who never ran a varsity race in his life called a one-minute, twelve-second 600-yard race Your Auld Author clocked while eking out a very *narrow* win over Jamaican Olympian George Rhoden and the fast-finishing Ernie Billups of Loyola in Ann Arbor in February 1960.

Those deprecating words that the sportswriter wrote inspired your angry Auld Author to wish fervently, after he read them, that he could some-how be permitted to *horsewhip* the hapless scribe all the way around the track with a riding crop, meanwhile exhorting him, "Now let's see *you* run a "good-but-not-*gaudy*" 1:12 600, you ink-stained S.O.B.!"

GOOD, GOODNESS — *See* **DEMOCRACY; MACKINAC ISLAND FUDGE; MINCE PIE; "WHITE" WITCHCRAFT** (good *sometimes*)

GOOD LISTENERS — Folks who listen *discerningly*.

Old Men have learned of long experience to *listen* to their loquacious ladies with real *care*. In fact, they have learned to *go out of their way* to ask their conversant mates *deeply considerate questions*.

For example, they know to ask their ladies frequently, "How do you feel?," and "How did your day go?," or "What was today's big crisis?"

Or perhaps on suitably jocular occasions, "What did you say your *name* was?"

This last question is a great one to ask your young lady as she's clutch-ing her overnight bag in a crowded hotel or motel elevator with your fond, familiar old arm around her. And the prime time to ask it is 11:30 on a Saturday morning when you're riding down with her to check out. She'll enjoy being kidded.

However, never *ever* ask her whether she *came* (especially if you're still in the elevator). Not only is such a question indicative of abject geriatric insecurity, it's *very* bad *form*. And if you're as sensitively attuned to her as you should be (and she's not an accomplished *faker*), you'll *know* she did, anyway.

If you *aren't* in tune with her, she may well reply (in the crowded elevator), "Yes, I have come *many* times—but not with *you*, you limp-peckered old goat."

See **COME** (*verb*); **"CUM"** (*noun* and *verb*)

GOOD MAN — Someone a good woman usually tries hard and often to find, before finding him—if she *ever* finds him.

(Often, though, he is *right under her nose*—but seldom in her *pants*.)

GOOD NAME — Something Old Men have dearly earned over time through many *good deeds*—and something they can lose forever through *one bad* one.

"GOOD NIGHT, MRS. CALABASH, WHEREVER YOU ARE" — And *good night, Mr. Jimmy Durante*, wherever *you* are.

Also, we wish a *good night* to the former Ms. Bonnie Manhart of Detroit's Linwood Street circa 1941-1948, *wherever you are*.

My house on Sixteenth Street is gone, my grade-school girlfriend Bonnie's little four-family flat on the corner of Linwood and Marquette Street is gone—and fittingly, the land they occupied is now part of a new school-ground near where our *old* schoolground once stood. ("My Bonnie lies over the ocean, my Bonnie lies over the sea. . . .")

GOOD OLD DAYS — Old Men know that *these* are the good old days. ("This is the day that the Lord hath made; rejoice and be glad in it." – *Psalms 118:24*.)

Still and *also*, however, to *ruminate* on some old days (and on some old *romances*) is good, too. Such *ruminations* can warm an old boy's winter-weathered bones. (Thank you, unnamed ladies, for loving one *specific* undeserving, unappreciative, wild, roguish young reprobate.)

But above all, your *grateful Old Author* must give thanks *most* of all to one particular (and *particularly gorgeous*) *young* lady named *Gina*, a.k.a. *Mrs. John Telford* (if he knows what's *good* for him).

See **MEMORIES**

GOOD WOMAN — A veritable *queen* worth *thrice again* her weight in *rubies*.

(I'll bet *you* think I got *this* definition from Omar the Tentmaker or some other old Middle Eastern guru, but I wrote it *myself*—honest.)

G.O.P. — The "Grand Old Party."

(Except these days, there aren't too many things that are particularly *grand* about the "Grand Old Party"—other than that most of its "leaders" are insufferably *grandiose* and/or also have *grand*children).

GRACE LEE BOGGS (age ninety-six) — *See* **GIANTS; Old Women; WISE OLD WOMEN (W.O.W.)**

GRAMMATICAL RULE AGAINST ENDING A SENTENCE WITH A PREPOSITION — (Better to end it with a *proposition*?)

As my main man *Sir Winston* relevantly said, "This is *nonsense* up with which I will not *put*."

See **WINSTON CHURCHILL**

GRAND-DADDY — What most of us geezers become several times over if we live long enough.

Alternative definition: The *Ultimate Flying Orgasm* (UFO), sometimes spelled g-r-r-r-a-n-d-d-a-d-d-y, with two extra r's and punctuated with two exclamation points; e.g., "Baby, you just gave me a *colossal grrrand-daddy*!!"

GRAND-KIDS — The *rarest* of blessings.

Many grand-kids are grubby little gremlins who love it when their grand-pa tells them *stories*. A good story for Grandpa to tell them is the one about Herbert the Friendly Lion who *humped* all the other animals in the zoo. (No—on *second* thought, maybe that's *not* such a good one.)

See **HUMP** *(transitive verb)*; **ZOO**

GRAND MARNIER ("Grand MarnYAY": pronunciation aid for the benefit of Republicans) — A feisty orange-based liqueur best taken in a snifter, *straight up*—with a chaser of iced water, a *great* see-gar, and a great woman whom you're trying to get to drink *lots* of it with you. If you're *serious* about the great *woman*, though, it's best to *eschew* the cigar (and not to *chew* it, either). Yay for MarnYAY!

See **ESCHEW**

GREAT — A grossly *overused* adjective.

That is, it's *overused* unless it's applied in describing Thurgood Marshall, Mother Teresa, Nelson Mandela, Jesse Owens (zoom!), Jim Thorpe, Secretariat (*double*-zoom!), Gordie Howe, Sugar Ray Robinson, all individuals listed in this towering tome under the categories Giants and Sages for the Ages (or in describing a great *cigar*).

Here, however, is a *caveat*: You (yes, <u>you</u>) do indeed have the *potential* for greatness. As The Bard wrote 400 years ago, "Our fate is not in the stars, but in *ourselves*."

Also, as the great Scottish essayist and Aged Sage Thomas Carlyle said, "A great man shows his greatness by the way he treats [people who are *less* 'Great']."

It is well to remember, too, that all great men aren't *celebrated*, and all *celebrated* men aren't great. (See the tribute to Dr. Mel Barclay under [On] **DYING**.)

See **YOU**

The **"GREAT BEYOND"** — Where most Septuagenarian Sages' childhood chums and friends from young adulthood have sadly gone.

Many of our family, *some* of our lovers, and *all* of our grandparents, parents, mentors, uncles, and aunts have sadly gone there, too.

The "Great Beyond" is also called "The Happy Hunting Ground" by the noble, sometimes now *ceremoniously* befeathered, indigenous folk from whom *illegal immigrants* from Europe called "settlers" stole this once gloriously green and fruit-filled land.

Descendants of these very first *"illegal immigrants"* ultimately black-topped much of it for parking lots, begriming much of the rest of it with smokestack soot, and polluting our rivers and streams with all sorts of foul industrial byproducts "from sea to shining sea."

The **GREAT "RECESSION" OF 2008** — Actually an economic *depression* for those at the bottom of the *race* ladder and the *class* ladder.

The great "Recession" of 2008 marked the outset of an era of high joblessness that has only just *begun* (and I wrote this item before the disastrous 40,000-barrels-per-day oil spill in the Gulf of Mexico).

In October 2009, the nation's *reported* jobless rate was 17.4 percent, the highest rate since Your Auld Author was a pre-schooler growing up on Sixteenth Street and McGraw in Depression-time Detroit, where the *un*reported jobless rate *now* actually exceeds *50 percent*. It also exceeds 50 percent in other suffering inner cities all across America, as well as in rural areas and even in some sizable *suburban* enclaves.

When unemployment insurance finally runs out, *comes* the Revolution.

See **GEORGE W. BUSH**

GRIEF — An increasingly frequent and inevitable emotion of Old Men.

See **THE "GREAT BEYOND"**

GRUDGE-HOLDING — A state of mind which, if it endures for long, can utterly destroy the *grudge-holder*.

Often, grudge-holding also does *virtually no damage*—or at least, far *less* damage—to the "*grudged-against*"; thus grudge-holding really is entirely counter-productive. So, *forgive* those who wronged you. (Then, per JFK—smack the s--- out of them.)

See **ANGER**

GYNECOLOGIST — The *dream job* of <u>Old Men</u> (when they were young).

H

HAIR — Something that with <u>Old Men</u>—particularly old *Celtic* men—their *heads* lose but their <u>ears</u> gain.

This mysterious hair-transference happens to the point where one can sometimes actually *comb* those big, elongating shells (along with their eyebrows).

Old Celts' thick old white nose hairs in their thick old white noses can get pretty long, too. (So can their thick old white noses.) And hair also sprouts on their *backs* and *shoulders*—hair which, before, ne'er e'er was *there*.

See **HEAD HAIR**

HAITI — A nation born two centuries ago in bloody revolution against its Napoleonic oppressors.

Haiti was nearly destroyed by the 2010 earthquake and therefore has a chance to make a *brave new beginning*. Haitians must revolt again and create a self-government unlike the dictatorial government they have had for far too long—one that has cared nothing for its people's welfare but only for the lining of its own pockets.

The heartbreak of hunger and hopelessness accelerates there as these words are written, but better times will come for Haiti as its people rise up once more and seize their fate into their own hands from the hated hands of the oppressor.

HALLOWED GROUND — Anywhere American soldiers have suffered and died defending their country. . . .

. . . Or have suffered and died *believing* that they were defending their country.

In Iraq, they have been suffering and dying *protecting the acquisitive interests and investments of the* international corporate puppeteers *who sent them there by* governmental proxy—a crime and a disgrace.

HALLUCINATION — What Your Auld Author's alcoholic but otherwise admirable Auld Papa experienced when he saw large spiders crawling up the wall after a weekend drowned in whiskey.

Also, what a young man should maybe try to tell his wife that she was experiencing when she caught him pants-around-his-ankles and pumping atop a lady whose legs were wrapped high and tight around his waist. (Well, it's worth a *try*, isn't it?)

The *wisest* of Old Men don't have to tell their wives a lie like this (anymore), having learned that adultery hurts everyone concerned, and so they don't *commit* it, even if they are physically capable of it and have the opportunity.

See **ADULTERY**

See also **LEPRECHAUN**

HAPPINESS — The state of being a *giver* and being *good.*

Old Men try to be *happy* and they try to be good. (They also try not to see being *happy and* being *good* as a contradiction.)

See **GIVE, GIVING**

HARD MAN — Someone *good* for a woman to find.

At least, this is so according to American Aged Sage Mae West, who wittily switched the words "good" and "hard" in the venerable old saw, thus: "A *hard* man is *good* to find."

However, the aging diva was probably talking about a hard young man—and *surely* a Democrat. (Sorry, you Republican geezers, and some *Democrat* geezers, too—you-all need to go get your Viagra.)

Marvelous Mae also famously inquired of an admirer, "Is that a *gun* in your pocket or are you just glad to see me?"

HARDER (*adjective, a* comparative *of the adjective hard*) — More *difficult to do;* or firmer to the *touch—not soft.*

Yeer Auld Author trruly trusts that y'all find that this here empurpled publication be harder for y'all to put down and pass up than a luscious *piece of tail* (lobster tail, that is—which with the oil spill in the Gulf is going to be a lot scarcer than the *other* kind of *tail*).

Also (in the exemplified sense of *erectile firmness*), *harder* is what you young Republican roosters only wish you could be, as compared to us diamond-hard Old Democratic Stallions. *Neighhh! Snort! StampStampStamp!*

Some indulgently tolerant ladies of our acquaintance have confided to us that there *are* a *few* young members of the Pachydermous Party who can stay reasonably hard for ten or twenty seconds, though. In that vein, you've all heard the story of the young Repub who said to his psychiatrist, "Doctor, please help me—I suffer from premature ejaculation," and the psychiatrist answered, "I *can't*, son. You're a *Republican*, remember? But I *can* introduce you to a woman with a *short attention span*."

Well, you youthful, whumping Repubs, at least your *noggins* are hard. Could that be because some of you have got *rocks* in them? (I'm just kidding you young Elephantine fellers a little bit, okay?)

HARD-ON — A word Old Men sometimes use figuratively with an amused chuckle and a shake of the head to refer to what a young maverick's got who won't back off on a hotly disputed issue which can sometimes be crucial but more often *isn't* and can be settled peaceably.

Also, American slang for penile *erection*.

See **ERECTION; HARDER** (*adjective, a* comparative *of the adjective hard*)

See also **WOODY**

HARPAXOPHILIAC — Someone who is sexually aroused by being *robbed—* a psychological cousin to the masochist.

See **MASOCHIST**

HATRED — A "madness of the heart." (So wrote Lord Byron.)

Hatred has induced misguided men to commit *murder*, and it has led misguided *nations* to commit *mass* murder.

Hatred is also the most *psychically expensive* of all self-indulgences. In essence, it can also be the ultimate self-*punishment*.

See **ANGER; ENVY; GRUDGE-HOLDING; WAR**

"HATTISM" — The often overwhelming psychological urge to *nuke* upon donning a *general's* hat.

"Hattism" is also the urge to have one's *ring* kissed after donning the hat of a *bishop* or *cardinal*, or to be too quick to *mace* or swing a *night stick* after donning a *policeman's* blue hat with a black bill and a silver badge, etc.

"Hattism" is a term first presciently coined by Philip Wylie over half a century ago in his biting book *Generation of Vipers*. Many <u>Old Men</u> of high and distinguished position know all too well that the siren song of *hattism* is a song that must be resisted fiercely.

See **"ROBEISM"**

"HE WHO WANDERED BY THE SEA / OF MIDDLE EASTERN GALILEE . . ." — The greatest Revolutionary of them all.

Even though Jesus didn't wander there long enough two thousand years ago in His earthly form to become *Old*, His *teachings* are *timeless*.

See **CREATIVE INSUBORDINATION; SOCIAL ACTIVIST; "UNREASONABLE" MEN**

HEAD HAIR — Something that, if it's *fake* head hair in a bottle or can, <u>Old Men</u> have found that to spray or shake it on their heads takes more and more *spraying* and *shaking* every year after sixty.

This is because there's usually a whole lot more bald skin to cover after sixty. In fact, it's good to use a *salt shaker* with extra-huge *holes* (or else a <u>garden hose</u>!).

Actually, fake head hair is at best an affectation. So is *beard-dyeing*.

Ordinarily, it's best to try to look and act one's age, even though Your Auld Author often eschews his own Sage Advisement in this regard.

See **BEARD**

HEALTH CARE (Government-mandated) — Something that former vice-presidential candidate Sarah Palin stated she doesn't *want* for the American people.

President Obama got the Health Care Bill passed *anyway*, the boorish cad. That was *exceedingly inconsiderate* of the lady's wishes and feelings on his part, don't you think? For *shame*, Barack—you should have just left all those millions of little children to *languish without health care* instead. (You *betcha*!)

HEALTHY IRREVERENCE — A *mental posture* which all Old Men have been *passing wise* to assume toward all of the earthly *"powers-that-be"*— as well as perhaps toward most of the *un*earthly ones that there *may* be.

A HEALTHY MILE — The distance that all Old Men try to keep between themselves and *hospitals* (unless they're *visiting*).

Or unless they *work* in one.

Or unless they're reincarnations of Hollywood's old world-class drinker/ womanizer W.C. Fields, who after recuperating for two days in one, "took a turn for the *nurse*." (As my old Uncle Alfie would have said, "I *love* that joke.")

The **HEART** — A "lonely hunter," according to the timelessly Sagacious Carson McCullers.

The human heart sometimes has reasons *beyond* reason.

"HEART" — A multidimensional attribute of Old Men and Old Women (as contrasted with mere *old* men and *old* women).

"Heart" consists of three basic components: *courage, perseverance,* and *caring.*

World War II Congressional Medal of *Honor*-winner (and later film star) Audie Murphy had great <u>*courage*</u>.

Barefoot Olympic marathon champion Abebe Bikila of Ethiopia had great courage and great <u>*perseverance*</u>.

But while "heart" demands both *courage* and *perseverance,* its third essential component is the one that perhaps is paramount—a rare and deeply *self-sacrificial* kind of <u>*caring*</u> for *another* or *others.* The deaf and blind Helen Keller, the activist boxer Muhammad Ali, and the humanitarian Albert Schweitzer all have or had all three. Thus, they prototypify Aged Sages who have or had "heart."

Mother Teresa possessed *prodigious* "heart." (So do *great* <u>*educators*</u>.)

See (the second of) "The Two **ALBERTS**"; **GIVE, GIVING; "LIVE HERO-ICALLY!"; TEACHER**

HEART ATTACK — *See* **WHAT HAPPENS WHEN AN OLD MAN TRIES TO PLAY FULL-COURT BASKETBALL**

HEAVEN — A place that some <u>Old Men</u> (and *old men*) warily suspect is an antiseptic, sweeping cloudscape where (gasp!) there is *absolutely no* <u>*beer*</u>!

Nope—no beer at all. (And maybe not too many *politicians,* either— or at least, perhaps not too many *Republican* ones.)

(For some reason unrelated to *Heaven,* this recalls the old saying, "Whiskey on beer; never fear. Beer on whiskey; mighty risky!")

See **BEER**

See also **POLITICS; REPUBLICAN**

HELL — A place it's way too easy to <u>*go*</u> to.

(It's the *coming* <u>*back*</u> that's hard.)

See **BAD MARRIAGE; JEALOUSY; <u>*REX REBORN*</u>; WAR**

HENRY DAVID THOREAU — A true Sage for the Ages.

One of America's greatest all-time, *old*-time essayists, Henry David Thoreau was jailed for refusing to pay the poll tax as a protest against the 1848 Mexican War, which led to his writing *Civil Disobedience* while in jail. (This set the precedent for another great civilly disobedient American to write a landmark letter from a jail in Birmingham, Alabama a little more than a century later.)

A Thoreau quote: "Under a government which imprisons *unjustly*, the true place for a *just* man is in *prison*." And, he might have added, "in prison *with my mighty pen in hand*."

The Mexicans' great "sin," which caused the United States to go to war with them during the Polk administration, was that they had land which the United States *wanted* in order to expand *slavery*. Another Sage whom you may have heard something of *also* spoke out against that war (when he wasn't quite so Aged). His name was Abraham Lincoln.

Where are the Old Lincolns (not the car) and the Old Thoreaus of today?

One, thank God, inhabits the ironically named *White* House at this writing, and although *non*-white Barack Obama isn't an *Aged Sage* just yet, we all must pray every day that he lives to *become* one. Martin Luther King, Jr.—the Birmingham jail letter-writer—tragically *didn't*, and neither did Robert F. Kennedy. In 1968, our divided nation suffered two irredeemable losses which still affect it adversely four long decades later.

We need many more *Aged Sages* of Obama's caliber in this suffering world, we need them *now*, and we must keep them *healthy*.

See **GIANTS; SAGES FOR THE AGES**

HERO — Someone who isn't celebrated as such by mealy-mouthed bureaucrats and other hypocritical honchos until he's *safely dead*.

Malcolm X is one loudly and mendaciously lauded example.

(A *hero*, of course, is also a *sandwich*.)

HIBERNIANS — The ancient Irish.

(Did you know that the word *Scot* means *Irishman* in Gaelic?)

See **CALEDONIANS; IMBIBERS; IRISHMEN; LEPRECHAUN, SCOTS**

"HIDES IN THE WEEDS" — *See* **PSEUDO-EDUCATOR**

The **HIGHEST-STRESS JOB** — *Urban high school English teacher*, as desig-nated in a ten-year-old study.

A doting mother tells her twenty-three-year-old college-educated
   daughter: "This new young fellow of yours sounds *neat*, honey.
   What does he do?"
Daughter: "He's a *high school English teacher* in *Detroit*."
Silence. "Mom? . . . Mom? . . ."
The girls' father comes on the line: "Sweetheart, it's Dad. What did
   you just say to your mother?"
"Why, Papa? Is something wrong?"
"She just *fainted*."
"I told her my boyfriend is a *high school English teacher* in *Detroit*."
Silence again, followed by a dial tone.

The ten-year-old study ranked *urban police officer* as the second most
stressful job. As I write this item on May 3, 2010, five Detroit cops have
just been shot, one fatally. I think we need a follow-up study. In that
one, *urban cop* would unquestionably become *first* (unless *U.S. combat
soldier* in Iraq or Afghanistan were included in it).

HIPS — *See* **KNEES**

HISTORY — An impure social *"science"* tainted by *ethnocentrism*.

Ergo, a chronological recounting of *fables* as created and then written
as *gospel* by the "winners" of wars.

See **ETHNOCENTRISM; WAR**

HOME — The timeless dwelling place of the *heart*.

Home is a *house* like the one in old Indianapolis that the late, great Aged Sage Kurt Vonnegut *returned to* in forlorn longing and nostalgically reminiscent dreams of when he was *nine* and had a *mother* and a *father* and a *sister* and a *dog* . . .

. . . Or like the *house* on *Sixteenth Street* at *McGraw* in old Detroit that a certain <u>Old Man</u> returns to in dreams of when I was *ten* and had a *mother* and a *father* and *cousins* and *sleek black cats* and a *plum tree* to *climb up high in* and *squirt-gun* fights with *Gussie* and *Jeanie* and *Dickie* and *Skip* in the alley next to the house on sultry summer nights and had a girlfriend named Bonnie and a slingshot and a *Red Ryder bb rifle* to shoot the few rats our cats didn't catch and a poor dumb old *mutt* named *Rapscallion* whom Bus McCracken shot to death because Rap was howling at the *moon* at midnight because my mother made him sleep out in the yard one night to *punish* him, or to punish *me*—I can't remember *which* now, sixty-five tumultuous years later.

But the house isn't there anymore; it isn't *there* anymore—except in dreams, except in *dreams*. . . .

HOODOO — A variation of *Voodoo*.

("You remind me of a *man*." "*What* man?" "A man with *power*." "*What* power?" "The power of *Voodoo*!" "<u>Who</u> do?" "<u>You</u> do!" "I do *what*?" "Remind me of a *man*. . . .")

See **VOODOO**

HOPE — A "thing with feathers," according to the divine Miss Dickinson.

> If *hope* no longer *flies*,
> That's <u>when</u> the <u>Old Man</u> dies.

HOPELESSNESS — The most dangerous, despairing, and potentially *terminal* emotion any man or woman—old or young—can ever experience.

See **ANOMIE; CLINICAL DEPRESSION**

HORIZON — Where the road rises to merge with the sky.

Just before that ultimate rise in the road, Old Men metaphorically or metaphysically become *the road itself* in that distant dip beyond the hill where reality becomes *illusion* and illusion *becomes real*. In that magical place, *one* consciousness flows into *another* and *another* and *another*. The *real* then melds with the unreal, the *what-once-was-real*, and the *not-yet-*real.

It is *there* that a Septuagenarian Sage can win a world middleweight championship and an Olympic sprint race and write a best-selling book that will save the world for its children. It is also there that he may forever prance with primal princesses in palatial gardens, under a pale moon.

See **DEATH; EUCLID; INFINITY**

HORROR — *See* **ABOMINATION; REX REBORN; A RIDDLE TO PONDER; WAR**

"HOSE" (*plural noun*) — Misspelled Ebonic slang for *"ladies of the evening."*

(Correct spelling, *ho's.*) Also misspelled *hoze*.

"Ho's" is a word that *disreputable* young men and women disrespectfully call *reputable* young women. They need fathers like *me* or like I *had* to teach them never to do this.

HOSTAGE — A person being detained against his will (unless he's an innocent Arab being held by the CIA or the FBI—then he's a "suspect").

HOUSEKEEPER — A long-term wife with a good *divorce lawyer*.

HOW (NOT) TO FIGHT A WOMAN — Old Men have painfully learned that the best way (*not*) to fight an angry woman is with your hat and coat.

Grab them and *run!*

HOW OLD IS "OLD"? — A *major* cosmic question.

Also, what *is* "old"? (This vaunted but daunted *Dictionary* can only leave such questions to *you* to try to answer definitively for *yourselves*.)

See **OLD; QUESTIONS TO CONSIDER**

HOW TO LOSE WEIGHT — That's quite simple—keep your <u>mouth</u> closed. When we long-winded Old Democrat dudes really want to lose weight, we manfully strive to just keep our mouths *closed* for a while—except to drink lots of *prune juice*, smoke lots of cigars (without any *whiskey*), and tell jokes about Republicans.

That will work for you <u>young</u> Democrat dudes, too—if you can possibly manage to keep your <u>mouths shut</u> (save for the cigar)—for a reasonable span of time, and also eschew the whiskey.

See **ESCHEW**

HUBRIS — Insufferable and self-destructive *arrogance* that—like the Biblical pride—"cometh before a fall."

Just ask my ex-mayor buddy Kwame Kilpatrick of Detroit to define the word: As I write this particular *Definition*, Kwame is sitting in the Wayne County slammer for the next few months for, among other things, lying under oath about his adulterous relationship with his female chief of staff, and he could be locked up in a federal prison for much longer when the feds get through with him.

I am one of the few folk who happen to hope and believe, however, that Kwame will bounce back some day and still do something great with his life, and I remain even more convinced that *she* will, too. Only *time* will tell.

See **TIME**

HUGS — Something we <u>Old Men</u> know to give our *loved ones* (a whole *lot* of times).

We also know to tell them we *love* them, a whole lot of times.

As author George Eliot (who incidentally was a *woman*) said, "The *eternal silence* is *long enough* to be silent in" (and never again to *hug* in).

HUMANISM — *Humanitarianism; ergo,* any democratic system or mode of thought or action in which both individual and collective *human interests* predominate over <u>*corporate*</u> interests.

See **SOCIALISM**

HUMANIST — Someone who wishes the best for all humankind— a humanitarian.

See The **"GOLDEN RULE"**

HUMANITARIAN (*noun*) — A *humanist,* and an unflaggingly hopeless and *hopeful* <u>optimist</u> in regard to the underlying and untapped goodness of our often *sorry* but sometimes *soaring* species.

See **OPTIMISM, OPTIMIST**

HUMILITY — Something in extremely short supply, particularly among all politicians and physicians, many overpaid and ultra-*flattered* athletes, and *some* school superintendents and professors of education.

<u>Old Men</u> know that humans are obliged to attain at least a *modicum* of humility sooner or later, unless like one particular recent American president, they're among that vast multitude who are too dumb to recognize their limitations or correct their misdirection.

Humility is what old King Canute learned at the moment he confidently commanded the waves in the River Thames to go backward (they *didn't!*—how *dare* they *not?*).

Humility is also what—like old King Canute—Yale's most famous "C" student *may* finally have learned when his waves-to-go-backward, *No* [rich] *Child Left Behind* edict had <u>*zero*</u> *positive effect* on urban schools' <u>*test scores*</u>.

HUMP (*transitive verb*) — *See* **BOINK**

HUNTERS — Folks who should be required to wear antlers and buckskin. Fair's *fair*.

HYDROGEN BOMB — The potential Destroyer of *Nations*.

Some rank *idealists* maintain that *all* nations should *share* the hydrogen bomb. Some rank *pessimists* like Your Auld Author maintain that some day soon they all *will*.

See **APOCALYPSE**

HYPNOTHERAPISTS — Professionals that Old Men don't care to patronize.

Old Men know to avoid *particularly* those who swing a pendant under your nose and enjoin *you* monotonically: "Repeat this mantra after me: '*Hypnotherapy* is worth $200 an hour; *hypnotherapy* is worth $200 an hour.' . . ."

I

I — Here, *definitely* and <u>*Definitively*</u>, follows what I call *"The* <u>Old Man's</u> Mantra" (T<u>OM</u>M): "The biggest troublemaker *I* have ever had to deal with regards me bemusedly in the *mirror* every morning."

It is well for all of us <u>Old Men</u> (and *old men*) to repeat T<u>OM</u>M seven times daily at precisely 7:00 a.m. (Then we can take precisely *seven minutes* to *pee* seven droplets and go sleepily back to bed.)

See **ME;** **A** <u>*RIDDLE*</u> **TO PONDER;** *YOU*

IDEA — The *deepest root* of human creation. (<u>*Ideate*</u> on that.)

Also, the acronym for the Kettering Foundation-sponsored Institute for the Development of Educational Activities (whereof your unassuming Auld Author was named a Fellow in 1982).

IDEALS — The guideposts whereby we endeavor to chart our life's course, as by the stars in the night sky.

Indeed, our *ideals* are *like* those stars we will never ever quite reach but can see and thus know that they are there for us to *strive for*, and try thereby to steer our lives.

IDEOLOGUE — An *"ogue"* (pronounced "awg", to rhyme with *dog*) who is neither *ideal* nor *ideational*.

Doctrinaire old *"dawgs"* to a *fault*, those old ideologue *"dawgs"* won't learn any *new* <u>*tricks*</u>. They detest new and creatively *contrary* and *progressive* ideas.

Ideologues are also *scarily* susceptible to the spell of divisive "awgs" called *demagogues*, like Black Muslim leader Louis Farrakhan, Michigan's racist Royal Oak radio priest Charles Coughlin, and Coughlin's contemporary, the Depression-era Louisiana Governor Huey Long.

See **DEMAGOGUE; PEDAGOGUE**

IDIOSYNCRATIC — For a contextual reference regarding the use of this word, revisit Dr. Wayne Dyer's Introduction to this tumid tome. Otherwise (if you're a card-carrying member of the Pachydermous Party), you might simply want to check your *Webster's* (xyW).

See **QUIRKY**

IDIOT — *See* **A-- H---; CHIP SALTSMAN**

IGNORANCE — A *voluntary* misfortune.

See **INCOMPETENCE**

"I'LL MISS YOU" — Three little words a long-suffering Old Woman says when her pestiferous *old man* tells her he's going to make her the *happiest woman in the world.*

IMAGINATION — The ruler of the universe. (*Ponder* that definition for at least a few days—or better yet, for a few *years*.)

IMBIBERS — Your Auld Author wishes all you happy Hibernians a most *celebratory* Saint Patrick's Day in advance.

Let's *tip a glass* to *Saint Andrew*, too—as well as to Saint George, Saint James, and Saint John, and then to Saint Matthew, Saint Mark, and Saint Luke, and then to Saint Paul, Saint Christopher, Saint. . . .

See **IRISHMEN; SCOTS**

IMMATURITY — A state of lengthy duration in a few young four-legged forest animals and *most* young *two-legged human* animals.

See **young men**

IMP — A mischievously mosquito-like disciple of The Devil.

An imp insidiously plies his pitchfork to poke righteous and unrighteous mortals alike, causing them considerable consternation and discomfort —rather like the Shakespearean Iago (pronounced ee-AH-go) from *Othello*.

Also rather like the insidiously impish Karl Rove. (*See* **KARL ROVE**)

IMPOSSIBLE THINGS — Phenomena that Miguel de Cervantes' old sixteenth-century knight Don Quixote believed in, and that little girls and boys believe in—particularly on Christmas Eve.

Many Old Men also believe in *impossible things*. In fact, *this* Old Man still harbors the hope that on some magic day in the year 2020 he might shed thirty pounds and win the Olympic 400, his unattained goal of the 1950s. (I have actually had this dream several times recently— talk about the *impossible dream*!!)

Do you *really* think that Santa Claus is just some old dude whose heavy travel schedule and compulsive gift-giving are his way of compensating for having no kids of his own? No way! The magically *soaring* Santa of song, story and *childhood* lives! Yes, Virginia, he really *does*. But he *lives* only if we *breathe life into him*—and not just on December 24, but throughout the year.

When practical little Alice said in *Through the Looking Glass* that it's impossible to believe in *impossible things*, the Red Queen replied, "Fiddlesticks! I've believed in as many as six *impossible things* before *breakfast*!"

This time I've got to go with the Queen.

See **HOPE; HORIZON**

IMPOTENCE (with the accent on "<u>IMP</u>") — A dysfunctional political (and allegedly *physical*) condition suffered by young (and *old*) affiliates of the G.O.P. —the *(in)*famous Party of "No."

See **DETUMESCENCE; FLACCID; G.O.P.; IMP; INEFFECTUAL**

INCOMPETENCE — A characteristic *far* too likely (and *unfortunately*) to get one promoted in an academic or governmental bureaucracy.

(Sad to say, sometimes it's *bad* to be *good*, and *good* to be *bad*.)

See **BUREAUCRAT; IGNORANCE; SUPERORDINATE**

INCORPORATED STATES OF AMERICA — *See* **CORPORATOCRACY; A *RIDDLE* TO PONDER**

INEFFECTUAL — *See* **IMPOTENCE; REPUBLICAN**

INFINITY — An *infinitely* <u>uncommon</u> concept, subject to the three dimensions within the *common* spheres of human divination—height, width, and depth.

(*Eternity* is the word that is more accurately used in referring to the realm of *time*—the *fourth* dimension.)

Infinity can be found in a fleeting rainbow that disappears before one can sufficiently admire its perfection, or visualize its nether arc. The most Sagacious of Aged Sages can't discover the rainbow's *end*, because in the 3-D environment wherein we mortals reside, it *has* none. (But if it *did*, I'm sure there'd be a *pot of gold* there!)

The miracle of the rainbow is that it's the *visible* half of a half-*unseen*, *perpetually perfect* circle of the panoramic colors formed by sunlight and liquid and air—like the guardian angel some of us think maybe we fleetingly *half*-saw when we were little and we turned very suddenly to try to catch her off guard. (Did you ever do that when you were a little nipper?)

Some relatively simple questions about infinity still stump even the most accomplished mathematicians. For example, prime numbers such as 5, 11, and 29—which can be evenly divided by themselves and 1—tend to occur in *pairs* separated by two units: 5 and 7; 11 and 13; 41 and 43; 101 and 103. The ancient Greeks found this mathematical method of attempting to conceptualize *infinity* to be so threatening to men's sanity that they actually forbade any further study of it. In the Third Century B.C., the great Aged Sage Euclid risked studying it *anyway*.

Euclid was able to prove that the number of prime numbers is *infinite*. However, mathematicians even today aren't sure whether there's an infinite number of these *pairs*, called "twin primes."

Far and deep within even the near-*infinite* reaches of an Aged Sage's cosmically curious mind, for him to attempt to address and to grasp the concept of *infinity* is for him to confront the *universal labyrinth*, the *ultimate abstraction*.

Actually, the word "infinity" *is* an *abstract noun* conceived by old, Old Men long ago in an attempt to encompass the maddening concept of what it would be like to fly up, up, and away from Planet Earth like *Superman* and sojourn straight out into space in a single direction forever and ever and ever and *ever*. This is the mystery within the riddle inside the enigma of the ages that even we as-yet-veritably-*Earthbound* and Earth-*bonded* Aged Sages have tried and tried and tried *in vain* to *solve*.

Endlessly and *endlessly* and *endlessly* we ponder the darkling puzzle of *infinity*'s physical manifestation: The mirror within the mirror within the mirror within the mirror within the mirror within the mirror within the . . . Stop! For God's *sake*, stop. . . .

See **ETERNITY; EUCLID; LEPRECHAUN; TIME**

See also **STRING THEORY** (if *you really* want to *blow your brain*)

INFLATION — The immediately impending American and world currency-crash that common folk aren't anticipating and only gold-hoarding multi-millionaires are even *semi*-prepared to cope with.

For the only *practicable* (but admittedly psycho-genetically *improbable*) solution, *see* **RESOURCE-DRIVEN AND *TECHNOLOGY*-DRIVEN ECONOMIC SYSTEM**

INFLUENCE — The power of producing *effects* via means that aren't necessarily *visible* or *sensate*.

Old Men's thoughts and actions are influenced *lastingly* by everywhere we've *been* and everyone we've *met*—and everywhere we've been and everyone we've met are a lasting part of us.

You can "take the boy out of the *country*," but *you* can't "take the country out of the *boy*"—whether the "boy" be *young* or *old*.

INJUSTICE — Unjust action or treatment.

Since *caped crusaders* (that is, sane ones) exist only in comic books and fantasy films, *We the People* ourselves must take on the fight against evil *ongoingly*, or evil *will* prevail—*guaranteed*—and it won't need *Kryptonite* to do us in. In real life, there *ain't* no Superman soaring like some savior in the sky. Nor is there a Batman in a Batmobile, nor a Silver Surfer, nor a Billy Batson shouting "Shazam!" to summon the lightning bolt that transforms him into Captain Marvel. (Blessedly though, we *do* have a *Barack Obama*.)

See **CREATIVE INSUBORDINATION; DRAGON; EVIL; FASCISM; JUSTICE; OBAMA; "RRR"**

The **INJUSTICE OF THE *FAUX-JUST*** — An entire additional *Definitive Dictionary* could be composed on this topic—perhaps Your Auld Author's *next* one (if he is to survive beyond a lifetime of good whumping and bad whiskey to *have* a next one).

Note: This item could also be titled *The Injustice of the "Just"* (note quotation marks).

See **DETROIT PUBLIC SCHOOLS**

See also **WHUMPERER, WHUMPING**

The **INQUIRY PROCESS** — A procedure that involves reformulating aspects of current high school and university curricula into the form of *questions* to which students are guided toward *deriving and articulating their own answers.*

Here are some sample questions:

What, if anything, seems to you to be worth _dying_ for? How did you come to believe this? At the present moment, what would you most like to be able to _be_, or _do_? _Why_? What would you have to _know_ in order to be able to do it? How can _good_ be distinguished from _evil_? What kind of _person_ would you most like to be? How might you get to _become_ this kind of person? What are the most important _changes_ that have occurred in the past ten years? _Twenty_ years? _Fifty_ years? In the _last_ year? What will be the most important changes _next_ year? Next _decade_? What makes you think so? What would _you_ change if you _could_? How might you go about it? Of those changes that are going to occur, which would you _stop_ if _you_ could? _Why_? _How_?

Here are some more:

What are the most dangerous _ideas_ that are popular today? Why do you think so? Where did these ideas _come from_? How might humankind's _survival-activities_ be different if we didn't have _language_? What meaning does the word _infinity_ hold for you? What is the _meaning_ of _meaning_?

In _Conversations with God, Book II_, Neil Walsche states, "Right now, schools exist mainly to _provide answers_. It would be far more beneficial if their primary function were to _ask questions_. What does it mean to be _honest_ or _responsible_ or _fair_? What are the _implications_? For that matter, what does it mean that $2 + 2 = 4$? What are the _implications_?"

Okay, _what are you waiting_ for? Get a pencil and paper and start _answering_ (or at least _trying_ to answer) these questions!

(Send _me_ your _answers_, too—as well as _new questions_, c/o my publisher, Harmonie Park Press in Sterling Heights, Michigan.) Walsche correctly implies that the _treasure_ should be in the _question_ as well as in the _answer_.)

INSANITY — The sad state of our entire civilization, which suffers not only from not being rational—but from not knowing that it is _irr_ational.

See **LUNACY; RACISM**

INSIPID — Lacking _distinction_, or lacking interesting or attractive _qualities_.

See **DOGGY DIAPERS**; The **DUMBING-DOWN OF AMERICA'S TEXTBOOKS; PUTTING CUTE LITTLE COATS AND HATS ON CUTE LITTLE DOGS AND CATS; "VALLEY GIRLS"**

INSTINCT — The *"bloodhound"* of the human brain.

Instinct is *untaught ability*. It is also a genetically *protective gift* from the Creator.

See **INTUITION**

"INSTRUCTION MANUALS" — The intentionally boring label that shrewd Old Men paste on their file folders to keep curious intruders from snooping in them.

This is particularly the case if they don't want their wives nosing into their surreptitious stash of clipouts of Playboy bunnies or surreptitiously-hoarded hundred-dollar bills they've slipped into the folders.

INTEGRITY — The rarest wealth a man, whether he be young or old, can possess—to be guarded like gold; and paradoxically, to be generously *spent*, yet never to be risked or sacrificed.

The **INTERNET** — *See* **FREEDOM OF THE PRESS**

INTERPLANETARY (AND ULTIMATELY INTERSTELLAR) SPACE — The *sky's* the limit *no longer*!

If our species survives and advances, Man will be on Mars in this century and beyond our solar system near the end of the next one.

INTOLERANCE — In a strictly *ethnic* sense, the curse of every human *era*—and of more than a billion *errant* humans.

INTUITION — Something women erroneously suppose that they possess *more of* than men do.

See **INSTINCT**

IRAQ WAR — America's illegal, immoral, expensive, and catastrophic conflict in the Middle East, over *oil*.

So-called "preemptive" aggressions like the Iraq War can only be avoided when we build a brave new movement to create a more *just*, more *caring*, and more *sustainable* democracy.

See **ABOMINATION; AFGHANISTAN; DECEPTION; *RESOURCE*-DRIVEN AND *TECHNOLOGY*-DRIVEN ECONOMIC SYSTEM; VIETNAM WAR**

IRISHMEN — Natives of Ireland, or *descendants* thereof who claim (or rather, *boast*) predominately Irish heritage.

As Scots actually aren't people who invariably greet you with an ex-claimed, "Hoot, mon!," neither are Irishmen people who always greet you with an exclaimed, "Top o' the *mairnin' t'* ye, laddie!"

In actuality, too many Irishmen—quaint tales of thatched cottages and pints of brown ale and leprechauns and shamrocks *aside*—are contentious folk who have felt impelled to kill *each other* (while they weren't also killing a host of *Englishmen*) over *religious disagreements* (absurdly) and also *national sovereignty* (sadly and understandably).

See **IMBIBERS; PATRIOTISM; RELIGIONISM; SCOTS** (*noun*)

"IS YOU *IS*, OR IS YOU *AIN'T*??" — "*Are* you or *aren't* you ('for real')?"

"Is you *is*, or is you *ain't*??" is one of the more challengingly pointed samples of American Ebonic dialectical idiom uttered by the late, lamented Gracie Kemp and many wonderful others among Your Old Author's Detroit high school and junior high school students over the past half-century.

(Is *you* really for *real*?—don't answer *me*, answer *yourself*.)

ISIS — The sacred Egyptian goddess of life, and of the moon.

Isis accordingly consecrated the pre-eminent sacredness of sable-hued, night-stalking cats—a pre-eminence whereof Your Auld Author's finicky and utterly *indulged* long-haired, sable-hued feline *Mindy* is fully convinced.

Isis is also distinguished by the *solar disc* on her head, as the spouse (and *sister*) of the god Osiris, whose *eye* was the *sun*.

See The **"EYE OF OSIRIS"**

IT AIN'T NO FUN LYING SEDATED IN A HOSPITAL BED . . . — *See* **CANCER; TOBACCO**

J

JACKAL — See **BLACK REPUBLICAN; BUREAUCRAT; LAPDOG; "YES-MAN"**

JACKIE ROBINSON — A fellow who just happened to *long-jump* over *twenty-five feet* as a *track* (and *football*) All-American at UCLA.

(Oh, yes—he also integrated major league baseball.)

See **DODGERS; GIANTS; ZACK ROBINSON**

"JC-ICBM" — A poem about murderous missiles named for ancient Greek gods.

No way should American missiles be named for ancient Greek gods, since the United States is one of the world's so-called "Christian" lands. The "JC" represents the initials of Someone no *deadly missile* should *ever* be named for.

Hint for hawkish Republicans: That *Someone* is the *Prince of Peace*.

See **ABOMINATION; MURDEROUS MISSILES NAMED FOR ANCIENT GREEK GODS**

JEALOUSY — "The injured lover's *hell*." – John Milton.

Jealousy is also sometimes the *uninjured* lover's hell.

See **ENVY; HELL**

JEKYLL-and-HYDE (*hyphenated adjective*) — A Robert Louis Stevenson-inspired expression, and now *syndrome*, depicting an *illness*/"*wellness*" *bipolarity*—a personality split between "good" and of "evil."

This all-too-common *syndrome* denotes a crack in the mirror that best had been *patched*—and the best of men have that "crack." In the worst of men (and of women), that crack is a *gaping hole*, but even those of us who are ninety-nine parts Dr. Jekyll remain *one part Mr. Hyde* until we're absolutely *ancient*, and some of us even *beyond* then. It's particularly ingrained in violent *masculine*-human nature, just as it's in our masculine nature to spread our seed indiscriminately. Ask any sane, plain, decent, honest woman how hard it is for (some) men not to act on the latter impulse. We'd spread our seed beyond the *stars*, if we could. (Actually one day, we will *have to* spread our seed beyond the stars if our currently earthbound species is to *survive* beyond the demise of our planet).

The true (and truly *cosmic*) conundrum here is whether *Homo Sapiens* *deserves* to survive beyond the demise of Planet Earth.

Even though a misogynistic answer to this conundrum presently pounds implacably in Your Auld Author's aging brain and beats and bubbles in his heart and mind, at this point I shan't attempt to offer (or *impose*) that answer. The so-called "cosmic jury" is, after all, still *out* on us and how we might evolve to a more peaceable, non-"bipolar" species.

See **A *RIDDLE* TO PONDER**; **SEED**; **"SEEDS"**

JESTER — A playing card.

Also, someone who utters a risky truth—often (but not *always*) with *impunity*. The late Lenny Bruce, the late Richard Pryor, the late George Carlin, and the very-much-alive Bill Maher are prime examples.

(Republicans, for your information, "impunity" means "exemption from punishment." Let *me* use "impunity" in a sample sentence for *you*: "Bush and Cheney shouldn't have been granted *impunity* for their treasonous war crimes." Your Auld Author isn't always going to be so helpful defining words *you* should already be familiar with. Often, I'm simply going to say "Check your *Webster's*—xyW.")

JOGGING — A curious part-*run*, part-*walk*, and *all-shuffle* form of *perambulation* (Repubs, check your *Webster's*—xyW.)

Old Men have painfully learned *never* to jog very *far*.

Besides, jogging is *boring*—especially for old, formerly lightning-fast ex-sprinters, who were accustomed to *out-racing the wind*. The only destination for old joggers is the *toilet bowl* when they eat and drink too much—and sometimes this turns into an urgent *semi-sprint* rather than a *jog*. (As the old Scots drinking song goes, "*Oop Comes Yeer Supper!*")

My old buddy Buster McBunnigan, who drinks to *pass the* time, passed into the *twenty-second century* last night.

Or rather, he passed *out* into it.

See **KNEES**

JOHN BOEHNER — An Ohio Republican who at this writing is currently the House Minority Leader in the Obama administration.

In the March 24–30, 2010 edition of the *Metro Times* (www.metrotimes. com), *semi-Aged* Sage columnist Jack Lessenberry called Congressman Boehner a "sleek, tanned *pseudo-fascist.*"

Along with Mr. Boehner's lockstep G.O.P. congressional colleagues—all of whom enjoy excellent health insurance—Boehner (naturally) voted against Obama's victorious bill for health-care reform. "If we don't stop this so-called health-care reform, we're going to spend our sunset years telling our grandkids what it was like in America when men were *free*." (*Oops*—it wasn't *Boehner* who said that! It was *Ronald Reagan* in the 1960s, badmouthing Medicare, which George (H. W.) Bush called "socialized medicine" in 1964!)

Dr. Lessenberry also wrote, "It's interesting that neither Reagan nor George H. W. Bush breathed a word about repealing [Medicare] when they got to the Oval Office. [Years later,] Bush *minor* did start muttering about making Social Security 'voluntary.' That made sense to him. After all, Republicans had denounced Social Security as a plan right from the Kremlin when it was passed in 1935. Yet when Bush started talking about getting rid of it, [the] Republicans—who then had a majority in Congress—sent him a message even *he* could understand: '*Shut up.*'"

See **PSEUDO-FASCIST**

JOHN KERRY — A man who should have been president of the United States.

See **AL GORE**

john powell (uses no capital letters in his name) — *See* **AGED SAGES; FEDERATED REGIONALISM**

JOKE 1 — Two very old men hobbled into a house of ill repute. Noting their age, the madam decided not to waste any of her ladies on the geezers and instead provided them with inflatable dolls, figuring they were too decrepit to tell the difference. Hobbling home, one geezer told the other,

"I think my gal was dead."
"Dead? What makes you think so?"
"She never moved or made a sound the whole time."
"Could be worse—mine was a real *witch*."
"A *witch*? How?"
"When I kissed her on the neck I gave her a little nip, and I lost my teeth—and they stayed *stuck* in her!"
"That doesn't mean she was a witch."
"Yes it does—when I bit her, she *farted* and flew out the *window!*"

JOKE 2 — An Army lieutenant driving down a muddy road a mile from the barracks encountered a mud-mired jeep with a red-faced old colonel at the wheel.

"Are you stuck, sir?" the lieutenant asked.
"No, *you* are," the old colonel replied, coming over and handing him the keys.

JOKE 3 — Old Jumping Jack Humper was sunning his wrinkled old hide by a pool in a posh condo complex with his young buddy Jealous Joe, and despite Old Jack's obvious age, he still was sexy enough to be attracting 100 percent of the nubile poolside honeys. When young Jealous Joe asked him how this could be happening, Old Jumping Jack confided, "The secret is to put a *potato* in your swim trunks."

Gratefully, young Joe followed Old Jack's advice. The next day at the pool, Old Jack was still getting all the girls. His disconsolate young friend asked him again even more plaintively how this could be. Old Jack responded, "Joe, you little peach-fuzzy dummy! You're supposed to put the potato in the _front_ of your swim trunks."

JOKE 4 — An old fellow was getting remarried, and one day when he was at his fiancée's drop-dead-_gorgeous_ younger sister's house, the sister threw her panties down the stairs and called for him to come up to her bedroom. He fled hurriedly out the front door only to find his fiancée's whole family out there waiting for him. It had been a _test_—which he had thus passed with flying colors and much back-slapping and congratulating from his new family.

The moral to the story? Keep your rubbers in your _car_.

JOKE 5 — What do you call forty guys watching the Super Bowl on television? The winless 2009 Detroit Lions. (Courtesy of the January 2009 _Reader's Digest_.) But just _wait_ until 2019—_Detroit_'ll show 'em! (Hope indeed springs external.)

JOKE 6 — How did the nation know that New York's ex-Governor Eliot Spitzer is a Democrat? Answer: He was caught with a woman.

JOKE 7 — "Well," snarled the tough old Navy chief to the befuddled seaman, "I imagine that after your discharge, you'll just be waiting for me to die so you can come and _pee_ on my _grave_."

"Not me, Chief—once I get out of the Navy, I'm never going to _stand in line_ again."

JOKE 8 — God told a particularly righteous Old Man that He wanted to grant him his fondest wish. The Old Man was a motorcyclist who still was wont to traverse the country on his Harley, so he asked God to build him a bridge from California to Hawaii so he could ride there across the vast ocean on his cycle and feel the sea breeze.

God responded, "I can *do* that, of course, because I'm *God*—but I would have to put girders deep on the ocean floor to grant that wish. Besides, I was hoping you'd wish for something more *socially conscious*."

The Old Man replied, "Well, God, then give me the power to be able to understand all of my young wife's *ever-changing moods* and show me a way to empathize with her regarding '*today's* crisis'."

God pondered for a moment and then asked the Old Man, "Do you want the highway to be *one* lane or *two*?"

JOKE 9 — A young Scottish couple whose respective clans had different familial plaid tartans were getting married. A friend of the prospective groom who was in the wedding party asked him,

"What's the *tartan*?"
The groom replied, "She's in just a *regular wedding dress*."

(Some of you regressing Repubs are going to have to *reflect* for a bit on Joke 9. Think "*tartan*" / "tart *in*.")

JONAH — A Biblical figure who survived being swallowed by a "big fish," according to the beliefs of many Judeo-Christian fundamentalists (perhaps including a recent American president and probably including a significant number of his party's senators). 'Twould perhaps be far better had they believed in *Santa Claus*—and faithfully *practiced* that belief. (And *no*, Repubs—this *isn't* Joke 10.)

See **FAITH; FUNDAMENTALISTS; IMPOSSIBLE THINGS**

JOY! — A rapturous, exhilarating, exclamatory, intoxicating, tingling, fantastic, physical yet *deeper*-than-physical, far-too-*fast*-fleeting *phantasm* that can only dwell deep in one's very own *heart of hearts*.

Old Men also know that *fortunate* are the folk who know *joy!*, if only for a moment or two in a lifetime. It is truly tragic that many men and women live out their days without ever drinking a solitary *droplet* of *joy!* This *phantasm* isn't a mere feeling of *infatuation*, or even an *obsession* to be sipped until one is eventually sated of sipping: After experiencing *joy!*, one is never *ever* the same again.

Joy! encompasses an entire *foreverness* in one's memory, and too many relevant nostalgically recollective revisitations can sometimes actually drive an <u>Old Man</u> mad.

JUSTICE — An *abstraction* representative of a "commodity" that is ever in *short supply*.

Fragile, life-affirming oases of justice are ones that have survived only fleetingly between the *sweeping wartime deserts* of the ages. While *establishing* justice and maintaining *peace* can often be mutually exclusive, the only kind of peace that is sustainable for long is *peace with justice*.

See **INJUSTICE; PEACE WITH JUSTICE**

K

KARL ROVE — Can *you* spell e-v-i-l g-e-n-i-u-s?

See **BUSH'S BRAIN; IMP**

KHARTOUM — The capital of Sudan, south of the Sahara Desert. Also, the setting of a Hollywood film of the same name.

When some *Republicans* overhear some fellow say he's going to Khartoum, they think he's about to draw a picture. (Get it?)

KID ROCK'S FOUR S's — *Sex, Supper, Silence,* and *Support.*

These are what Kid Rock looks for his ideal woman to provide him with.

(Hey, ladies, don't blame *me. Kid Rock* said it—*I* didn't.)

KIDNEY STONES — (Owwwww!!!)

You better believe these are some sharp-cutting little devils which it's far better never to get *cut* by. Your Auld Author speaks from bloody experiences he would have vastly preferred not to have had.

See **PASSING**

KILTS AND TARTANS — What the brraw, claymore-totin' Highland lads hae trraditionally worrn to imprress the lassies, scarrrify the *Lowlanders* and the *English* in ancient times, and terrrify the *Huns* in the Argonne Forest in 1917 and in North Africa in 1942.

See **"LADIES FROM HADES"; SCOTS** (*noun*)

See also **ETHNOCENTRISM**

KISMET — *See* **COINCIDENCE**

KNEES — Joints that can really *hurt*, if the pain-wracked old pisser in question was a *jock* in his frisky young years.

Oww! Oww! <u>Ow</u>-woo! Guess *what*, Gramps—*replacement time* be jest 'round the corner. (You know, as I write this, I'm suddenly having trouble arising *from my rocking chair*. Someone give me an Advil. No, make that the *whole damn bottle*, and let me take it with *another* bottle—of *Crown Royal*, or *150-proof rum*.)

KNOWLEDGE — Something that even Aged Sages can never sufficiently and totally attain, because since *knowledge* is *infinite*, nearly its entire eternal aggregate remains perforce <u>unknown</u>.

Knowledge is also the wisdom of knowing that we *cannot* know (a paraphrase of Socrates), since most cosmic *knowings* are beyond us.

See **AKASHA**; The **ANCIENT WISDOMS**

See also **SOCRATES**

"KUM" (*noun* and *verb*) — An alternative spelling: "cum."

Note: Both of these spellings are phonetically simplified for Republicans.

See **COME**—a third (and correct) spelling, for *grownups*.

KWAME KILPATRICK — Detroit's nationally <u>in</u>famous and now unhappily yet *fortunately* very <u>former</u> mayor.

See **HUBRIS**

L

L. BROOKS PATTERSON — The attorney who represented Irene McCabe and the other Pontiac, Michigan parents in their successful efforts to block the busing of black children from Detroit to their neighborhood schools in the 1970s and thus prevent racial integration.

A Republican, he is now the longtime Oakland County Executive whom the late, great *Detroit Free Press* columnist Jim Fitzgerald customarily called "L. Bizarro Patterson." Mr. Patterson once mockingly referred to Your Auld Author in print as "the *eminent* Sir Telford." Methinks he was just jealous because I'm not as pie-faced and squinty-eyed as he is. Someone should have told Mr. Patterson that the knightly appellation "Sir" is supposed to precede the *given* name, not the *surname*. Still, *I did* appreciate his knighting *me*. (If *you* members of that particular Pachydermous political party aren't sure what "*surname*" means, figure it out by its context, or check your *Webster's*. While you're at it, check out "Pachyderm" and "*context*", too.)

See **REPUBLICAN**

LABOR — *Wealth*. Work. A *job*.

<u>Old Men</u> know that labor is the truest and most honorable "currency." The fruits of a man's (and a *woman's*) labor *must* be a <u>living wage</u>.

It was a nineteenth century American president, Benjamin Harrison, who said, "I pity the man who wants a coat so cheap that the man or woman who produces the cloth will *starve* in the process." These are words wise and fair that the Congress of the United States needs to act upon again now in the twenty-first century. Most ordinary citizens are suffering financially and are struggling to earn a living wage.

See **RESOURCE-DRIVEN AND *TECHNOLOGY*-DRIVEN ECONOMIC SYSTEM**

"LADIES FROM HADES" — What German soldiers called the kilted Scots charging headlong amid the shrilly keening kirl of bagpipes in World Wars I and II (except they used the word *frauleins* and *Hell*).

Which brings to mind a *limerick*—although perhaps we should call it a *glasgow*, too, or maybe a *prestwick*:

> You tell us the *pipes* you abhor!
> You're just *one* among so many more!
> I believe in the past that the bagpipes were classed
> As a terrible weapon of war!

See **BAGPIPES; KILTS AND TARTANS; SCOTS**

LANGUAGE — The *apparel* of *thought*.

Like our garments, *language* is that which *defines* us, and it also divides us from the *lower* apes (sometimes).

Indeed, as Your Auld Author has *repeatedly* told thousands of students within lo this past fifty-three years, the *limits* of our *language* are also the limits of our *world*.

See **LOGIC**

LAPDOG — *See* **BLACK REPUBLICAN; JACKAL**

LAUGHTER — A great *healer*.

Laughter is the dancing sunlight that lifts the wan shadows from our faces. (This is one of my favorite *Definitions*.)

LAW ENFORCEMENT — The due implementation of the law as impartially carried out (sometimes) by police, judges, courts, and attorneys. Old Men know that a good law *un-enforced* amounts to just *words on paper*, and a bad law *enforced* is tantamount to *tyranny*.

Abraham Lincoln once said, "The best way to get a *bad law repealed* is to *enforce* it *strictly*." Indeed, *repeal* is *one* way, but perhaps not the *best* way. Arguably, Gandhi and King had a *better* way in peaceful *resistance*, and that *failing*, the young Malcolm X—in the spirit of this country's revolutionist Founding Fathers—then offered us the *best*.

See The **MARIJUANA LAW**

LEADERSHIP — "The art of getting *someone else* to do something *you* want done because he *wants* to do it."

LEARN *(verb)* — To master an element or body of knowledge.

(To *teach* is *also* to *learn*.)

LEARNED *(adjective;* "LERN-ud": pronunciation aid for the benefit of Republicans) — It is *good* to be "LERN-ud," but unfortunately not all the *learned* are *good*.

(Consider Werner Von Braun, Hitler's *enfante terrible*, who had devised and was preparing—using the labor of concentration camp prisoners— to launch the horrifically destructive V-2 rocket against the British in World War II. Rent the old Peter Sellers film *Dr. Strangelove: How I Learned to Stop Worrying and Love the Bomb*. The film, in which the gifted Sellers plays multiple characters, including a very thinly disguised Von Braun, is eerily contemporary again.)

LEGACY — An *inheritance* for all *posterity*.

The *legacy* of all Aged Sages, and indeed of all human beings, should be to have worked to make the world *worthy* of its *children*.

A **"LEGEND IN HIS OWN MIND"** — What some wags used to call the late great announcer and sports journalist Howard Cosell (and what some could probably also call *Your Auld Author* with more than a modicum of accuracy).

See **ARROGANCE**

LEISURE — The *end* [as in "goal"] of labor.

See **LABOR;** *RESOURCE*-BASED AND *TECHNOLOGY*-BASED ECONOMIC SYSTEM

LEPRECHAUN — ("How are *things* in Glocca Morra?")

See **HALLUCINATION; MYTH**

LIAR — Someone who damn sure better have a *good* memory!

The liar who lies *really* well numbers among the most dangerous persons on this earth. A pathological liar actually begins to believe his own lies and often can pass lie detector tests with relative ease.

LIBERTARIAN — One who advocates *liberty*—especially regarding thought or conduct.

Prior to the election of Barack Obama, a significant number of Aged Sages (and some young not-yet-Sages) had begun to believe that the political party that goes by the name *Libertarian* is the party that perhaps should take over from the Republicrats and the Demopublicans and lead a *revolution*—if the 'publicrats and the 'opublicans in elected office don't begin to recall that America purports to be a democracy.

If all oppressed Americans—namely blue-collar whites, women, Hispanics, blacks, Arabs, and some Asians—had found a Libertarian leader and united under him/her, the "corporate cats" would really have had to *look out* (not to speak of the domestic sectarian demagogues who trade on the miseries of their own oppressed *brothers and* sisters, as do many preachers and politicos (and as have some central office honchos in the Detroit Public Schools).

Now that we have miraculously found that Libertarian-style leader in Barack Obama, his long arm is hopefully going to reach out and fix things in a whole lot of places—including in the Detroit Public Schools and other similarly beleaguered school districts across the land, with the help of a freshman Congressman from Michigan by the name of Hansen Clarke.

See **"CORPORATE CATS"; DEMAGOGUES**

LIBERTY — Along with *justice*, the only *state* worth *dying* for.

Patrick's Henry's words still ring true across the centuries. Paradoxically, *liberty* is the only thing you *can't* have unless *you* give it to *others*.

See **DEMOCRACY; GIVE, GIVING**

LIFE — A tragedy for those who _feel_; a _comedy_ for those who _think_; a tragi-comedy for those who _feel and_ think.

Actually, one's life is something that is only important in terms of the positive impact it has on others. This is a paraphrase of UCLA track and football star Jackie Robinson, the giant (actually a _Dodger_) who broke baseball's color barrier in 1947.

In a more _cosmic_ sense, _life_ itself—the _existence_ thereof and _our_ existence _therein_—is the greatest of all puzzles.

See **DODGERS; DEATH; GIANTS; GIVE, GIVING; JACKIE ROBINSON**

LIFE'S GREATEST SECRET — To give is to _receive_.

Most _Old Men_ and _Old Women_ alike sooner or later (usually _later_) discover the truth of this remarkably simple _paradox_, but too many merely _old_ men and _old_ women _never_ do.

See **GIVE, GIVING**

LIGHT — The symbol of truth _and learning_.

"LIKE TO FIGHT" — _See_ **SCOTS** _(noun)_

LIQUIDITY — An old man's act of _enuresis_ when he checks the scant balance in his _retirement account_. (Repubs, xyW.)

LITERATURE — Speech, _immortalized_.

Example: The _timeless tome_ you are reading at this precise point in time-space. What _Old Men_ Know is something _you_ may well read _completely_ and then return to and read again, and still _again_—and then eventually _re-read_ it from yet a still _deeper_ perspective long after its Auld Author is dead. Some day your children and grandchildren may read it, too, and marvel at the deep wisdom and the _depthless_ folly that we—their multifaceted progenitors—manifested.

"LITTLE GIRL IN HIGH CHAIR GUZZLING FROM BEER CAN" — Title of a sometime-to-be *famous* sometime-to-be *painting* sometime-to-be-*painted* by Your Auld Author.

My model is *sometime-to-be* a famous family photo taken *sometime* in 1975 of our two-year-old daughter Katherine by my first wife, Lynn— to the horrification of my poor mother, who thought the can had been *full*. (See Photo 16 in *A Life on the RUN* (www.AlifeontheRUN.com.)

(Indeed, the can *had* been full until Your Auld Author gulped down its lip-smacking contents before giving it to his little angel.)

"LIVE *HEROICALLY!*" — An *auld* Celtic adage Your Auld Author's fighter father lived by *invariably*.

It is also one his son has earnestly endeavored to live by as well (although oftentimes with considerably more reflective and *reflexive* trepidation —not to mention occasional abject *failure*).

LOBBYIST — Usually, *jackal*.

See **PARASITE; POLITICIANS, POLITICOS; WORMS AND MAGGOTS**

LOGIC — The *anatomy* of *thought*. (*Think* about it.)

See **LANGUAGE**

"LOLITA" — A precociously seductive pubescent girl.

Old Men know (or should have learned) never to succumb physically to the emotional blandishments of a teen (or post-teen) "Lolita" to which the actually *not-so-fictitious* old Humbert Humbert fell prey. (Check the James Mason/Peter Sellers movie on DVD, and the landmark— and evidently semi-*autobiographical*—book by *Aged Sage* Vladimir Nabokov.)

"Lolitas" abound in junior high schools and high schools and have ruined the careers of many a susceptible and wayward "teacher."

LONELINESS — The desolate pain of isolation.

Loneliness is the major cause of suicide among the elderly, who have by far the highest incidence of suicide of all age groups.

There are some things worse even than loneliness, however.

See **ANOMIE; BAD MARRIAGE**

LONGEVITY — See **MARRIAGE**

LOQUACITY — The frequent companion of *error*.

Those who err are often extremely *garrulous* in their erring. (Your thoughtful Auld Author added this sentence so you smarter Republicans can grasp the meaning of *loquacity* in *context*.)

See **REPUBLICAN**

LOST WORLDS — See <u>Old Men's</u> **CHILDHOODS AND YESTERYEARS OF YOUTH**

LOVE (*noun*) — "The morning and the evening star."

That metaphor comes courtesy of Burt Lancaster in the title role of the great 1960 film *Elmer Gantry*, based on the Sinclair Lewis novel.

True romantic love is something you can't purchase with money, because it's not for sale. To be truly loved is the greatest boon, bar none, in all of Christendom, in all of Pagandom, in all of Islam, and in all of every other realm beyond.

But *you* can *express* love with money! This is true even when *you don't know you're spending* the money, as many <u>Old Men</u> like me will ruefully acknowledge. As the Muppets' practical porker Miss Piggy opined, "When you love someone, you want to be near him all the time— except when you are out buying things and charging them to him."

Also, it must be noted: As the Aged Sage and great playwright Plautus wrote two thousand years ago, "Love is that entity which first devised the *torturer's* profession."

Nonetheless, *love* (for any human being with a *heart*) is also something that, like death, is utterly *inescapable*.

LOVE (*verb*) — Something the ancient Roman *Aged Sage* Publilius Syrus claimed that we can't *do* and be *wise* at the same time.

Amen to Publilius Syrus.

LOVE AFFAIR WITH LIFE — The Aged Sage's relish and seasoning.

Old Men and Old Women have a *love affair with life* in defiance of *death*. Remaining open to new experiences instead of rocking backward and forward and backward again in the same old rut ensures that what we lose *physically* we can gain *experientially* a thousand-fold as our lives lengthen imposingly like shadows near sunset.

This kind of gain is effected via constant, *consciously-willed* cognitive input to the brain. *Increase* that input and we actually increase and broaden our brains' neural pathways. As we age, taking on new tasks (such as learning a foreign language) becomes more difficult; yet it offers a "reason for the season," as it were. *Neglect* to do this and both mind and body *diminish*.

Thus *with* age must we grow in the two most important ways— *intellectually* and *spiritually*.

LOVE AND WAR — All's *fair* there, right? Wrong.

This time-tested axiom simply means that in love and war (as in life), far too often *nothing* is fair.

LOVE OR HATE — "Your woman loves you or she hates you—there is no in-between."

One of Your Auld Author's favorite ancient Roman philosophers and Aged Sages—my oft-quoted Publilius Syrus—wrote that, in his *Maxims*.

Actually, though, your woman *can* love you *and* alternately hate you, if she is what the psychologists now classify as *manic-depressive*, or *bipolar*—or has a similar (unmedicated) personality disorder.

Life with such a woman (or man) can be a *manic* and *maniacally schizophrenic* roller-coaster ride (to say the least).

LOVED ONES — People who don't necessarily love you back.

(When they do, it's a double blessing.)

LOVER — Someone to whom one must never give a written intimate testimonial, or take nude photos with, or make any kind of cozily explicit videotape with.

This is especially so for anyone who some day intends to enter politics, education, the ministry, or the Miss America pageant.

LUCK — The mechanism whereby one's *rivals* gained their *success*.

LUNACY — *See* **RACISM; WAR**

LUNATIC — Anyone making less than $300,000 per annum who votes Republican.

This definition obtains particularly in presidential elections and for candidates for other national offices.

LUXURY — An eventual killer of *kings*—and of *kingdoms*.

M

MACKINAC ISLAND FUDGE — *See* **GOOD, GOODNESS**

MAKING THE FIRST MOVE — When John Alden told the Pilgrim Priscilla that Captain Miles Standish was interested in her, she memorably asked, "Why don't you speak for *yourself*, John?"

Old Men long ago learned the wisdom of making the first move, whether in:

a) romance, or in
b) *necessarily* hostile *aggression*.

Here are some hopefully helpful seductive opening lines courtesy of an Old Seducer for you reticent *young, would-be* seducers:

"Sex *bores* me. Want to play Trivial Pursuit?";
"You carryin' any protection?";
"Been *tested* yet?";
"Wanna *screw*?" (Maybe you better pass on that one.)

In fact, probably you better pass on *all* of them except the second one.

In b) *necessarily* hostile *aggression*, it is best to get in the first punch—and make it a *good* one, as my fighter father taught me on Sixteenth Street in the teeming Zone 8 of mid-twentieth Century Detroit.

MALCOLM — The martyred, Michigan-bred Malcolm Little, a.k.a. Detroit Red, a.k.a. the spellbinding and great civil rights icon Malcolm X, a.k.a. *Denzel Washington* (in the biopic).

See **GIANTS; HERO**

MALE CHAUVINIST — An arrogant and ignorant man who has base (and *baseless*) contempt for women's intellects and abilities.

Many non-chauvinistic Old Men have learned, however, through hard and frustrating living with the ladies, that no matter how appreciative, admiring and empathic a man is (or *tries* to be) toward the fair (*unfair?*) sex, he's frequently going to be *unavoidably* classified by the mad and *maddening* damsels as a *male chauvinist anyway* (even by the reasonable ones) if:

a) He's *heterosexual*, and
b) He has a *penis*.

See **ROMANCE** (*noun*)

The **MAN WHO NEVER FAILED** — The man who never *tried*.

Even Jesse Owens lost a few races, and Sugar Ray Robinson lost fights (although never to anyone in his natural weight class or in his prime).

"MANASSA MAULER" — The appellation his many admirers conferred upon 1920s world heavyweight boxing champion Jack Dempsey, the Scots-Irish hobo and miner from a Manassa, Colorado mining camp whom Your Auld Author's Auld Fighter Father asserted could at his peak have flattened any heavyweight in history (except Jack Johnson) inside two rounds.

Having observed Dempsey, Louis, Marciano, and Ali all in action (on film), Your Auld Author always tended to disagree with his Auld Fighter Father (but wisely kept this disagreement to himself in his Fighter Father's perenially Formidable presence).

MANNERS — A set of *genteel* (as still too-often prejudicially associated with *gentile*) behaviors that *mature* to become *morals*.

And yes, per the preceding parenthetic aside, Your Auld Author is a confirmed *Judeophile* who has often become galvanized to act against some of his "*Christian*" compadres' brutish behaviors—both historic and recent, and *overt* and *covert*, toward our Jewish brethren.

The **MARIJUANA LAW** — A law banning the sale, use, and distribution of *cannabis* ("weed," "pot," etc.).

This ill-advised law has created and imprisoned thousands of harmless "criminals" and deprived our indebted nation of billions of dollars annually in potential taxes.

MARRIAGE — A good marriage is the key to longevity; a bad one presages an *early grave*.

See **ROMANCE** (*noun*)

MARRIED MAN — Someone whom many particularly *sadder* and *wiser* Old Men would advise to look in the mirror, take serious stock, and recognize that the syllable that sounds like "me" is the most important syllable in *monogamy*.

The same goes for the married man's distaff partner.

It's all about *self-control, loyalty,* and responsibility. As Your Auld Author's war-hero cousin Dick cautioned him long ago, "If you're going to be married, be *married*." This goes double and triple for married folks who are *parents*—and all parents ideally should be *married* (to each *other*).

See **ME**

MARTIN LUTHER KING, JR. — The martyred crusader who was the lead-off runner, the symphony conductor, the quarterback, the point guard, the absolute *lodestone* of the American civil rights movement.

Now King's dream is on the threshold of realization, but *make no mistake*: Despite America having now elected its first black president, much egalitarian work remains for us Old Men to do, and for you Young Men (and Young Women) to do even *more* of. The sacred egalitarian crusade must be carried on.

See The **OLD CRUSADER'S CREDO; GIANTS; MARTYR; MOHANDAS GANDHI**

MARTYR — A rare seer whose so-accorded status is engendered not by his death but by the *nobility* of his cause.

MARVA COLLINS — The savior of countless Chicago schoolchildren who weren't getting appropriately educated in the public schools.

See **GIANTS**

MASOCHIST — *See* **BLACK REPUBLICAN; LAPDOG**

MASTODON TUSKS — Billiard balls.

"The tusks that clashed in mighty brawls / of mastodons are billiard balls." A fine poet wrote that line, but Your Auld Author forgets who he/she was, as we geezers tend to do with greater and greater frequency. That doesn't necessarily mean that now the *forgotten poet* is just a "billiard ball," too—although methinks that by now he has probably joined his ancestors. (My proofreader, the intrepid Karen Simmons, researched the forgotten, unnamed poet as I write this item— his name is Arthur Guiterman.)

See **FORGET**

ME — *See I;* The **"ME" GENERATION**

The **"ME" GENERATION** — A generation of Americans born in the years immediately following World War II.

They are known alternatively as "baby boomers."

Their professed anthem: "Me, me, *me*—it's all about *me*."

See **GIVE, GIVING; A *RIDDLE* TO PONDER; YOU**

MEDICINE — *Ideally* (and to the *patient*, perhaps *nervously*), the only *profession* whose practitioners strive (if they are honest) to *remove the reasons* for their patients' need to continue to <u>retain</u> them.

And if they *aren't* honest . . .? (<u>*Think*</u> about it!)

"MEDIOCRITY" — The word (and the _condition_) most detested by the great Wayne State University track coach David L. Holmes—Your Auld Author's second father.

See **DAVID L. HOLMES**

MEDIUMSHIP — The (_occasionally legitimate!_) art and practice of helping and guiding those who are experiencing _genuine_ hauntings to enable them to exist with the spirits.

This practice includes how to help _psychic children_ exist with spirits. It also includes teaching the _haunted_ how to protect themselves and defend their families from their sometimes dangerous or unwanted "guests." (Yes, Matilda—many _entirely lucid professionals_ have little doubt that they _do_ exist, entrapped within some shadowy nether plane beyond the third dimension.)

MEDUSA — The ferocious mythological lady with _snakes_ for hair.

A considerable number of Aged Sages can opine on good authority that metaphorically, this unlikely and unlikable lady may not have been entirely _mythical_ (particularly if said Sages happened to have had the misfortune to be _married_ to her).

See **ERECTION-INHIBITORS; TERMAGANT**

MEMBERS OF THE POLITICAL PARTY THAT USES AN _ELEPHANT_ AS ITS SYMBOL — These _Elephantine_ folk are of course the _Republicans_.

(THE FIVE MISCREANT) **MEMBERS OF THE UNITED STATES SUPREME COURT WHO VOTED IN 2010 TO PERMIT CORPORATIONS TO HAVE EQUAL STATUS WITH INDIVIDUAL U.S. CITIZENS** — Traitors.

MEMORIES — _Re_collections.

"God gave us our memories so that we might have roses in _December._" Your ever-_un_remembering author has unfortunately forgotten the source of that lovely quotation. (My resourceful proofreader and researcher, Karen Simmons, has now come to the rescue [again] and informed me that the author is J. M. Barrie.)

Our *memories*—and our *imaginations*—are two wonderful "time machines." It's not for nothing that the Beatles' song "Yesterday" has been played on the radio 6.5 million times, making it the most frequently-heard pop song in history.

Our memories are the only pleasure palaces wherefrom we can *never* be evicted, except (unhappily) by death. Conversely, they are also the only *torture chambers* wherefrom we can never *escape, except* (hopefully) by death.

See **Old Men's CHILDHOODS AND YESTERYEARS OF YOUTH; TIME**

MERCY — *"Nobility's* true badge." – The Bard

MERIT — A quality that *should* be closely united to *good fortune* and *just rewards*.

Tragically, too often it isn't.

See **DETROIT PUBLIC SCHOOLS**

M-F (Metal/fire—plus one other more *common* definition) — Two abbreviate letters and the two *nouns* they begin, meaningfully conjoined.

Old Men note that metal/fire (M-F) are perennial resources and manifestations of war that have been wrought into forms increasingly fearsome over the cruel centuries. Metal rips flesh; fire sears it.

Alternative definition, noun: A much-too-universally-applied American dialectical acronym for an insultingly incestuous twelve-letter word (variation: two six-letter words, hyphenated to make one) that merits no further reference, as it obscenely insults sons and their mothers.

Adjectival usage of *alternative definition*: M-F'ing.

See **ABOMINATION; WAR**

The **MICKEY MOUSE CLUB** — *See* The **"500" CLUB; INSIPID**

MILLION-DOLLAR LEGS — What Betty Grable and Anna Pavlova swayed so alluringly upon—and danced so divinely upon.

Also, what a high school athletic coach who once coached Your Auld Author (until he tried to boink Your Auld Author's high school girlfriend) once said that Your Auld Author possessed. Specifically, he said, "Telford has *million-dollar legs* but a *two-cent brain*." Well, those "million-dollar legs" got Your Auld Author's "two-cent" brain educated via a four-year college track scholarship. However, whether that education was ever of any use in getting him some plain, ordinary *common sense* remains debatable—particularly among *many* Republicans and *some* Democrats, plus a few of his former ladies (and occasionally his *present* one).

See **BOINK**

MINCE PIE — *See* **GOOD, GOODNESS**

MINISTER MARY EDWARDS — A great Detroit lady who organized a lively widow-support group called Widows With Wisdom (WWW).

See **WISE OLD WOMEN (W.O.W.)**

MINUTE (my-NOOT; *adjective*) — Small, tiny, infinitesimal; *or* (MINN-it; *noun*) — *Sixty seconds* in duration.

"*Minute*" also can imply *short, brief, premature*—as in "Hang on; I'll be with you in just a minute"; or in "Holy cow, that ol' *minute-man* was done jack-rabbiting away on that gal in less that *sixty seconds*. Must be either a my-NOOTly endowed *Republican* or a boy in a god-awful hurry to get somewhere else!"

The measure of time that Rudyard Kipling in his poem "If" called "the unforgiving minute" is the sixtieth part of an *hour*. The *minute hand* on your watch makes one full revolution in a minute. In his profligate youth, Your Auld Author was able to get a quarter-mile's worth of sprinting approximately one second outside three-quarters of a minute. "Every minute starts an hour" are the words whispered by then-six-year-old Paul Gandola of Rocky River, Ohio, as he peered quizzically at his father's watch and puzzled at the grownup mystery of *telling time*.

"*Every minute starts an hour*": Old Men and Old Women (and Young Men and Young Women, too) have learned it's never too late to *start* _over_. Also, it's never too late to explore, or to risk. Since you (may) live only once, with no dress rehearsal, you should tend to unfinished business, or try things you may never have tried, _to wit_:

Write a book. Or a poem. Roller-blade. Study a foreign language. Make marvelous early-morning love with your spouse or significant other. Sip champagne at noon. Learn to square-dance, or fence, or play an instrument. Put up multi-colored lights in midsummer. Read— or re-read—_Penrod_, by Booth Tarkington, and Mark Twain's _Tom Sawyer_, and Alexandre Dumas' _The Three Musketeers_, and _A Life on the RUN_ (www.AlifeontheRUN.com), by Yours Truly, and the poignant poetry of Robert Frost, John Keats, Emily Dickinson, and Vachel Lindsay ("The Bronco That Would Not Be Broken Of Dancing").

Or, browse through a _conventional_ dictionary—and an _encyclopedia_ and a thesaurus (no, Repubs, remember?—it ain't a _dinosaur_). Then read every volume of _The Story of Civilization_ by Aged Sages Will and Ariel Durant (they married when she was fifteen and he was twenty-seven, and they completed their work when he was in his _nineties_).

Attend a séance. Attempt telepathy. Burn incense and turn off the lights and recite Poe's poetry aloud by the flame. Throw a costume party. Look for a good used-book sale. Attend a high school athletic event. Eat an entire minced pie at one sitting. Wear cowboy boots. Whittle dildos. Then sell them. Keep a few and use them for more than just paperweights (but be careful of slivers). Join the Shriners and get one of those marvelous bejeweled, tasseled hats. Run for a school board. Hang wind chimes. Follow that impulse and call her (or him) _right this minute_ and tell her you're sorry and you want to see her again —and if you don't know where she is, hire a missing-persons tracer or seek her on the Internet. Fly your ancestral flag(s). Fly to Scotland. Or Denmark. Or the Greek Isles. (I hope your arms don't get too tired; it's a long drop to the ocean.)

Or steam down the Rhine. Or go to a special green place on an island in the middle of a huge equatorial lake in a tiger preserve and have an affair with a native girl—or a native _guide_—or a native girl-guide! (But watch out for the tigers.)

Also, make a "Bucket List" of twenty more things you want to do before you die. Regardless of what you mid-life "almost" Sages and you silver-haired (or scant-of-hair) _Aged_ Sages—whether Old Man or Old Woman —do in your "middle years" and your "golden years," it has to be uniquely worthwhile, because you all are of the maverick breed that must do the utmost to live life in such a manner that your epitaph should read, "No regrets."

See **ETERNITY; INFINITY; PYGMY** (adjectival usage); **REPUBLICAN PRIVATE PART; SECRETS OF THE CENTENARIANS; TIME**

"MINUTE-MEN" — One of a group of eighteenth century blue-clad American militiamen just before and during the Revolutionary War.

The "minute-men" were armed with muskets and stood ready within the span of a "minute" for instant battles against the British Army—then commonly called the "Redcoats." (Get ready for my history quiz.)

Alternate Definition in twentieth century American slang: Premature ejaculators.

In addition, men with minute (my-NOOT) penises (usually Republicans).

(Incidentally, in the first "minute-men" item, I was just blowing smoke about the history quiz.)

See **MINUTE** (adjective); **REBEL** (noun); **REPUBLICAN; "RRR"**

MIRACLES OBSERVED, EXPERIENCED, IMAGINED, KNOWN, OR ANTICIPATED — The Biblical account of the Transfiguration, ancient Greek sculptor Phidias' Parthenon and "Winged Victory," and Michelangelo's "David," "Moses," and the Sistine Chapel frescoes.

Also, the Pyramids in Egypt, the 8-foot high jump, the 20-foot pole vault, the 30-foot long jump, the 19-second 200-meter dash and the 43-second 400-meter dash; the Theory of Relativity; Rembrandt van Rijn's "Self-portrait"; Beethoven's Fifth Symphony; anything composed by Debussy; the intricate contrasting symmetries of a bass violin vis-à-vis a skyscraper; and the sleek, powerful physiognomies of a panther and a champion racehorse.

Also, the similarly sleek musculature of Jamaican Olympians George Rhoden (1952) and Usain Bolt (2008), American Olympians Jesse Owens (1936) and Detroiter Henry Carr (1964), tennis sisters Venus and Serena Williams, unparalleled boxers Sugar Ray Robinson and Muhammad Ali, Dallas receiver and Olympian Bob Hayes (1964), Detroit Pistons guard Isiah Thomas, and Red Wing hockey legend and transplanted Canadian (and descendant of Scots) Gordie Howe.

In addition, the gargantuan rocket ship that one day will propel our descendants to Mars and thence ultimately to the farthest stars; Stonehenge; the human brain; the lacy delicacy of a snowflake; the geometric circularity of the sun; the perfect half-circularity of a rainbow; Saturn's massive, porous rings; and a newborn's smile.

MISANTHROPE — Someone who believes that most male *non-adulterers* never had the _opportunity_ to become *otherwise*.

See **CYNIC, CYNICISM; YOUR AULD AUTHOR**

MIS-EDUCATED — What way too many of our young folks *are*—morally and spiritually.

Our schools are relentlessly teaching a belief in the predominant importance of personal success, individual achievement, the competitive race for recognition, the inequitable distribution of human wealth, that only things that "can be *counted*" count, and that education's true function is as a vehicle to sort and select *winners* and *losers*. Our children need and deserve an education that awakens them to a life of greater purpose and meaning than the one most American schools currently offer.

See **PURPOSE; SCHOOLS**

MISPRONUNCIATION (*noun*) — A word widely misspelled and mispronounced.

When *mispronunciation* is mispronounced and misspelled, it is invariably mispronounced and misspelled "m-i-s-p-r-o-n-O-u-n-c-i-a-t-i-o-n") by former Republican vice president Dan Quayle and one-fourth of the country's fifth-graders.

See **GEORGE W. BUSH; "NUCULAR"; QUAYLE; REPUBLICAN**

MISSION — *See* **PASSION**

MISSPELL (*verb*; often misspelled "mispell") — Something the former Republican vice president who is cited in the mispronunciation item did *repeatedly* with hard words like "potato" when he wasn't swinging a golf club or criticizing the *Murphy Brown* TV show.

(To be fair: What else have Republican vice presidents—other than the shadow *president* Dick Cheney—ever really had to do?)

MOB — Rampaging beasts with many heads but without any brains.

Also, when prefixed by the article *the*, a reference to the Sicilian and Sicilian-American Mafia, or *Cosa Nostra*.

MODERATION — "A *fatal thing*: Nothing succeeds like <u>excess</u>." So said Oscar Wilde.

Your *Immoderate* Auld Author nonetheless disagrees with the erudite Oscar on this (in *certain* contexts).

See **EXTREMISM; "RRR"**

MODESTY — <u>Honesty</u> among those of *average ability*; <u>benign hypocrisy</u> among the *highly talented*.

Also, as the historic Hibernian Sage Jonathan Swift said, "Modesty can make a *fool* seem a man of sense" (that is, if he remains *taciturn*).

MOHANDAS GANDHI (the *Mahatma*) — The Aged Sage who freed India from the Brits with his mantra of passive (peaceful) resistance.

The great Gandhi was the precursor of the great MLK.

See **MARTIN LUTHER KING, JR.; MARTYR**

MOLARS — *Crunchers.*

Trust your old author—*lose* one and the sharp corners of the teeth adjacent to where it was will ulcerate your tongue and make you definitely *wish* you still *had the tooth* (unless you get a bridge or an implant).

MONETARY ECONOMIC SYSTEM — The obsolescent, dehumanizing, corrupting, ultra-competitive, currency-based, enslaving economic system currently, capitalistically, and *historically* in place—*globally*.

See **RESOURCE-DRIVEN AND TECHNOLOGY-DRIVEN ECONOMIC SYSTEM**

See also **UTOPIA**

MONEY — A historic and current *currency that <u>costs</u> too much*.

MONOGAMY — An essential component of a happy marriage.

In an *unhappy* marriage, *monogamy* is a state that can devolve into *celibacy*—or possibly worse, become <u>*non*</u>-*monogamy*.

See **CELIBACY**

MONSTERS — The ancient Roman emperor *Nero*; centuries later, the Soviet Union's *Josef Stalin* and Nazi Germany's *Adolf Hitler*.

Others were Uganda's *Idi Amin* and Cambodia's *Pol Pot*.

Recorded human history offers us far too many similarly unspeakable examples of *monsters*. At certain points in recorded time, all of them appeared to be winning, yet all of them thankfully have bitten the dust. We can only hope that this *dust-biting* trend is *perpetuated* for their awful ilk.

Torturers—including those who torture *animals*—are *monsters*, too, whether they do the actual torturing or merely *authorize* it. So are *child molesters*—a particularly despicable form of chronic criminal that makes Your Auld Author almost rethink his opposition to capital punishment (or to *castration*).

See **DICK CHENEY**

See also **PEDERAST**

MONUMENTS — *Mausoleums*, minus the *corpse*.

Great and mighty *deeds*, rather than *mere marble*, are mankind's *true* monuments that tower and resonate across the centuries.

See **ABRAHAM LINCOLN**

"MORAL MAGGOTRY" — A multi-faceted term Your Old Author coined.

Examples of "moral maggotry" that Aged Sages could cite include the centuries-long Native American genocide and the centuries-long enslavement of kidnapped Africans and their descendants in this country, the unconstitutional Nisei and Guantanamo confinement camps, American mega-corporations' world-wide exploitation of their own countrymen, all of America's wars except World Wars I and II, the Civil War, the War of 1812, and the Revolutionary War, and our country's shabby and shameful treatment of our Vietnam veterans.

See **WAR**

MOST DOGS — Uncreative Subordinates (with apologies to Lassie, Rin-Tin-Tin, and my family's smart, rough-and-ready, home-defending German Shepherd mix Kyra, God rest her valiant wolflike soul).

See **CATS**

MOTHER TERESA — Simply a saint—and a *giant* among giants.

See **GIANTS**

MOTHERS OF SOLDIERS KILLED IN IRAQ — Folks to whom "W" and Dick should humbly and repeatedly apologize.

MOTHERS OF SOLDIERS KILLED IN VIETNAM — Folks to whom Vietnam-era Secretary of State Robert S. McNamara did finally apologize, decades after the war.

(But he couldn't get them back their tens of thousands of beloved, formerly alive, bright and vibrant sons.)

MULTI-NATIONAL CORPORATIONS — The rulers of our "brave" new world who are still busily and brutally shaping and pulling it in what is a *daft and dire direction* for all the *rest* of us.

(Shades of the visionary Aldous Huxley, author of the prescient and ironically titled mid-twentieth century novel *Brave New World*). Can

President Obama curtail them? Can they be stopped *at all*, short of bloody revolution? Time will *tell*, and _soon_.

See **OBAMA; VISIONARY** *(noun)*

MURDEROUS MISSILES NAMED FOR ANCIENT GREEK GODS — If a "Christian" nation is going to build bombs designed to decimate other nations, it shouldn't name these horrific weapons after some ancient people's deities, but rather after its *own* predominate deity, right? (At least the thirteenth century Crusaders who invaded the Holy Land wearing their crosses over their chain mail in ironic "tribute" to the Prince of Peace weren't as hypocritical about it.)

As the savagely sardonic 1961 poem "JC-ICBM" went,

> The ancient heathen *Norsemen* didn't fashion—
> With steel, and Satan's godless, blistered hands—
> Such hatred-heated forces of destruction
> As these we've made in modern *Christian* lands.
> Don't name new, high-priced "*Messerschmidts*" for *Odin*,
> Nor million-dollar missiles after *Thor*—
> A plane will be _Christ_-blest as it's unloading,
> If _Jesus_' name adorns its bomb-bay door.

Ten, nine, eight . . . *Jee-zuz Christ . . . Intercontinental Ballistics Missile . . .*

Three, two, one . . .

Boom.

See **A-BOMB; ABOMINATION; HYDROGEN BOMB; "JC-ICBM"**

"MUSTANG" — Your galloping and gamboling Auld Author's high school nickname.

Also, a *spirit* that must run wild and free (and additionally, a magnificent, memorable, truly *classic* car that debuted in 1964).

See **REBEL** *(noun)*; **"RRR"**

MYTH — A common collective belief having *no proven foundation in _fact_*.

Example: Since the mystically misty medieval era, French women have always reigned supreme as the world's best *lovers*. (_Not_!)

N

NAGS (of the *human—*not the *equine—*variety) — *See* **ERECTION-INHIBITORS**

NAPOLEON'S PICKLED PECKER — A blackened speck of shriveled flesh rumored to be desolately resting in an old bottle of formaldehyde on a back-room shelf in the Smithsonian Institute.

Napoleon Bonaparte was the Corsican-born early nineteenth-century emperor of France who set the example that Hitler (fortunately for the world) foolishly followed thirteen decades later—*unwisely attacking Mother Russia in the* <u>*winter*</u>. Napoleon is also a historic *personage* whom a few institutionalized lunatics still grandiosely fancy themselves to *be*. (Clinical cases of patients who suffer this curious delusion still abide, but far less numerously than in the 1920s and '30s.)

See **SHRIVELED** *(participial adjective)*

See also **REPUBLICAN**

NATIVE AMERICANS — Historic victims of homeland-theft and genocide at the hands of invading "illegal immigrants" from Europe.

Native Americans are the original and truest Americans, although of course they originally didn't *call* themselves "native Americans."

They didn't call themselves *Indians*, either. They called themselves Apache, Kiowa, Shawnee, Pawnee, Lakota, Cherokee, Seminole, Chippewa, Ojibwa, etc. They were already here thousands of years before Columbus "discovered" America and long before Amerigo Vespucci was even *born*, and they regarded themselves not as *owners* but as conscientious _stewards_ of that sacred and then-bloomfully-abundant continent now known as _North America_.

NELSON MANDELA — The South African human-rights legend Your Author took his dauntlessly egalitarian daughter Katherine to Detroit's now-demolished Tiger Stadium to hear in 1991 when she was an impression-able seventeen-year-old high school junior. Power to the people!

See **GIANTS**

NEPOTISM — _See_ **DETROIT PUBLIC SCHOOLS**

NEUTRALITY — Staying out of quarrels and controversy.

Those men who habitually remain neutral are most often those men who profit inordinately (and often _unfairly_) from the _status quo_.

See **_STATUS QUO_**

NIAGARA FALLS (also sometimes referred to as "_Viagra_ Falls") — The magnificent waterfall on the Niagara River.

Most <u>Old Men</u> who've seen the Falls from an eleventh-floor window or anywhere else within close viewing range will testify that they are a scintillating sight, day or night.

A Niagara Falls honeymoon can be wondrously blissful for a wheezy geezer with a lusty young wife, but the hoary old humper had better take plenty of _Viagra_ to _Niagara_! (Repubs, you'd better xyW for the word _hoary_, lest you mistake its meaning.)

See **VI-<u>AGG</u>-RA!!; WHEEZY GEEZER**

NICCOLÒ MACHIAVELLI (1469–1527) — One of the _darker_ Sages for the Ages.

Machiavelli's book _The Prince_, which details the ruthless political de-vices of the would-be nationalist/imperialist tyrant Cesare Borgia—his contemporary and the illegitimate son of Pope Alexander VI—is a cautionary exegesis to be carefully read and studied, not by those tyrants who would seek to imitate the sinister methods and machinations of the Borgias, but by those who would contemplate avenues to thwart their evil ilk. Forewarned is forearmed. (To see Orson Welles' chilling portrayal of Borgia, get the hard-to-find film *Prince of Foxes*, based on the great Samuel Shellabarger novel.)

Machiavelli teaches us that *to know thy enemy* is to become enabled *to prevail over him*—and to do so, as the prevalent Motown-originated slogan goes, "by any means necessary" ("BAMN").

NINETEEN EIGHTY-FOUR (1984) — George Orwell's nightmarish novel wherein "war" is called "peace" and "truth" is called "lies."

We didn't arrive at the totalitarian state Orwell predicted in his 1950s novel that we would be in by the year 1984, but we were drifting ever-too-close to that state during the Bush II administration between 2001 and 2008. (Restore our democracy, Barack, if you can.)

See **GEORGE ORWELL; GIANTS**

NON-REBEL (*noun*) — An *Uncreative Subordinate*.

A *non-rebel* is an obsequiously unquestioning conformist. The first words out of an infant non-rebel's mouth are, "What would the *neighbors* think?" The non-rebel's guiding rule is, "Never disagree with the boss." Non-rebels are also slavish adherents to Lynch's Law: "When the going gets tough, *everybody leaves*." Like the died-in-the-wool, sheep-like bureaucrat and the conniving jackal, the non-rebel would make a truly *excellent* Nazi.

A distaff example of a non-rebel would be any Caucasian female over the age of sixteen who still answers to a name like "Bambi" or "Muffy." If *you* can't bear to stand free and alone, never get into any kind of serious trouble or controversy whereupon you need to call upon your friends for aid if most of your friends are *non-rebels*. The non-rebel isn't free. Freedom *frightens* him.

See **BLACK REPUBLICAN; BUREAUCRAT**

See also **SHEEP** (*noun, singular* and *plural*)

"NORMAL" — Something many psychologically normal folk have been induced by the self-styled "experts" in the National Institute of Mental Health to fear that they *aren't*.

Psychiatry has been able to sneakily and self-servingly narrow the defining borders of what's "normal." The National Institute on Mental Health recently reported that in any given year over a quarter of Americans— and over a lifetime, *half* of us—suffer from a "mental disorder," but *this* particular Aged Sage has a *contradictory bulletin* for *you* potential (but non-Aged-as-yet) Sages.

Here is that bulletin: Ordinary sadness is not *clinical depression*, boyishness is not "attention deficit disorder," and shyness is not "social phobia." Actually, those who manifest flaming paranoia often insist on their "normality"! (Well, *gee*—*anyone* would be nervous if the entire world were plotting day and night to <u>kill</u> him, right?)

Also, most *mood disorders* are common and largely treatable. The westward-rolling, pioneering women and men of the nineteenth century, our soldiers fighting in Iraq and Afghanistan, twenty-first century policemen and high school English teachers on the front lines of America's inner cities, waitresses in roadside diners and workers on assembly lines have little time to be "depressed." Only unemployed, empty-nest housewives whose corporate-honcho husbands provide them with amenities unimaginable to the pioneers (or permanently unemployed victims of Bush II) can indulge that mental luxury.

See **CLINICAL DEPRESSION**

"NUCULAR" ("NEWK-you-ler"; one Republican president's pronunciation) — A common mispronunciation of the word "nuclear."

This mispronunciation is often enunciated with disquieting relish by many Republican politicos and almost as many generals and admirals, as well as by the ubiquitously hawkish George W. Bush and other remarkably incisive individuals already cited herein.

(Republicans, please check this term under the spelling "nuclear" in your *Webster's Dictionary* [if you have one] and take note of its *correct* pronunciation.)

See **"HATTISM"**; **MISPRONUNCIATION** (*noun*); **NUKE**

NUKE (*noun* and *verb*) — What many of the old white wowzer politicos and military brass who are referenced in the "nucular" entry would <u>do</u> (in the *verbal* usage) or <u>use</u> (in the *nominative*) to solve many major international confrontations, given half a horrifying chance.

See **"BY GOD, WE'LL *FIGHT!*"**

OBAMA — Hopefully, The *Restorer*. All *hail*. (That includes *you*, O great ungrammatical, unwashed, and omnipresent Teapartyers.)

Barack Obama is the statesman-president who can save America and the world from fascistic corporate rule and lead us out of war, as the revolutionist Robert Kennedy would have done forty years earlier had he not been assassinated.

See **"TEAPARTYERS"**

OLD — As the lamentive Yiddish saying goes, too soon old; too late smart (or, in the vernacular, "*shmart*").

See **AGED SAGES; Old Men**

The **OLD CRUSADER'S CREDO** —

> If I <u>engage</u> in the Crusade, <u>follow</u> me.
> If I <u>hesitate</u> in the Crusade, <u>push</u> me.
> If I should <u>err</u> in the Crusade, <u>correct</u> me.
> If I should <u>falter</u> in the Crusade, <u>uplift</u> me.
> If I'm <u>unaware</u> in the Crusade, <u>inform</u> me.
> If I should <u>betray</u> the Crusade, <u>kill</u> me.
> If I should <u>hunger</u> in the Crusade, <u>feed</u> me.
> If I need <u>aid</u> in the Crusade, <u>assist</u> me.
> If I should <u>die</u> in the Crusade, <u>remember</u> me!

> —Author unknown (adapted from
> *The Window 2 My Soul*, the memoirs
> of my young crusading comrade
> Yusef Shakur—www.yusefshakur.com)

OLD FOOL — The saddest kind.

As the saying goes, "There's no fool like an old fool." (Except an older one.)

OLD GOAT — See **CODGER; COOT**

The **OLD MAN'S ALL-TIME HEROES** — Old Satchel Paige (may have been fifty when he finally got his chance to pitch in the major leagues), Old Archie Moore (won the light-heavyweight title at forty), Old George Foreman (regained the heavyweight title at nearly forty-six), historian Will Durant (still wrote and lectured into his 90s), octogenarian architect Frank Lloyd Wright, Will Robinson (assistant general manager of the Detroit Pistons when he was in his 90s), Detroit Red Wing Gordie Howe (played during five decades in the NHL), George Burns (made a booking for his 100th birthday at ninety-six), ninety-six-year-old Detroit activist Grace Lee Boggs, painter Grandma Moses (absolutely), and Clara Peller ("Where's the beef ?!")

Also Methuselah (particularly Methuselah!).

See **GRACE LEE BOGGS; Old Women**

The **OLD MAN'S BEST TEACHERS** — His mistakes.

The **Old Man's FIRST AXIOM** — "What will ultimately kill you is not what you're eating, but what's eating you."

This is true at any age but particularly among oldsters, whose aging nervous systems are more physically vulnerable to emotional stress.

The **Old Man's SECOND AXIOM** — "Don't drink and drive."

Have you ever tried to turn a car while holding a martini? (Actually, some half-blind old geezers shouldn't be driving at all.)

The **Old Man's THIRD AXIOM** — "Avoid surgery" (unless you're a surgeon).

My recently departed and revered friend Mel L. Barclay, M.D., once told the story of the venerable sawbones the nurses dubbed "Dr. Whoopsy" (not to his face). When Dr. Whoopsy cut and sawed a tad too deep, "Whoopsy!" was his customary comment, whereupon his *whoopsied* victim frequently took flight to a better world. 'Twas well past time for Dr. Whoopsy to retire.

Indeed, surgical errors are increasing. The Joint Commission on Accreditation of Healthcare Organizations has patient-safety tips on its website at www.jcaho.org.

The **Old Man's** FOURTH AXIOM — "Avoid *shrinks*."

Psychiatrists *have* successfully "shrunk" *some* patients' noggins. My old buddy Mackie went to one for five years, and five years ago Big Mack wouldn't even answer his phone. Now he answers it whether it rings or not.

Also, his ears are stuck together, with what's left of his brain poking up out of the top of his head.

The **Old Man's** "FRIENDS" — Old "Al Hymer" hangs around the Old Man more and more often. "Will Power" helps the Old Man get out of bed. "John" is where the Old Man spends a lot of quality time sitting reading the newspaper. When "Charlie Horse" is around, he takes a lot of the Old Man's time and attention, and the Old Man spends some time with "Ben Gay" then, too. When "Charlie" leaves, "Arthur Ritis" shows up and stays the rest of the day.

(This item comes courtesy of my fellow *Michigan Chronicle* columnist, the erudite Hugh Burrell.)

The **Old Man's** GREATEST *ACCOMPLISHMENT* — *Survival.*

The **Old Man's** GREATEST *FEAR* — To become *irrelevant.*

The **Old Man's** GREATEST *MASTERPIECE* — His <u>next</u> one.

The **Old Man's** LIQUID VIAGRA — For pouring himself a <u>stiff</u> one.

The **Old Man's** MOST PRECIOUS POSSESSION — His *health*.

He who has *health*, has *hope*—and he who has hope, has *everything*. (Arabian proverb.)

See **HOPE**

The **Old Man's** SECRETS AND ADVICE FOR CONNUBIAL BLISS — First, stay *healthy*. Play Scrabble together. Write poetry to each other. Don't get fat (unless your spouse prefers that you have a lot of meat on your bones—and then don't get morbidly *obese*).

Also, don't drink to excess (alcohol has ruined millions of marriages). Arrive at an agreement regarding how the money is to be managed, and by whom. Take your meals *together* at home and dine out together frequently if you can afford it. Share with or read to each other things that you find interesting. Take turns choosing what movies and television shows you're going to see, and then watch television together, attend movies and plays and concerts together, and frequently visit libraries and bookstores together. Shop for food, clothing, cars, and furniture together. Take walks and bicycle rides in the woods together. Volunteer for worthy causes together. If you are church-going folk, attend church together.

Further, socialize with each others' friends and family, and try not to *criticize* each others' friends and family. Also, try not to be *moody*. Cultivate an interest in your spouse's interests—and find hobbies or activities for mutual involvement. Attend most of each others' functions (even if they bore you). Conversely, allow each other a little time and space to be alone to "do your own thing."

Never hold grudges toward each other—and never, *ever* play The "Blame Game."

Moreover, never criticize each other to third parties—always keep a united front to the world. Praise each other *to* each other—as well as to the *world*. Never use the silent treatment as punishment—always talk things out. Also, don't raise your voices to each other or *interrupt* each other—and *listen* to each other with your *hearts*. (Make love a lot via a *variety* of techniques, too.)

Finally and above all, *never* go to bed *angry*—or *alone* (or with *anyone else*).

See The **"BLAME GAME"**

The **Old Man's** SECRETS AND ADVICE FOR LOSING WEIGHT HEALTHFULLY —
Exercise regularly. Eat spicy foods if you can tolerate them (it makes you eat slower). Eat smaller portions. Eat rice and beans (low in fat, high in fiber, and they stabilize blood-sugar levels). Avoid seeds, rice, and corn on the cob if you have diverticulitis.

Fast occasionally. Eat *out* less: cook and eat healthier food at home. Eat fresh fruit and vegetables and fish and nuts. Use plain vinegar for salad dressing. Always eat breakfast. Poach or boil your eggs, and avoid pork sausage and red meat. Eat turkey bacon—and beef ribs in moderation. Eat one bar of dark chocolate per week.

Exercise regularly following meals, and consider taking up Nordic walking (an activity that involves using walking poles for a full-body workout). Eat a daily bowl of muesli (oats, fruit, and nuts—it digests slowly and makes you feel fuller longer). Raise your own garden vegetables.

Make lunch your largest meal (rather than dinner, which is the last meal before bedtime). In fact, if you can, eat just one full meal per day, and instead of having the other two meals, snack on whole grain crackers, sugarless cereals, raw carrots, radishes, asparagus, potatoes (including the skin), apples (including the skin), pieces of orange, and non-hothouse tomatoes or cherry tomatoes.

Get fifteen minutes of sun every day if you're in a climate where you can, and if you *can't* (or even if you *can*), take 1,000 IU of vitamin D and 1,000 mg of calcium on a daily basis. Also, drink a glass of low-fat milk and take an aspirin every day. Drink lots of water, and go very easy on drinks containing alcohol, except for one glass of red wine with an aspirin before bedtime.

Following the counsel contained in these secrets will facilitate living well and long.

See **Old Men's** EASY TECHNIQUE FOR LOSING WEIGHT WITHOUT EVER GETTING OUT OF BED and **SECRETS OF THE CENTENARIANS**

The **Old Man's** SECRETS AND ADVICE FOR STAYING OUT OF DEBT —
Maintain a budget and stick to it. *Save.* Travel very *little.* Don't take
expensive trips, and reside as close to your work as you can.

Also, take advantage of today's attractive real estate bargains, and
establish equity in a home. If you already *have* a home and your mort-
gage is "under water," re-negotiate it. If you're a senior citizen who
owns a home and has considerable equity in it, get a "reverse mort-
gage" for a lifelong source of income.

Hire a trusted expert to manage your investments. Buy "off brands"
rather than "name brands." Don't use a debit card; if someone steals
the number and empties your bank account, you have no recourse.
Use a credit card, but have only one—and *always pay it off in full every
month.* That keeps you out of debt and also builds up your credit rating.

Buy previously-owned late-model cars for *cash.* Shop in thrift stores.
Don't make loans to relatives or friends.

Never own a big boat. (Take it from Your Auld Author—the main-
tenance and docking costs are *astronomical,* and so is the cost of
gas.) Instead, rent one for an occasional afternoon of cruising, book
an occasional passage on a cruise ship, or go for rides on your friends'
boats and help them pay for the fuel (and/or get yourself a little pedal
boat and pedal it on a little lake).

old men (not capitalized) — Ordinary, mediocre, uninspiring *hombres*
who guzzle lots of beer, watch lots of football from their easy chairs,
and envy productive Old Men's success. (Not that there's anything
wrong with an Aged Sage drinking beer or watching football now
and then—even if he's a *Lions* fan.)

See **Old Men**

Old Men (with a capital "O" and "M") — Aged Sages: The Old and Wise.

Sadly, Old Men real and true *per this* timelessly *authoritative source's
definition* of *them* are relatively *rare.* Thus, we oldsters are a precious
resource, but we are often ignored by the young and not-yet-wise
or *never-to-become-wise.* We are Super-Sagacious cosmic beings
made of thinking, breathing *star stuff* who yet remain *miraculously
alive* late in life for a far-too-infinitesimal flicker of cosmic time.

Old Men know and can teach young men and women much of what's written here, and much more. Conversely, many *unwise and chronologically* old men—in contrast to those Men who are wise through experience as well as being chronologically *Old* with a capital "O" —don't, can't, and probably never will.

Also per this definition, we wise, witty, well-seasoned *Old Men* are what *young men* ultimately can *become* if they live *long* enough—and live *receptively* enough.

See **Old Women**

Old Men's CHILDHOODS AND YESTERYEARS OF YOUTH — Dimly glimmering, dream-driven moonscapes.

These yesteryears are veritable lost worlds peopled reflectively by hordes of loved ones long dead. Yet, Old Men's memories can breathe into those lost loved ones the miraculous breath of life once again and bring them into the resurgent sunlight of our minds' eyes and our recollective reveries.

Beloved cousins Carl and Dick, can we truly play "war" in the woods just one time again, or dive for turtles at Sand Lake? Carl is gone— but at this writing Dick and I still can, *in our minds' eyes.*

Beloved Cliff and Ralph and "Bullet" Billy, can we relive those victorious big-time relay races again? Cliff and "Bullet" Billy are gone, but Ralph and I can, *in our mind's eyes.*

When Old Men and Old Women consciously relive their many triumphs and joys in their mind's eyes, it wondrously warms their Old Bones.

See **MEMORIES**

Old Men's EASY TECHNIQUE FOR LOSING WEIGHT WITHOUT EVER GETTING OUT OF BED — Healthful, enjoyable, and natural, O.M.E.T.F.L.W. Without Ever G.O.O.B. is an *extremely pleasurable technique* that stretches the muscles, accelerates the heart rate, and uses up calories.

If you're a reasonably comely female who would like to learn more about this technique, send me your letter of inquiry and resumé (and picture), and maybe we'll go on tour demonstrating it—if you pass the blood test. (Just *kidding*, Gina. *Ouch!*—Hey, I <u>*said*</u> I was *kidding*, didn't I?)

Old Men's SPIRITS — The principal animating *essence* that pervades and tempers <u>Old Men</u>'s thoughts, feelings, and actions.

<u>Old Men</u> know that our *spirits* never grow old. Wrinkles may be written upon our brows, but never upon our *hearts* (or our *behinds*).

OLD POET — An Aged Sage with a lyrical bent who harbors a fierce heart.

The *old poet*'s therapeutic poeticizing can help to heal intense emotional and psychological wounds both in himself/herself and *in those who* read *and* <u>*digest*</u> *his/her verse.* Old poets who have suffered viscerally can initiate deep healing and change.

OLD *VIOLINS* — "The older the violin, the sweeter the music."

This is true of the *violinist* as well! (Note: Your Auld Author has been a violinist for sixty-six years, and sweet sounds still sing from his trusty old fiddle—especially at Christmastime.)

See The **VIOLIN**

old women (not capitalized) — Aged *non*-Sages.

See **Old Women**

<u>Old Women</u> (with a capital "O" and "W") — Aged Sages—the wise and sacred counterpart of and complement to <u>Old Men</u>.

A rare W.O.W. prototype of the author's acquaintance is ninety-six-year-old Grace Lee Boggs (wwwboggscenter.org), the Asian-American widow of Jimmy Boggs, a lauded African-American civil rights activist. Grace Lee Boggs still lives at this writing in her decaying eastside Detroit neighborhood despite her national celebrity status among civil libertarians. For three-quarters of a century, Grace Lee Boggs has been an implacable foe of the materialistic culture, the inequitable distribution of wealth and opportunity, and the emphasis on celebrity in every part of our society.

See **MINISTER MARY EDWARDS; WISE OLD WOMEN (W.O.W.)**

OLDER — You've never been *older* than *you* are today. (Think about it.)

OLDEST — So far this is the *oldest* you've ever been—but hopefully, not the oldest you'll *ever be*!

(Personally, in the spring of 2008, Your Auld Author *reveled* in his septuagenarian status as the oldest educator working full-time in the beleaguered and desperately needful Detroit Public Schools.)

OLDSTER — A "senior citizen."

Note to Republicans: This word is not to be confused with "roadster" or "holster."

See **ELDER** (*noun*)

OPINION — Something that almost *never changes* about <u>anything</u> among the *foolish* and the *close-minded* (right, Repubs?).

OPPORTUNITY — An entity ordinarily to be *seized* the instant it materializes. (<u>Carpé diem</u>!)

Nonetheless, many <u>Old Men</u> have agonizingly learned at some point in time that when opportunity knocks, it isn't always *safe* to open the door.

Down a darker avenue, *opportunity* is also the major engine that drives destructively adulterous behavior in married males—and *stealing another man's wife* is a despicable theft. (*See* **ADULTERY**)

See **CYNIC, CYNICISM; SECURITY**

OPTIMISM, OPTIMIST — Optimism *exemplified* and *personified* was Old George Burns at ninety-six booking the gig for his 100th birthday, or any opponent of Sugar Ray Robinson between 1940 and 1950 who imagined that he might be able to pull off an unlikely upset.

When an optimist's alarm clock jars him awake at six o'clock on a gusty week-day winter morning, he awakens, throws open the window, and shouts, "Good *morning*, God!"—in contrast with the pessimist, who opens his eyes at six a.m. and moans, "Good God, *morning!*"

Like Voltaire's *Candide*, the *optimist* maintains that we dwell in the *best of all possible days*, and the pessimist is certain that the *worst of all possible* days is nonetheless *about to dawn*.

See **PESSIMIST**

ORGASM — Old Men and Old Women know that ultra-orgasmic places can be reached and touched in the *mind* as well as the body. For many old (and young) poets or poets-at-heart, writing or discovering the *perfect poem* approaches an orgasmic level of intensity; many old jocks recall that a sweet *victory* can actually *surpass* it.

So, too, for social activists, can the successful subversion of an *unjust system*.

See **COME** *(verb)*; **GRAND-DADDY**

OUTER SPACE AND THE NEAREST PLANETS — Inevitably, the next victims of *urban sprawl*.

OWL — A poor, put-upon feathered creature that old Cowboy Earl caught out on the prairie one night and had his way with when the sheep were skittish.

Cowboy Earl's sidekick Cowboy Clem remarked to him the next morning, "Earl, iffen y'all don't tell nobody 'bout me and that purty little heifer, ah won't tell nobody 'bout you and the *owl*."

See **SHEEP** *(noun, singular and plural)*

OXYMORON — A contradiction in terms. Example: *"Productive* committee."

To quote A. *Nonni Mouse,* that wry and oft-cited old rodent: "To get something done, a committee should consist of three members, *two* of whom are *absent.*"

Further examples of *oxymorons:* "*Sweet* sorrow" (from Shakespeare's *MacBeth*—right, Republicans?), *jumbo* shrimp, *honest* lawyer. . . .

(Yes, *I* know—you megalomoronic Repubs thought *oxymoron* meant "a *dumb ox,*" *right?*)

"Sweet sorrow" wasn't really from *MacBeth,* either—it was from *Hamlet, right?*

(Actually, "sweet sorrow" *really* was from *Romeo and Juliet.* I'm telling *you* suspicious GOP fellers the *truth* this time—honest!)

See **ANONYMOUS**

The **OZONE LAYER** — A very thin, frighteningly *fragile* layer of oxygen in the outer stratosphere at an elevation of about twenty miles.

There's a huge and growing *hole* in the *ozone layer* generated by the carbon-emitting gases from the giant industries of greedy corporate moguls and from the cars and trucks that we all ride in to work every day, and from the aircraft that some of us fly in *almost* every day back and forth across the country and throughout our ever acceleratively *warming* globe.

See **AL GORE**

P

PACIFISM — A policy which sadly must remain *anathema* to American men *young* and American <u>Men Old</u> so long as there exist within America *undemocratic* <u>men</u> and undemocratic <u>institutions</u>—and so long as there exist dangerous, *non-democratic* <u>nations</u> around our globe that mean America no good and indeed *intend* America <u>harm</u>.

Evolutionally for some time yet, *war* will still inevitably *follow diplomacy* when efforts to effectuate a fair compromise *fail*.

PAGAN — An oftentimes *mythic polytheist*. One who practices *Paganism*.

See **PAGANDOM**

PAGANDOM — A little-understood cosmotheistic, pantheistic, often mythic and polytheistic (and incidentally usually <u>democratic</u>) *realm* whereof a few metaphysically aware and *ultra*-Sagacious Aged Sages are *well-acquainted*.

Therein dwell some of the most enlightened, lucid, contemplative, progressive, sometimes only *semi*-sane and yet always challengingly *inquisitive* of mortals—who claim to have attained a kind of cosmic communion with the universe. They are thus also some of the least understood and most-often *persecuted* of mortals—misunderstood and tormented by elements within the traditional societal establishment that ignorantly tend to hate and fear them. (Repubs, most of you probably shouldn't even *read* this and similar items herein, let alone try to *grasp* them and try to *empathize*, but go ahead and try if you want to, and *maybe you can*.)

See **PAGAN; PANTHEISM; WICCA**

PANTHEISM — A doctrine that perceives an infinite, living Eternal Presence as a transcendent reality, of which the material universe and all living beings within it are panoramic and perpetual manifestations.

Pantheism repudiates what it sees as the infantile practice of literally "personifying" God as a male humanoid in the clouds with a long, white beard (other than *allegorically*), and it expresses a tendency to identify God with "nature." (Interestingly, it doesn't profess [but neither does it *reject*] the proposition that *death* could also *conceivably* trigger a transfer to another dimension or even to a physically reincarnate earthly existence.)

Within pantheism, aspects and elements of mythicism, mysticism, and sometimes animism and polytheism can also be found. This *Definitive Dictionary* is far too limited in scope to delve further into this area (and these *areas*) of theology.

See **HUMANISM; THEOLOGY**

PARAPSYCHOLOGY — The scientific study of the supernatural and the paranormal.

It should be noted here that many *seemingly unearthly phenomena* which we regard as *paranormal* are actually quite *normal*. We just don't know enough *about* them yet. Had men seen someone flying an (as-yet-then-uninvented) helicopter one hundred years ago, they would have thought that the pilot was either an *intergalactic traveler*, some sort of *deity*, or *both*. *Other* such events *are* truly unearthly.

See **VOODOO**

PARASITES — See **FEDERAL REGULATOR; POLITICIAN; WORMS AND MAGGOTS**

PASSING (*gerund; verb intransitive* and *transitive*) — In both the *gerundive* and the *intransitive* verbal usage, a euphemism for *dying*.

This is a rather ironic contradiction, because death may be *no "in-transition"* but rather *possibly* a *transition* from the fleshly (carnate) to the *non-carnate* and the *dateless*. Shakespeare in his Sonnet XXX alliteratively refers to "death's dateless night."

In a prize poem Your Author penned in 1966, I refer to *death* as "that pre-chaotic cancelling of mind—foreverlasting darkness, *undesigned*."

Grammatically, *passing* as a *transitive* verb takes a *direct object*; e.g., Old Men ruefully discover that as they *age*, passing *gas* ("gas" being the direct object) gets embarrassingly easier (and embarrassingly *louder*); passing urine gets harder; passing *kidney stones* gets *hardest*.

See **DEATH; FLATULENCE; GAS; KIDNEY STONES; URINE** (Your Auld Author speaketh *experientially* regarding the latter *four* of these and *quasi*-experientially regarding the *initial* one, having grievingly *died* a little at funerals of twelve old friends within the past four years.)

PASSION — A high-intensity personal characteristic that, for example, distinguishes a *great* teacher from a *good* one.

Passion is also the characteristic that distinguishes a great *anything*— e.g., athlete, singer, author, lover, school principal, pipe-fitter . . . even a great *Scrabble* player—from a mere *good* or *mediocre* one.

Further, *passion* is something that all Old Men must maintain and nurture in *themselves* in order to remain for *long* on the *up*side of the grass.

This is true whether it be passion for a cause, passion for a woman (or simply passion for the ancient Scottish *game of golf*—which incidentally is a game that, like a woman, can prove to be either *maddening* or else *fulfilling* and tranquilly *relaxing* for a man, depending on his temperament).

See **TEACHER**

The **PAST** — The Aged Sage and gifted poet Carl Sandburg somewhat surprisingly called the *past* a "bucket of ashes," and Henry Ford famously (and erroneously) called history "bunk."

Quite to the contrary, the *past* remains perhaps the best subject of study for designing a *preferred future*.

PAT ROBERTSON — *See* The **"500" CLUB; FUNDAMENT; FUNDAMENTALISTS;** The **MICKEY MOUSE CLUB** (also, the "Foot-in-Mouth" Club?)

PATRIOTISM — A *virtue* than can become a blindly nationalistic <u>vice</u> unless accompanied by humanistic principles. (We must *never* forget how the "patriotic" Nazis ascended to power in Germany.)

It was the white-bearded Sage and playwright George Bernard Shaw who said, "We'll never have a quiet world until we knock the *patriotism* out of the human race." While your Old All-American Author regards himself as a patriot, he does not subscribe to the blindly fanatical adage, "My *country*—right or <u>wrong</u>." (*See* **DEMOCRACY**)

PEACE — Historically, a mere brief interlude between *wars*.

Peace is something as fleeting as a will o' the wisp, as elusive as a butterfly. Mankind is genetically, generically, and *fatally* programmed for war—not peace; yet peace is the *one* and *only* condition for the *ultimate survival of the planet* in this terrifying nuclear age.

See **WAR**

PEACE EVERLASTING — See **DEATH**

PEACE OF MIND — Something *more precious* than <u>platinum</u>. *Peace of mind* is attainable only by those who have an entirely *clear* conscience (unless they're virtually conscience-<u>less</u>).

PEACE WITH *JUSTICE* — A condition that is even scarcer than either peace or justice *alone*.

While peace with *justice* is *elusive*, it is not <u>*illusive*</u>. It is the only *true* kind of peace on this earth that there can—or will <u>ever</u>—be, for humankind. Without *justice*, there can never be real, lasting peace.

See **BALANCE** (*noun*); **JUSTICE**; *RESOURCE*-**DRIVEN AND *TECHNOLOGY*-DRIVEN ECONOMIC SYSTEM**

PEDAGOGUE — A *too-rigid* proponent of the more esoteric tenets of the *education profession* (in the context of this prescient publication).

Many practicing professors in ivy-walled colleges of education and their slavish sycophants high in the central offices of many large public school districts are arrantly dogmatic, ideological pedants and peda-gogues—confessedly and occasionally but (*mostly*) *formerly* including Your Auld Author.

See **PEDANT; SCHOOLS**

PEDANT — An unperspicacious pseudo-educator who inflexibly adheres to a narrow set of arbitrary pedagogical rules (and uses big words).

A *pedant* would genuflect obsequiously to a senior colleague's "magnum opus" even if it proved to be based on a flawed premise.

See **IDEOLOGUES; PEDAGOGUE**

PEDERAST — *See* **MONSTERS**

PEE (*verb*) — Old Men know all too well that waking up to pee five drops in five minutes five times a night can get *passing* tiresome (pun intended).

See **PASSING; URINE; WEE-WEE** (*verb*)

PEE-PEE — What small boys and many male Republicans call their private parts.

See **WEE-WEE** (*verb*)

PEE-WEE WEE-WEE (hyphenated *adjective* modifying a hyphenated *noun*) — A male Republican's private part.

PENIS — The organ most likely to get a man in deep doo-doo at *any* age.

Some commonly-used synonyms for "penis" are "prick," "dick," "dong," "dork," "putz," "peter," "phallus," "pecker," "schmuck," "schloin," "schvantz," "member," "*male* member," or "*Republican*."

The preceding list of synonyms is only a *partial* one. It's truly remarkable how many words we male humans actually have in our language to describe our "head with no brain"—our most prized, pampered, in-dulged, and *troublemaking* organ—which the Creator attached to us for the elimination of liquid waste and the production of progeny, not for self-induced *"disaster."*

See **DICK; PYGMY** *(adjectival usage)*; **REPUBLICAN; SHRIVELED** *(participial adjective)*

PENIS ANXIETY — A malady suffered by minuscule-membered male affili-ates of the political party that uses the *elephant* as its symbol.

In actuality, it's been rumored on good feminine authority that *most* male members of that particular party accordingly do indeed have *minuscule* members. (Repubs, xyW.)

See **MEMBER**

PENIS UNEASINESS — Synonymous with penis anxiety.

See **PENIS ANXIETY; REPUBLICAN**

PENNILESS — *See* **POET**

PEOPLE <u>Old Men</u> **HAVE FROM LONG EXPERIENCE LEARNED TO AVOID** — These include most former guests of Jerry Springer, moochers, a goodly number of lawyers, and all bigots.

They also include proctologists, fundamentalists, "'Greeks' bearing gifts" (allusive to the fabled Trojan Horse), garrulous women (Republicans, xyW), *some* Republicans; *most* politicians, any preacher wearing a platinum pinky ring and a $500 suit who drives a late-model Bentley (Jesus wouldn't like that).

In addition, they also include many rappers, some timid Democrats who *talk* a good game, arrogant authors, grudge-holders, drunks, Wayne Newton fans, Wayne Newton, xenophobes, divas, vacuous pedants (a redundancy),and vacuous bureaucrats (a redundancy).

(On second thought, cancel *Wayne Newton fans* and *Wayne Newton* —many people actually *like* Wayne Newton.)

See **BUREAUCRAT; DIVAS; RAP; REDUNDANCY; YOUR AULD AUTHOR**

PEOPLE WHOSE COMPANY Old Men ARE COPACETIC WITH — Nurses, *some* doctors, teachers, war veterans, social workers, secretaries, forest rangers, fishermen, boxers, ex-boxers, most ex-sprinters (*current* sprinters are too high-strung), carpenters, airline stewardesses, barmaids, bartenders, Willie Horton (old Detroit Tiger), Libertarians, and octogenarian Pete Petross —the Aged Sage who ran on the Detroit Track Club sprint relay team with Your Auld Author that miraculously took the silver by a whisker at the nationals in Madison Square Garden in 1958 after *dropping the baton*!

These also include benevolently divergent thinkers, most high school principals in urban ghettos, *some* policemen, Judge Greg Mathis, Judge Judy (maybe), marathon runners, most Wayne State University alumni, *many* University of Michigan alumni, our cat *Mindy* (thinks she's a person—and actually, she *is*), the *newly-repentant* Tiger Woods, the old, _un_repentant Tiger Woods—and maybe *you*.

The **"PEOPLE'S REPUBLIC" OF CHINA** — A nation that, frighteningly, has become *America's banker*.

China is also the farthest thing from a "republic" imaginable but is rather a *pseudo*-communistic (actually a *totalitarian*) nation.

We went in hock to the tune of $800 billion to China alone during the Bush II administration. China's espionage efforts to obtain U.S. secrets and technology for the benefit of its military and its economy are accelerating. Its stepped-up cyber-espionage and cyber-warfare capabilities constitute a growing threat to U.S. computer networks. Its use of subsidies and other trade-distorting measures are in violation of its international commitments. It played a major role in the creation of the economic imbalances that helped engender the global financial crisis during the Bush II administration. Its expansion and modernization of its navy and the resultant effect on U.S. access to the waters around it and around Taiwan increase the likelihood of a maritime arms race.

Nonetheless, for the common good (and ultimate survival) of the planet, we must try with all our *might* (no pun intended) to link *arms* (no pun intended) with this stirring behemoth *that sleeps no longer*.

PERCEPTION — Dangerously, for some folks *perception* is *reality*—even when it isn't *real*.

See **WIZIANS; "YOU'LL *SEE* IT WHEN YOU *BELIEVE* IT"**

PESSIMIST — Someone who upon *winning the lottery* immediately expects to be *robbed*.

This is in contrast with the *misanthrope*, who upon winning the lottery expects a *robbery* attempt.

(Cheer up, Mr. & Mrs. Pessimist—the *worst* is yet to come.)

See **CYNIC, CYNICISM; OPTIMISM, OPTIMIST**

PETTY TYRANT — *See* **BUREAUCRAT**

PEZZONOVANTE — A spine-tingling word that sounds "godfatherly."

See **DICK CHENEY** (He was a *malevolent* pezzonovante. Republicans, check your English/Italian dictionary—if you *have* one.)

PHILOSOPHICAL QUESTIONS POSED BY THE Old Man ON THE MOUNTAINTOP — "Who needs *another woman* (or man) when you've already got a perfectly *good* one?" and "Who needs *sex* when you've got *love*?"

See **ANSWERS to BOTH of the PHILOSOPHICAL QUESTIONS POSED BY THE Old Man ON THE MOUNTAINTOP**—as offered by Your Helpful Old Author

PHILOSOPHY — Perhaps the *most salient science*, because it's based on *pure reason*.

The Aged Sage Aristotle grandly proclaimed *philosophy* to be the only science which contemplates *The Truth unwaveringly* (an unsurprising proclamation, since Ari was, after all, a *philosopher* by profession).

PICTURES OF BULLFIGHTERS PAINTED ON VELVET — *See* **BARBARISM**

PICTURES OF ELVIS PAINTED ON VELVET — *See* **BARBARISM**

PILGRIMS — Some of the earliest *illegal immigrants* (circa 1620) to this once abundantly green and pristine continent, which we Euro-Americans have *abundantly abused* and are *still* abusing, ecologically.

"PILLAR OF THE COMMUNITY" — An inveterate advocate of the *status quo*.

A "pillar of the community" is a euphemism often applied to a non-rebel or an anti-rebel—and one who sometimes plays a dishonest "double game."

See **ANTI-REBEL; NON-REBEL;** *STATUS QUO*

PITY — An emotion unfortunately foreign to *too many* men (and *women*)— young *and* old. Perhaps they were behind the door when the Creator handed out the *hearts*.

PLACES Old Men HAVE FROM LONG EXPERIENCE LEARNED TO AVOID (OR *SHOULD* **AVOID)** — Biker bars, casinos (except to eat), parts of Philadelphia (except during the Penn Relays), and much of Cleveland.

These also include Beirut, Baghdad, Afghanistan, hospitals (except to visit), rock concerts, karaoke bars, the Detroit suburb of Madison "Whites" (Heights), and Samara (at least, *appointments* there).

Also, the *nursing* home in Saint Augustine, Florida whose insensitive owners named it after Ponce de Leon, the unsuccessful seeker of the fabled "Fountain of Youth." (Talk about rubbing salt in the wound!— unless, of course, we were to somehow learn that the nursing home actually *did* have some of those Yippee Yummy Youth Pills on hand that had been peddled by a Halloweenishly-garbed, spike-bearded, olive-skinned, breast-plated hombre sporting a shiny plume-topped helmet, who had been sought by the Saint Augustine *Gendarmerie* and later its *Police Department* for "fraudulent sales," dressing *ana-chronistically* [Repubs xyW], and toting a *blade* ten times longer than the legal four inches in 2010, 2001, 1990, 1981, 1968, 1922, 1898, and 1849—and then getting nabbed again in 1786, 1650, 1520. . . .)

See **THINGS Old Men HAVE FROM LONG EXPERIENCE LEARNED TO AVOID**

PLACES Old Men HAVE FROM LONG EXPERIENCE LEARNED TO FREQUENT OR WISHED TO SEEK OUT (OR *SHOULD* **FREQUENT OR SEEK OUT)** — These places prominently include a certain little lake in Shelby Township, Michigan, and a certain huge, Tudor-style house overlooking it.

They also include Traverse City at sunset, George and Joyce Blaney's quaint little cabin on a bluff overlooking Lake Michigan, the Hamtramck and Armada Fairs, the Au Sable River (great canoeing), the stately Detroit Yacht Club on Belle Isle (oldest in the United States), the island's Canadian shore in midsummer (a great place to eat Church's Chicken and watch the passing ocean freighters—but watch out for the omnipresent goose poop), small towns when they're celebrating the Fourth, rural roadside vegetable stands in August (great corn and tomatoes), Your Auld Author's godson Rick's rustic spread at the tip of the Mitten (where a persistent beaver keeps damming the pond), and anywhere else in Michigan in early fall ("in Michigan the maple leaves fall red and golden on the eaves, beneath a blue October sky . . .").

In addition, these places include Niagara on the Lake (Ontario: Shaw Festival); Chicago; Colorado; the beach at Ancona, Italy (great for woman-watching); the beach at San Diego (great for bodysurfing, but beware of sharks); *Florenzia* (Florence); Sorrento; San Francisco; the Florida Keys; Pearcy, Arkansas; Stratford, Ontario (Shakespearian plays); the Pina Palace on a mountaintop outside *Lisboa* (Lisbon); the Sistine Chapel; the vivid green of Ireland; Scotland's Western Isles; Toronto; *Venezia* (Venice); Williamsburg, Virginia; and Billings, Montana —where in 1993 every Christian family in the city put menorahs in their windows after a bigot heaved a hunk of cinder block through the window of a Jewish family's home decorated for Hanukkah. . . .

They *also* include *anywhere* in *Hawaii, American Samoa,* or the *Virgin Islands* (lots of *virgins* there).

See **THINGS Old Men HAVE FROM LONG EXPERIENCE LEARNED TO SEEK OUT**

PLAGIARISM — When you lift material from only *one* writer. (When you lift it from *many* writers, it's called *research*.)

Your Auld Author hopes you'll lift a whole lot of "research" from his *Definitive Dictionary*, whether you credit him or not. That's how knowledge and ideas are shared, for the ultimate betterment of us all.

PLAGUE! — Per this *Definitive Dictionary*, a contagious condition and circumstance that arises when groups who are supposed to be serving a *common cause* fractionalize and *factionalize*.

An example is the current infighting among Detroit activists over *individual school closings* when they should be uniting to save what's left of the *entire endangered, imploding school district itself*.

Another example is the myriad divisive denominations of the once united *Christian Church*.

A third example is the contentious positioning and posturing that Republicans and Democrats alike too often engage in even when it impedes our country's progress.

The familiar sayings "Divide and conquer," "If we don't *hang together* we'll all hang *separately*," "United we *stand*, divided we *fall*," "A house *divided against itself* cannot stand," etc., remain timelessly relevant.

Also, Shakespeare's ringing "a plague on *both* your houses!" (*Romeo and Juliet*) could well be contemporarily revised to read, "a plague on *all* your houses!" Let's get it *together*, people.

In *another context, see* **DIVAS; DRAMA QUEENS**

POET — A *perennially (and most un-poetically) penniless person.*

That is, a poet is perennially and un-poetically penniless if he depends solely on *selling his poetry* for his sustenance in the current economy (or in *any* economy—poetry just doesn't sell well). This is tragic for our society and our children, since every good poem is a unique treatment of human experience in a rare artistic form. Not only can poetry give us pleasure—it can also help us to understand ourselves, others, and the world around us. Through variant poems' very *variance*, they paradoxically reveal the essential *oneness* of humanity.

The relatively low marketability of the written and spoken word in *poetry* —language's most *sublime and divine form*—is rank testament to the level of barbarity to which most of the Western World has sunk.

See **BARBARISM;** A *(NON)*-**POETIC PARODY; "POET-*TENTIAL*"**

A *(NON)*-**POETIC PARODY** (an example) — *Note to the reader*: Those diabolical practical jokesters who passed off paintings a few years ago as the work of fine human artists (but which actually had been painted by *elephants* and *chimps*) to make *chumps* of "expert" critics are dudes dear to Your Auld Author's similarly *diabolical auld heart*. Indeed, their *"monkeyshines"* are the inspiration for this (*non*)-poetic parody (of a poem entitled "Lost Sonnet" that appeared in a prominent literary magazine):

"Lost Bonnet"

Its bunting frays too fast
these days, and *disappears*. Unwieldiness
becomes *unassumingness*, the trees
an entity to un-climb briskly.
You say your canny compartmentalizing
Is *fartless?* Well, then, *mine* is surely not,
Since I suffer your feckless *fartlessness*, you churlish whumperer!—
And your *ball*-lessness cries itself alive with *Nuevo disinterest*.

The cowpath always notes what's up ahead
Overhead—which is *resistance!* No booth
Or toll bar can undercut what is a *made man*
And hard to eff up. Wash the tenant's feet in cowpie,
The fallow old high-flyer fellow. *Gio* was his name
And heavens knoweth *we*-uns was/were akin to *brethren*,
Though we were/was *unacquainted*, utterly.

(Indeed, *compulsed* am I—the prodigal parodyist—to add:
Yow, now. *Yow! Yow!*
Yow!)

The actual published poem that the preceding "poem" parodies, which—closely imitating and *too* closely resembling it—can be found in the October 12, 2009 issue of the *New Yorker* magazine. The Emperor indeed has no clothes.

A POETICALLY PRESCIENT PRE-REQUIEM *REQUIEM FOR JAMAAL* — (Finney High School [Detroit], 4/14/06):

Once when Jamaal got sent to me, I said,
"Write that you won't throw pens in class."
He wrote, "I wont thow pent in class.
I wont thow pent in class, no moe."

Jamaal doesn't come to school much.
"It's 'cause I lost my bus card," he told me.

> "Get your butt up at 6 a.m. and *walk* the two miles.
> *I* did it—so can *you.*"
>
> "You like a father to me," he said.
>
> "Oh *no* I'm not—if I were your *father,*
> You can *bet* I'd be beating your behind."
>
> I don't *want* to be his father.
> I don't want to have to go one dark day
> To a Family Hour for a miseducated manchild
> Who "wont thow pent in class"
> Ever, *ever* again—
> No moe.

Jamaal was killed in a drive-by shooting in the summer of 2006. When will the tragic carnage in Detroit—and all across urban America—ever, *ever* again be "no moe"??

"POET-*TENTIAL*" — A *rare potential* that a very few Old Men possess to become *Platinum Old Poets* (POP's).

Truly precious, prescient *poeticizing* is the *ultimate and premier* oral and written art—what the ancient *Aged Sage* Plato called closer to *real truth* than mere historic chronicles.

POLITICIANS, POLITICOS — The *90 percent* of the people who get elected or appointed to public office who give the other *10 percent* a bad name. (Re-read that sentence, if you need to.)

Politicians are always there *when they need you.* (Re-read that sentence, too.) Also, most politicians are slavish poll-followers who always "lead" from the rear.

See **PARASITE; POLITICS**

POLITICS — A "profession" in which—according to the Aged Sage H. L. Mencken—it is necessary to *rise above principle.*

(The great Mark Twain also sardonically said that Congress is America's only *genuine criminal class.*)

Playwright P. G. Wodehouse once described a character in a tight spot as wearing the stricken expression of a U.S. senator who had just received a telegram saying, "All is discovered. Flee at once!"— leaving the bemused politico to try to guess which of his numerous transgressions had been detected.

A well-known politician once misspoke himself with this *Freudian slip*: "I'm not afraid of hiding anything." For once, he told the truth.

Or, to quote another politically memorable malapropist by the name of J. Danforth Quayle, "I stand by my *misstatements*" (if not by his *misspellings*).

See **PARASITE; POLITICIAN, POLITICO**

POOP (*verb*) — Something we doddering dudes feel the increasingly pressing urge to do at *decreasingly* opportune times.

(Here's a tip for all *you* loose-bowelled old poopers, free of charge: Avoid prune juice, grape juice, apple cider, too much hard liquor, and/or that second cup of morning caffeine.)

POORHOUSE — Where most of us are going if the price of gas resurges, or there are many more job losses and layoffs, or Wall Street and the country's banks aren't better-regulated, or pension funds go *kaput*, or unemployment insurance runs out, or the oil leak in the Gulf doesn't remain capped, or . . .).

The **POPE** (*il Papa*) — The old *signore* in the long white skirt-suit and funny pointed hat who should donate that big bejeweled gold ring he's wearing to the Salvation Army or Habitat for Humanity.

(Doesn't *Il Papa* know there's a pregnant Baptist lady with five hungry kids, no man, and swollen feet who's standing in the back of a crowded, bumping bus in Biloxi in 90-degree heat on the verge of fainting on her way to her job as a domestic in a downtown hotel that pays her less than $8 an hour and is about to lay her off?)

Somewhat embarrassing to say, your Egalitarian Auld Author was innocently photographed for magazines with the mid-twentieth-century edition of *"God's Emissary"* in the Vatican when I was a naive young sprinter on the U.S. track team. You remember Pius XII—the skinny, owlishly bespectacled old Pope who spoke thirteen languages but never *spoke out* against Hitler's and Mussolini's crimes against God and man.

PORPOISES — Playful, friendly, ultra-communicative sea mammals perhaps far *nobler* than humans.

Porpoises have been known to come to the rescue of men in trouble at sea.

One of mankind's major *purposes* should be to safeguard the porpoises. (Too bad British Petroleum didn't.)

See **PURPOSE**

POSITIVIST — Far from being a pessimist, the *positivist* is instead an *ultra-optimist* who believes that through the power of positive, progressive thinking, all good things for all of humankind can come to pass.

The appellation *positivist* was coined (in referring to *himself*) by Aged Sage john powell, who directs the Ohio State University's Kirwan Institute for the Study of Race and Ethnicity. In a decidedly *positivist* vein, Professor powell wrote the Introduction to Your Auld Author's scintillating 2010 memoir, *A Life on the RUN—Seeking and Safeguarding Social Justice* (www.AlifeontheRUN.com), which former Detroit Mayor Dennis Archer pronounced "Spellbinding!," and the *Detroit Free Press* called "sensational stuff." (In case you missed it in some other items within this wondrous work, Your Auld Author loves to sneak in some plugs for my memoir and some "advertisements for myself," à la the late, great Aged Sage, stormin' Norman Mailer.)

PRAISE — Something Aged Sages give lavishly as often as they can, when it's *reasonably* well-deserved (and sometimes even when it *isn't*).

We shall pass this way but once; any good, therefore, or any kindness that we can show to (*almost*) any human being, let us do it now, not only for the praised one's sake but perhaps ultimately for *posterity's*.

PREJUDICE — The murderer of *truth*.

PREJUDICED PEOPLE — Folks who size up other individuals and groups according to certain stereotypes; e.g., all Irishmen are habitually drunken, all Scots are habitually stingy *and* drunken, all blacks steal, all Jews are rich, all Italians are Mafia affiliates, all Mexicans carry switchblades, all jocks are dumb, etc.

Example 1—Flo (Florence), a Detroit candy store proprietress who banned your then thirteen-year-old Author from her store in 1949 for bringing in my two black buddies and one Mexican buddy because she had been blindly indoctrinated from childhood to believe the aforementioned stereotypes about blacks and Mexicans (and also because I was intentionally annoying her by warbling a then-popular song at the top of my lungs that went, "Up and down the *St. Lawrence*, a-hollerin' '*Florence!*'—Florence, O where can you beeee?").

Example 2—Folks such as Your Auld Author who poke unrelenting and sometimes unfair fun at people with political preferences contrary to theirs. (Yeah—since it's often so *obvious* here, I have to *admit* it, ok?)

And please don't ever *tell* anyone, but were truth to be *truly* told in this often *torrid* and *tumultuous* tome, eight of Your Auld, dyed-in-the-donkey-hide *Democratic* Author's all-time favorite folks just happen to be Michigan Governors William G. Milliken and George Romney; General Colin Powell; General (and later President) Dwight D. Eisenhower; Lawrence Hunter, the President of Alliance for Retirement Prosperity; the articulate North Carolina Senator Lindsey Graham; native Michiganian and *Moses*-impersonator Charlton Heston; old World War II hero and later President George Herbert Walker Bush (who wisely and *conservatively* departed the field in Iraq after the Gulf War was won); and former President Gerald R. Ford, the one-time Michigan Wolverine football star (for whom I voted)—*Republicans* all!!!

(Come to think of it, a certain melancholy martyr who *saved* and then *died* for the Union was a *Republican*, too—his name was Abraham Lincoln.)

Note: In the first draft of this vainglorious volume, I had Vietnam prisoner-of-war and presidential candidate John McCain on this list, but I was deeply disappointed in his opposition to the passing of the 2010 Health

Bill, so I removed him. Hopefully by the time I write my next *Dictionary*, I'll be able to put him back.

PRIDE — Something that *"goeth before a <u>destruction</u>. . . .*

(. . . And a haughty spirit before a <u>fall</u>)". *(Proverbs,* 16:18)

However, *pride* isn't always a *sin*—or at least not a *serious* one. When pride attains the level of *hubris*, though, it often becomes a man's most ridiculous (and also *too* often tragically *self-destructive*) trait.

See **ARROGANCE** *(noun)*; **HUBRIS**

See also **KWAME KILPATRICK; RICHARD NIXON;** *et al.*—*ad infinitum*

PROGRESS *(noun)* — Something often confused with *short-term expedience* and *material gain*.

Aged Sages know that genuine and lasting progress only occurs as *humankind* is helped to become more *<u>humane</u>*.

PROSPERITY — *". . . makes* friends; adversity *tries* them."

Your Author's favorite ancient commentator Publilius Syrus said this more than two thousand years ago; it is his memorable *Maxim 872*. Many "friends" made in prosperity are as quickly lost in adversity. If your prosperity returns, so will your "friends"—if you let them.

However, nowadays your prosperity is unlikely to return *any time soon* unless you're a big-bucks bank president, corporate executive, investor in prisons, or munitions manufacturer—or you compiled most of your wealth before the tragic onset and terrible onslaught of the Bush II administration. Contrary to the old Depression saw, prosperity is *<u>not</u>* "just around the corner"—due in large part to the eight devastating years of Bush's rogue regime.

Prosperity isn't even down the *street*, on the same *block*, or in the same *city, state,* or *<u>nation</u>*. In fact, the entire *<u>world</u>* is in trouble.

See **ADVERSITY; DEPRESSION; "FRIEND"**

PROSTATE (*noun*) — As an old man grows ever older, his pesky old *prostate* (undoubtedly pronounced "*prostrate*" by the 43rd President of the United States) gets ever *peskier*.

See **PEE; URINE**

PROSTRATE (*adjective*) — The physical position in which Nazi Germany's (but non-Nazi) Max Schmeling found himself in 1938 when Detroit's Joe Louis pulverized him in the first round of their second fight.

An often spoken (or rather, <u>mis</u>spoken) use of the word "prostrate" is actually a mispronunciation (and often a corresponding *misspelling*) of the noun "prostate" that is frequently uttered (and *written*) by the same cranially-concave cretins—both famous and infamous—cited under *athletics* ("ATH-uh-<u>LET</u>-ics"), "*nucular*", and, indeed, <u>*prostate*</u>.

See **PROSTATE** (*noun*)

PSEUDO-COMMUNISM — A form of fascism.

Russian (formerly *Soviet*) communism is a prime example of *pseudo-communism*. Top officials in Russia today are a kind of home-grown, governmentally instituted *Mafiosi*.

See **CAPITALISM; COMMUNISM; FASCISM;** The **"PEOPLE'S REPUBLIC" OF CHINA**

PSEUDO-EDUCATOR — See **"HIDES IN THE WEEDS"**

PSEUDO-FASCIST (sometimes more accurately called "*neo*-fascist") — *See* **JOHN BOEHNER**

PSEUDO-REBEL — A rebel *wanna-be*.

The *pseudo-rebel* makes a big show of breaking some superficial little rule simply because it's a *rule*. For example, he often *curses* a lot—loudly, obscenely, and publicly.

The potty-mouthed Andrew Dice Clay at the peak of his *blessedly fleeting* fame could be characterized as such.

PUBLIC-SCHOOL SEGREGATION — An illegality since 1954 that is still nearly universally pervasive in America's suburbs and great urban centers.

As recently as 2008, Your Sagacious Septuagenarian Author was doing some post-retirement teaching and administrating in a large, 100 percent-black high school in Detroit, where the swimming pool hadn't functioned for *nine years*. "Separate but *equal*?" No *way*—we're still entirely *separate* and egregiously *unequal*.

On that count, history will judged us harshly.

See **A SACRED DUTY OF ALL EDUCATORS**

PUNCTUALITY — "Never a *vice*; ever a *virtue*." – Your virtuously ever-punctual Auld Author.

PURPOSE — An intended or desired result.

Many Old Men know (or *believe* they know) that the universe itself is a divine product of purposeful, deliberate design. Whether or not this is true, the only real purpose of a *real* Old Man's life is to lead a life of *real purpose*.

Regardless of whether our lives' real *purposes* (as distinguished from *porpoises*) may or may not be divinely implanted, it's never too late for us to *discover* them or to *re*-discover them for *ourselves*.

See **PORPOISES**

"PUSSY-WHIPPED" — A pejorative term Old Men (and old men) have learned never to use (if we know what's *good* for us), because women *hate* the expression.

The correct, if rather archaic, term, is *hen-pecked*—à la the uncreative and subordinate cartoon and film character Dagwood Bumstead, who reigns as the veritable and pre-eminent *prototype* of *pussy-whipped non-rebeldom* if ever there *was* one.

PUTTING CUTE LITTLE COATS AND HATS ON CUTE LITTLE DOGS AND CATS —
   See **INSIPID**

PUTZ — *See* **MALE MEMBER; PENIS; REPUBLICAN; SCHMUCK**

PYGMY *(adjectival usage)* — *See* **REPUBLICAN** *PRIVATE PART*; **SHRIVELED**
   (participial adjective)

The **PYRAMID** — The symbol and physical manifestation of a magnificent
   hierarchy of ancient spirits in Egypt and *beyond*.

Q

"QUAIL" — 1940s and '50s slang for "a pretty girl ripe for the chase."

Also, a more *species*-specific variant of the *Frank Sinatran* expression "bird." (Note: In addition to its feminine denotation, members of singer/actor Sinatra's "Rat Pack" from the 1960s referred habitually to their *penises* as "birds" in jocular, rather juvenile banter.)

I feel compelled to relate an admirable incident involving Sinatra here. I first became his fan at nine when I was sitting in my elementary school auditorium in Detroit in 1945 with some of my black classmates watching a short film the singer had made in support of racial tolerance. That same year, he ventured into the lion's den to address 5,000 white students and their working-class parents at a high school in Gary, Indiana to try to get the kids to return to school after they had walked out to protest the "pro-Negro" policies of their new principal, who had let the school's few black students share classrooms with them, join the orchestra, and swim in the pool.

Sinatra consorted with mobsters early-on and continued to do so throughout his career, but he had a courageous commitment to racial justice and other righteous philanthropy that mitigated a multitude of his considerable sins.

QUAVER — What us old guys' voices begin to do at around say, age seventy-five.

Also, *quiver*.

QUAYLE ("Kway-yull"—not to be confused with "quail") — A *particular golfer* who also "played" at *politics*—and who spelled *potato* with an "e" and may still think Latin is the language of Latin America.

(Note: I didn't put former Vice President Dan Quayle in here alphabetically via his *first* name because I wanted to have at least five items that begin with "Q" to at least *partially* fill out the "Q" section of this here little old *Definitive Dictionary*.)

See **GOLF, GOLF COURSE; MISPRONUNCIATION** *(noun)*; **MISSPELL** *(verb)*

QUESTIONS TO CONSIDER — "How *old* is 'old'?"; "Who will watch the *watchmen*?"; "Who can *really* ever ultimately deceive a lover?"; "What is the size of the universe?"

And perhaps the most metaphysical/philosophical question of all: "So what?"

However, the question Your Auld Author is focusing all of his immense powers of concentration upon right now is, "Where in the dickens are my *glasses*?"

See **"SO WHAT?"**

QUIET *(adjective)* — What one's home would be without any children or dogs—or (perhaps) a loquacious housewife.

Even with no children or dogs (or a *loquacious* housewife—Repubs, xyW again), one's home would still be *unquiet* if one lived by railroad tracks, an airport, or on a certain block on Abington Street in Detroit—where the neighbors play their boom boxes full blast and party all night, and where the city has cut down all the trees to make it easier for helicopters to spot drug traffic.

QUIRKY — What Dr. Wayne Dyer correctly calls (some aspects of) this *Definitive Dictionary*.

See **IDIOSYNCRATIC**

"QUOD SUM ERIS" — "*I* am what *you* will be."

This is a mocking epitaph to the world, found on an old Roman tombstone. The writer of this epitaph is indeed what we *will* be, but blessedly in your case, dear reader, and in the case of Your Auld Septuagenarian Author, *not yet*—at this reading and writing.

See **CERTAINTY**

R

RACISM — "A fungus among us," per Melba Joyce Boyd, lyrical poet and Detroit Pershing High School distinguished alumna of 1966.

It was the often-quoted English peer and Aged Sage John Emerich Edward Dalberg, first Baron Acton, who wrote, "The most certain test by which we judge whether a country is really free is the amount of security enjoyed by its *minorities*." By that measuring stick, America still has some distance to travel on behalf of its black and brown citizens.

(Lord Acton, of course, was also the man who wrote the more famous and equally *portentous* words, "Power *corrupts*, and *absolute* power corrupts *absolutely*.")

See **ABOMINATION; LUNACY**

RACIST — What Your Auld Author publicly called the Rochester, Michigan, residents in the 1980s who protested my hiring black principals during my seven years there as the deputy school superintendent.

"Racist" is also what Your Auld Author publicly called the Madison Heights, Michigan, residents in 2009 who protested my bringing hundreds of Detroit students to the Madison District Public Schools when I was the superintendent there, and what I called the officials of the Detroit Athletic Club in 1958 when they wanted to sponsor me but wouldn't let me bring my three black relay teammates from the Detroit Track Club along with me.

("If it *looks* like a duck and *walks* like a duck and *quacks* like a duck. . . .")

Incidently, when that team later broke the world indoor record in the 880-yard relay, the DAC still stuck by its racist decision.

RADICAL *(noun)* — "A man with both feet planted firmly in the *air*," according to Franklin Delano Roosevelt, U.S. President, 1932–44.

"Radical" is what Detroit's FoxTV2 News anchor Huel Perkins once called Your Auld Author (as a compliment). Perhaps less accurately, he also called me a "renegade" (and a "Renaissance Man"). A *real* radical *renegade* is someone who is much more than a mere *insurgent*. <u>Old Men</u> know that the true radical is an *insurrectionist*, a *revolutionary*.

By the way, we old radicals remain intensely *passionate*. (Many of you radical young ladies have *undoubtedly* noted this.)

See **MARTYR; PASSION; *RENEGADO***

RAP — Short for *Rapscallion*, a scruffy mutt Your Auld Author had six decades ago on Sixteenth Street and McGraw in the bygone days when he was growing up in the once-mighty Motor City.

Whenever your then-very-youthful Auld Author tried to impress some pretty little West Side girl, big ol' Rap would pick that precise moment to break loose from the rope around his collar whereby Your Auld Author was trying to restrain him, and dash into the middle of the street and gobble up horse droppings, whether steaming wet or brittle-dry.

Ol' Rap also liked to help your then-very-youthful Auld Author impress the pretty girl by humping her leg or fetching her a crushed rat from the middle of the street.

Alternative definition: Originally a thuggish, raucously obscene form of urban-male-chauvinist patois nearly unintelligible to the civilized ear.

This once questionable cultural phenomenon has gradually evolved into a critically (albeit *hesitantly*) recognized *genuine art form* through the work of emergent young hip-hoppers like the frenetically eloquent Nas in his album *Illmatic*. Rappers' righteous anger manifests itself poetically in lines like Nas' clever "With more kicks than a baby in a mother's stomach" and his socially commentative "That buck that bought the *bottle*/Could have struck the *Lotto!*"

RAPTURE — *See* **ROMANCE** *(noun)*

"RAT PACK" — *See* **FRANK SINATRAN** (*derivative two-word adjective*)

READ (*present-tense verb*: pronounced "reed") — To observe and *comprehend* something written or printed.

If you can *read* even some modest portion of this exquisite exegesis and *comprehend* most of it as well, you may not be a *redneck* (or a *rank-and-file Republican*)—nor are you probably a young (or *not-so-young*), mis-educated Detroiter, Chicagoan, New Yorker, Philadelphian, urban Washingtonian, East Los Angeleno, etc.

Also, as the saying goes, you most certainly should *thank a teacher*.

REAL ESTATE — Something that in a good locale (even in 2011) remains a better investment than the stock market.

(Think "*lake-front.*")

See **STOCK MARKET**

A REAL *MENSCH* — Yiddish for a truly humane, righteous man.

All Aged Sages are real mensches.

"REALIO-TRULIO" — *Genuine.*

REBEL (*noun*) — Per this publication, one who righteously resists a specific *unrighteous, inept,* or *tyrannical* authority or control.

See **CREATIVE INSUBORDINATION; PASSION; RADICAL** (*noun*); **"RRR"; "UNREASONABLE" MEN**

REBELDOM, UNDER THE "REBEL DOME," REBELHOOD, REBELNESS, REBELRY — The Creatively Insubordinate world and all it stands for: The state of being a Creative Insubordinate.

See **C.I.; CREATIVE INSUBORDINATION**

REBELESQUE SYNERGY — The process whereby a mere two or four or a dozen rebels can pool their thinking to generate enough righteously rebellious and Creatively Insubordinate planning to foment and fuel *a thousand revolutions.*

Note: Aged Sages also refer to rebelesque synergy as *"Rebel Synergetics."*

REBELIZE — To radicalize, render *"rebelish."*

RECONCILIATION — The act of *repairing* an *estrangement.*

It is gratifying and rewarding to effect a *reconciliation* with an old adversary. And, as Yeerr Auld Caledonian Soothsayerr sayeth, "'Tis *guid* to forgive yeer' enemies. It messes with their _minds_."

REDUNDANCY — A needless repetition; *e.g., "radical* rebel," *"lying* politician," "under-endowed Republican."

Here is a *fourth example* of redundancy: *"verbose* writers."

In submitting this *fourth example,* your Frankly Politically Biased Auld Author has *particularly* in mind one very *old* "verbose writer" well-known to him who expounds politically, poetically, and philosophically upon *what _Old Men_ know* at loquacious length, and with rare *relish.*

REFORM — What "reformed" churches need to repeat, and what the Catholic Church and a goodly number of large urban school districts need *sincerely* to _begin_—because some are indeed _deformed._

REGAL REBEL — A majestic, battle-scarred Old C.I. (Creative Insubordinate)—an Aged Sage.

REGRETFUL *(adjective)* — A word now widely used *understatedly* to describe many folks who voted Republican in the 2000 and 2004 United States presidential elections.

"Regretful" is a word also used to describe a growing number of folks who voted *Democratic* in the 2008 election but at this writing are now selfishly upset over President Obama's and the Democratic Party's successful passage of the 2010 Health Care Bill that will give health insurance to several million previously uninsured American men, women, and *children*.

REGRETTABLE (*adjective*) — A word accurately descriptive of the outcomes of the United States presidential elections of 2000 and 2004.

Still, stronger words—such as *tragic* and *catastrophic*—would indeed be *better* ones.

See **CLARENCE THOMAS; IRAQ WAR**

RELATIVES — "Folks whom many 'rednecks' may need a *police scanner* to keep up with." So spake the as-yet-*un*-Aged Sage Jeff Foxworthy.

We Aged Sages didn't choose our relatives—nor <u>would</u> we have chosen some of them, had we been given a choice.

RELIGIONISM — Excessive religious zeal.

Religionism—particularly *Christian* religionism—has been responsible for countless wars and untold torturings and intolerances. Over the cruel centuries, The Earthly and Eternal Shepherd, now hopefully back in heaven at the right hand of God the Father after His storied too-short sojourn among us unappreciative mortals, has presumedly wept bitterly over His errant flock's intolerant transgressions.

REMORSE — The *conscience*-laden agony and burden of *sin*.

Those without conscience or capacity to *care* are utterly incapable of feeling *remorse* for their misdeeds.

See **SOCIOPATH**

See also **PITY**

RENEGADO — Synonymous with _renegade_: A far more intense version of _rebel_.

A _renegado_, in <u>Old Men's</u> palaver, is more than a "Real Righteous Rebel" ("RRR"). Rather, a renegado is a _righteous revolutionary_ who leads an armed guerilla or semi-guerilla movement in an attack upon an unjust _status quo_ so dangerously and fiercely that he becomes a hunted _desperado_, sought dead or alive by the government of his own country, <u>_within_</u> his own country.

The fiery abolitionist John Brown, the Scottish outlaw Rob Roy, the Scottish freedom fighter Sir William Wallace, the American revolutionary George Washington, the Haitian revolutionary Toussaint L'Ouverture, the Mexican revolutionary Emiliano Zapata, and the Cuban and South American revolutionary Ché Guevara are indeed prime examples.

The Thracian slave gladiator Spartacus and the renegade slave Nat Turner would more than qualify, too. (Repubs, check your _encyclopedia_ —if _you have_ one, or use your _library card_—if _you have_ one.)

REPUB — A Republican.

REPUBLICAN — Of or pertaining to the Republican Party.

It was Rutherford B. Hayes (incidentally an unwise president) who never-theless was wise enough to say, "He who serves his party best is the man who serves his _country_ best." Many politicos on both sides of the aisle need to hark to Hayes' words from way back in the nineteenth century. They are as applicable today as they were then.

Another, far better president also said, in the _twentieth_ century (speci-fically in 1962), "I know my Republican friends were gratified to see my wife feeding an _elephant_ in India. She gave him sugar and nuts. But of course the elephant wasn't satisfied."

(More serious note to Republican readers: Your Auld Author is really just having a little fun with you fellow-American folks, so don't send the NRA gunning for me, okay? As the cliché goes, some of my _best friends_ are Republicans, including my multi-decorated Vietnam War-hero cousin—retired U.S. Army Master Sergeant Richard J. Boudro, and my cousin Jeff Telford, a most *unretiring* though very *retired* Ford Motor Company executive whose later-in-life-turned-Republican father, Frank Telford, was a Hollywood producer/director who discovered Lee Marvin and directed Janet Leigh, Tony Randall, Helen Hayes, and other luminaries. Uncle Frank also directed television's *Sea Hunt*, featuring Lloyd Bridges and a very young Jeff Bridges, an Academy Award winner in 2010.

Also, Your Auld Author needs to say that I forgive all of you dumb Repubs out there for electing the dorkhead who used mendacious "information" about "weapons of mass destruction" to mire America in the Iraq war—even if you probably can't forgive *yourselves*. In a 2002 *Telford's Telescope* column in the Detroit-based *Michigan FrontPAGE* weekly newspaper, I warned everyone that this myopic and malevolent dork was going to do it, but nobody listened.

See **DORK, DORKHEAD**

REPUBLICAN PARTY — One of two major parties in an increasingly obsolescent American political system based almost entirely upon a benighted *fiscal* foundation rather than upon a sincere concern for the inalienable rights of all Americans regardless of race or class.

Less reactionary members of this party are sometimes called "Republicrats"—which, come to think of it, isn't all that bad a thing. Better to have a lot of Republicrats (Republic rats?) than have a few *Demopublicans* whom President Obama had to practically *beg* to support their own Democratic Party's Health Care Reform Bill.

REPUBLICAN *PRIVATE PART* — A *pee-wee wee-wee.*

See **PEE-PEE; PENIS ANXIETY; PENIS UNEASINESS; PYGMY** (*adjectival usage*)

RE*PUZZLED*CAN — Old Men's vernacular for "Republicans who *just don't get it*."

See **A-- H---; BUTT-HEAD; GEORGE W. BUSH**

RESOURCE-DRIVEN AND *TECHNOLOGY*-DRIVEN ECONOMIC SYSTEM — The ultimate evolution of the most advanced form of *true* socialism, in which every world citizen participates and to which each contributes a service accordant with his aptitudes and skills.

This could be the *ideal* worldwide economic system of the future, wherein "filthy lucre" (money) would become *obsolete* and *valueless*, and cooperation and the sharing and pooling of resources, goods, and artistic and technological talents and services would abound universally amid the permanent banishment of war, which even in our *present time* has become at least *semi*-obsolete. The love of (and dependence upon) money is *indeed* the Biblical "root of all evil." It engenders *gross* and egregious inequities among men.

For example, in our present unfair economic system, Africa can produce goods, but farmers in Europe and the United States are paid subsidies that enable them to sell similar goods at giveaway prices, wreaking insufferable havoc upon African countries' economies and upon other poorer countries' economies throughout the world.

In a *resource*-driven and *technology*-driven economic system, there would be no world bank and indeed no *money*, nor would anyone *need* any.

All we would *need* are *each other*.

See **UTOPIA**

RESPONSIBILITY — "The price of *greatness*," according to the great Aged Sage Sir Winston Churchill.

REVELROUS "RULES" FOR RETIREES — The First Revelrous "Rule" is: Create the word "Revelrous"!

The Second Revelrous "Rule" is: Just for fun, try sitting wearing sunglasses in your parked car with the headlights on and point a hairdryer at passing motorists to see them slow down.

The Third "Rule" is: In the memo slot for your checks, write "for *crack cocaine*." This will give the bank tellers and the police a chuckle.

"Rule" Number Four is: Pick up a box of condoms at the pharmacy and ask where the fitting room is—or else give the box back to the clerk and ask for a *larger size*.

The Fifth "Rule" is: Sit very low behind the wheel in your car while parked at a light with the window open and tell pedestrians crossing the street, "I'm a *little* person." If you happen to have a friend with you, have him or her sit low in the seat, too, and then inform the crossing pedestrians, "*We're* little *people*." (Actually, that's something my old buddy Bill Breen and I immaturely did when we were young teens.)

The Sixth Revelrous "Rule" is: Stand up on your seat and sing along loudly at the opera.

The Seventh and final "Rule" is: Flag down a police cruiser and shout, "Take me to the nearest casino!" If you like, you can substitute the word "casino" with the words "ho' house," "strip joint," "dope house," etc. Tell the cop you assume that he's a driver for the Policy Cab Company and compliment him on his sharp blue uniform.

If you're in Detroit, you could also confide to the officer that you have to get to the Canadian border *fast* because the FBI is hot on your tail.

You need to be cautiously aware, though, that if you include any of the latter optional components of the Seventh Revelrous "Rule," you may not be able to practice any of the earlier Revelrous "Rules" until after you've been read your Miranda rights and have called your lawyer to come and bail you out (if your bail isn't set at $1 million).

See **IMMATURITY**

REVOLUTION — In politics, the abrupt and often bloody toppling of a _mis_government.

This is something that your worried Auld Author fears may soon happen in this country when unemployment insurance runs out and desperate men can no longer feed their families by legal means.

It was President John F. Kennedy, no less, who warned the world forty-eight years ago, "Those who make _peaceful_ revolution impossible will make _violent_ revolution inevitable."

The **REWARD FOR A GOOD DEED WELL DONE** — Simply having *done* it.

At least, this is the *best* (and usually the *only*) reward.

Ergo, it was Clare Booth Luce who said, "No *good deed* goes *unpunished*."

See **DETROIT PUBLIC SCHOOLS**

See also **GIVE, GIVING**

REX REBORN (An Allegorical Poem, 1967) —

> Huger than the heaving ferns,
> Hulking higher than a hill,
> The Thunder Thing at night returns
> To *seek* and *find* and *pounce* and *kill*.
>
> Jungle fires in the night
> Flicker into spreading flame
> To cast their blazing, blood-red light
> Upon the hunter's hiding game.
>
> *Found*, the tiny quarry *flees*.
> Teeth like scimitars gleam wet—
> And drip, descending, pierce and *seize*:
> The killer gulps and rears erect.
>
> Body shining slimy red,
> Horrid red the staring eye,
> Tyrannosaurus turns his head
> To move against the midnight sky.
>
> Might once more in fiery glare,
> Over a primeval heath,
> A *brute* stalk forth to crush and tear
> And *cancel history* in its teeth?

Now in the twenty-first century, battlefields and war zones and suicide bombings and the probability of ultimate nuclear warfare all remain fearsomely extant, and they also thus remain societally *primitive*, *primordial*, and *primeval*, positing the absolutely certain potential to *cancel further human history literally* and with *grave* finality.

See **A-BOMB**; The **DEVIL**; **FASCISM**; **HORROR**; A *RIDDLE TO PONDER;* *SONNET FOR A SAFER SEA*; **WAR**

RICHARD CHENEY — A (thankfully) *former* vice president of the United States.

Also, someone to avoid going *duckhunting* with.

See **CROCODILE**; **DICK**; **DICK CHENEY**

RICHARD NIXON — A talented but tragically flawed Republican politician and former vice president and president of the United States.

Despite his talent, Richard Nixon nonetheless never would have attained the presidency had it not been for the world-history-altering assassinations of John F. Kennedy and his revolutionary brother Robert.

Nixon's overweening arrogance and misguided sense of entitlement caused him and his subordinates to commit illegal acts that fomented a national crisis of the first *water* (pun intended) and resulted ultimately in his resignation following the Watergate scandal.

See **HUBRIS**

A *RIDDLE TO PONDER* (poem) —

> "Now know thySELF," said Socrates,
> So tell me, WHO AM I?
>
> *You're mother to theocracies*
> *Autocracies, bureaucracies,*
> *And blinding-bright technocracies*
> *That tame the solar sky.*
>
> Why,
> I grant some ideocracies were buried by bureaucracies,
> But "Know thySELF," said Socrates, so tell me what I do!
>
> *You harbor old hypocrisies and arid aristocracies.*
> *You nurture corporatocracies that toll the end of you!*
>
> What, then, of my democracies?
> The highly moral minds among

My wiser children far outrun
The rank morass
Of vacuous <u>class</u>.
Next week I'll likely span
My seed among the stars!
Today I simply plan
To speed some sons to Mars.

(I wish they'd quit their *quibbling*, though,
And come and sit—
"The Sibling Show"
Is being re-run the thousandth time on late TV:
"The Backward *Gun*"! And now, "The Climb Back to the *Tree*"!

Yes, and <u>see</u>—
Suddenly,
"The Crime of Cain" begins again
(As forward runs the reel);
The cries of pain resound in vain.
Too far away to <u>feel</u>,
One errant offspring conjures up
A mighty "mushroom tree"—
Son Two cuts down the buttercups;
Son Three ignites the sea . . .

Thus each misguided brother
<u>*Annihilates*</u> *his <u>other</u>.*

So, after you've taken some time now to ponder this riddle and come up with the answer to it, tell me—Who <u>am</u> I? Who are <u>you</u>? Who—and <u>what</u>—are we?

Embedded within the answer to the riddle is the beginning of that vital and peculiar wisdom which is most crucial to the survival of our species—and perhaps to the longer-term survival of practically all life on our planet itself. Let us pray that as a sentient species we *collectively* discover that answer <u>*in time*</u>.

See **APOCALYPSE; TIME**

RIDICULE — A cruel and devastatingly effective weapon when wielded by a master wordsmith.

Thus, ridicule must never be unfairly and frivolously used—except for sometimes when it's aimed at rich Republicans (or dumb *poor* ones).

RIGHTEOUS INDIGNATION — An emotion Your Auld Author experienced at age seven when his teacher, Mrs. McGinity, grabbed him by the hair and knocked his head against the wall. When I went home and indignantly told my father about it, he asked, "Oh, like this?"—and grabbed me by the hair and knocked my head against the wall. (I never complained to him about Mrs. McGinity again.)

RISK (*noun* and *verb*) — A consistent initiative of any Creative Insubordinate.

Rebels are *risk*-takers, and by definition, risk-takers are *rebels*. This is because, as one anonymous Aged Sage has said, "Only a man who will risk is *free*."

See **CREATIVE INSUBORDINATION**

ROADKILL — Something *old rebels* never *eat*.

At least, they don't eat it *raw* (even if they're from Arkansas). Pseudo-rebels don't eat it, either, but they put smart-alecky signs on their pickup trucks urging *others* to.

Also, Old Men never *eat* on *empty stomachs*. *Drink*, yes—but not eat. Whenever my old Uncle Alfie drank straight Jim Beam on an empty stomach, he would wander around asking, "Whud the turtle say to the alligator? C'mon, tell me, whud he say?"

Then after a long forgetful pause, he'd opine, "Gawd, I *love* that joke," pass out under the kitchen table, and wake up seven hours later with nausea and a humungous hangover. (I never ever *did* hear the punch line. Maybe the alligator ate the turtle and then ate *roadkill*, too, as his second course.)

Incidentally, Old Men know that the best antidote for a hangover is a tablet or two of monoacetiacacidester of salicylic acid in a glass of milk. This also prevents *stroke*. The commercial name for this tablet is *Aspirin*. My uncle Alfie had to take it a whole lot (even though, despite the nausea, I don't think he ever ate roadkill).

"ROBEISM" — This intransigent tome defines *robeism* as "Yielding to the urge to accept bribes after ascending the bench and donning the *black robe*" (particularly at the circuit-court level).

Your cynical Auld Author is aware of an incident in which one Detroit judge boasted in a bar that he had demanded and received oral sex from a defendant in a forgery case and then ruled against her anyway. Talk about *"robeist"* perfidy! She should have bitten it off when she had the chance.

See **"HATTISM"**

ROBERT BOBB — An emergency financial manager appointed by the Governor in 2008 to fix the failing Detroit Public Schools.

After breakfasting at his invitation with Mr. Bobb one-on-one on Thursday, April 1, 2010 (April Fool's Day), Your Auld Author speculated that this seemingly able gentleman just might become the savior the school district and its suffering children sorely need. That is, if this speculation wasn't just another April Fool's joke it may turn out that I've played on *myself.* The students have already endured a long string of cruel "jokes" during the past *student*-exploitive and *student-destructive* decade.

Only time will tell.

Mr. Bobb also assured me that a high school track bearing my name will *retain* my name after the track is relocated. Only time will tell regarding *that*, too.

ROBERT F. KENNEDY — A giant.

RFK's tragic 1968 assassination changed the course of world history for the worse, for forty years. In 1968, we got Richard Nixon as our president —he of the illegal Cambodia bombings and the Watergate scandal. Getting Nixon instead of RFK as president can be likened to if we had got someone like the convicted felon *Liston* instead of the shining young warrior *Ali* as the *"people*'s champion."

See the allegorical poem with the alliterative title **REX REBORN**

See also **ALI; GIANTS; RICHARD NIXON**

ROBERT "THE BRUCE" — The fourteenth-century liberator who became king of a united Scotland—and Your Auld Author's reputed (and some undoubtedly would say *disputed*) ancient ancestor. When she was in her cups, my grandma would often repeat her claim that the Telfords were descended from an illegitimate daughter of Prince Charles Edward Stuart, a direct descendant of "the Bruce."

The film *Braveheart* portrayed "the Bruce" as having double-crossed Sir William Wallace, his comrade-in-arms—portrayed by Mel Gibson, a Scot by way of Australia recently gone sadly haywire over a woman (naturally)—but that inaccuracy was a liberty Hollywood took with Scottish history. No such betrayal ever happened. (I suspect my *grandma* may have taken a little liberty with Scottish history, too.)

"Scots what hae wi' Wallace bled, welcome to yeer gory bed . . ." so wrote Robert Burns, Scotland's greatest poet (on whose 177th birthday your proud Auld Author was born).

ROGUE REBEL — A societal renegade—a rebel gone bad.

A *rogue rebel* is one whose aims have become primarily selfish. Often, he is *profligate, prodigal,* or a *bully.* (Repubs, check your *Webster's,* and an encyclopedia.) Benedict Arnold is an example. Pancho Villa, Aaron Burr, and Errol Flynn were on the borderline.

ROMANCE (*noun*) — A realm wherein the *female* makes the rules.

This lamentably includes the rules for *sex.* Face it, gentlemen.

Also, y'all young fellers are soon going to learn that these rules—right or wrong, fair or *unfair*—are subject to change without notice, because the female is *never* wrong, understand? If she *does* happen rarely to be wrong, it is due to an understandable misunderstanding which resulted from something that you misunderstood. So you *really* were the one who was wrong, and mistaken, and a bad boy. (I hope all of you hapless young humpers are reading this diligently, because you can bet that your *ladies* are.)

See **SCHEMING; SEX**

The **ROYAL "WE"** — Referring to oneself in the plural—a historic practice of kings (and of *commoners* who carry <u>*mice*</u> in their waistcoats).

The alert reader may have discerned that Your Auld Author occasionally refers to <u>*himself*</u> in the plural. This isn't because he considers himself a *sovereign*—or at least, he doesn't consider it very *often* (although, as mentioned elsewhere in this revelatory exegesis, his frequently tippling old grannie once told him—while tippling—that there's a drop of royalty in his bloodline via the bar sinister).

He doesn't have a *mouse* in his pocket, either. The truth is that his big, beautiful, long-haired black cat, Mindy, sometimes sits beside him as he compiles this triumphal tome and helpfully supplies him with ideational items for it—and she's sitting next to me now coaching me as I write. Big, beautiful, long-haired black cats are <u>*seers*</u>, you know (and they also <u>*obviously*</u> boast an ancient royal bloodline).

"RRR" — A "Real *Righteous* Rebel," a Creative Insubordinate *extraordinaire*: An "RRR" is a righteously *reason*-driven, iconoclastic, dynamic, idealistic individualist who refuses to sit in his *"assigned seat."*

Does the *mustang running free on the plains* have an assigned seat?? Do <u>*you*</u> have an assigned seat???

Alternate definition of "RRR": The sound a lion makes when his nap is interrupted by a too-playful cub. Also, the sound our frenetic little black dog BeeBee makes when our big, pugnaciously playful black cat Mindy gives his ear an impertinent left jab.

See **ASSIGNED SEAT;** *YOU*

RUSH LIMBAUGH – The "American" who actually said on the air that he wants your, my, and *his* President's policies to <u>*fail!*</u>

See **SCHLOIN; SCHMUCK**

S

A SACRED DUTY OF ALL *EDUCATORS* — To critique educational structures and institutions and to offer alternatives within them (or *to* them).

Old Men recognize that this is a duty which *true educators* must discharge individually, collectively, and *continually*, in order that we may sustain the ongoing *survival* of our endangered democratic state. The fact that the institution we call "school" is regarded in some quarters as an *"agent* of society" does not absolve it from the responsibility to serve as an agent for *progressive societal reconstruction*. The American public school *is in the most visceral sense an agent of society*, but it is far from being an agent of the *state*—and this is a fundamental difference. It is not *democratic* but *fascist* political theory that would merge the will of society with that of the government and would bestow power to the government to determine what citizens should think and say.

It *definitely must not* be the function of the educational leadership in any democratic community to be *uncritical supporters of the status quo*. Some once-cherished practices of the past weren't always good or right. If we don't fulfill our charge as educators to anticipate and shape a productive and preferred future for our childen, we become, in the late Aged Sage Sydney Harris' words, "Mere tools of the state— or *prostitutes* trading our ideas for a dubious security, a precarious status."

The previous two paragraphs paraphrased from *A Life on the RUN— Seeking and Safeguarding Social* Justice, Harmonie Park Press, 2010 (google www.AlifeontheRun.com) are for folks who *care* about kids.

See **"HIDES IN THE WEEDS"; PSEUDO-EDUCATOR; PUBLIC-SCHOOL SEGREGATION; SLAVERY; *STATUS QUO***

SAD SHIT-UATION — What most of racially segregated urban America and much of the rest of America is *in* today. (Pun courtesy of my kindred crusader Yusef Shakur).

A *SAGACIOUS SECRET* SHARED BY THE OLD MAN ON THE MOUNTAINTOP —
"*Life* is a *fountain*."

When challenged incisively to explain the rare and lofty rationale behind this sacred secret, the Sagacious Old Man on the Mountaintop tugged at his long, white beard and then scratched his head in nonplussed perplexity for quite a while. Finally, he inquired of his interrogator, "You mean life *isn't* a fountain?"

Moral: Seek out no Sagacious Seer to find answers to your life's questions until you have checked his credentials—or better yet, seek *inside yourself* for the answers.

SAGES FOR THE AGES — In everlasting memory of some of history's most sacred (and *scarcest*) religious, scientific/mathematical, psycho-analytical, literary, political, and philosophical thinkers and creative artists, *this* Old Man invites you to lift a celebratory toast and recite this *Te Deum* for these *Sages for the Ages*:

Before we loose our restless ghost from clay mortality,
Let's lift our too-short glass in toast
To all this long, heroic host:

Homer, Plato, Franklin, Frost,
(Plus their peers whose works were lost);
Shakespeare, Cantinflas, Columbus
Intransmutable among us;
Paganini, Beethoven, Leonardo, Hume,
Touchstone of the Joyceans—genitor of Bloom;
Anna Pavlova, Pericles,
Abraham Lincoln, Sophocles . . .

Up brown hillocks spare of trees
Labored lank Pheidippides.

Sandburg, Lindbergh,
Hammerstein,

Gandhi, Strindberg
Conquered time.

The plunging depths of pain's frontier
Disgorged a pale pioneer—
Predestined Roger Bannister.

The Atom Bomb? No, that's a *thing*.
Instead, take Martin Luther King—
Or Buddha,
Or Someone by the sea
Of Middle-eastern Galilee.

("Who were *they*?" some will say. Some will wonder, "Who were *they*?")

Or our nameless Unknown Soldier in his faceless tomb.
But what if he were wakened in that marble womb
To be reborn
and claim he'd worn
an Iron Cross??!
Now your untossed
Goblets, *horrified*, you've thrown;
Thus my skoal I end alone:

O maker of Winged Victory,
O patriot John Kennedy,
O Robeson, Einstein, Schweitzer, Swift:
To *you* this final cup I lift!

And let us include *Confucius* and *Mohammed* in our *next* toast. They, too, are "intransmutable among us," and among the absolute Sages for the Ages, as are the prolific American inventor George Washington Carver, American satirist H. L. Mencken, Lutheran theologian Reinhold Niebuhr (who indeed confirmed your author's mother Helen at Bethel Evangelical & Reformed Church on West Grand Boulevard between Linwood and Grand River in Detroit in A.D. 1920), American Founding Father Thomas Jefferson, American statesman (and Detroiter) Ralph Bunche, and pioneering psychiatrist Sigmund Freud (sorry, Dr. Phil).

We must also toast iconoclastic German dramatist Johann Wolfgang von Goethe, the transformative Greek mathematician Euclid, American novelist Kurt Vonnegut, the eighteenth-century French philosopher Voltaire (born François-Marie Arouet), and violinist Isaac Stern. (I just had to get at least one more *fiddler* in here. The other—in the verse— is the nineteenth-century composer/violin virtuoso Nicolò Paganini.) He wrote violin concertos so difficult that only *he* could play them.

(Republican persons, you really need to crack open some encyclopedic passages about these preceding lauded luminaries, and on those to follow. Reading about them might even convert you into full-blown *liberal humanists* [a redundancy]—to the ultimate and infinite better-ment of our beleaguered nation.)

A Voltaire quote: "I disagree entirely with what you have to say, but I would defend your right to say it if it caused my death." That's the kind of sentiment that could incite a revolution, and *did*.

We must also toast the ancient Athenian philosopher Diogenes—who searched with a lantern (in vain) for an honest man.

Post-scripted note to any Republican readers and other miscellaneous baboons who are still trying to comprehend this tortuous tome:

Athenian refers to anything of or having to do with Athens, the Greek city that was in ancient times an independent city-state where was born and which embodied the liberating Periclean concept of *democracy*. This sublimely egalitarian concept is one which in all its starkly humanitarian splendor America's most recent ex-President (number 43) and *too many members of his Pachydermatous Party* have seemed utterly incapable of grasping. The Supreme Court of the Incorporated States of America briskly set about the repressive business of trashing our fragile, hallowed democracy with its Anno Domini 2000 ruling not to allow the *bent chits* to be counted in Florida in that pivotal presidential race, and its corporate-collusive 2010 decision to declare special-interest donations to political campaigns a *limitless enterprise* for those barons of big business who have the deepest pockets.

But America's *44th* President is not only *capable* of grasping the divine concept of democracy—he *personifies* it. Let all of us ordinary citizens pray now for the statesmanlike Barack Obama's safety—and that his Kennedyesque philosophies may once more prevail across the land.

See **EGALITIZATION; GIANTS**

SANSKRIT — One of the oldest recorded Indo-European languages.

See **AKASHA**

SARAH PALIN — *See* BAD BOOKS

SAVAGERY — A disquieting state that Old Men know and warn can appeal to mob instincts and subvert the more humane inclinations of even the most urbane culture.

To cite one horrendous example: During the decade which followed Hitler's ascension to power, events transpired which transcend the most pessimistic insights of any misanthrope of any era. The Buchenwald Concentration Camp was sacrilegiously constructed around Goethe's oak tree. The terrified processions of men, women, and children *who were marched en masse* into the Auschwitz gas chambers occurred even as elsewhere in the camp the orchestra was serenely playing selections from Viennese light music.

See MISANTHROPE; MONSTERS; PESSIMIST

SCHEMING — An endeavor wherein historically ancient Aged Sage Publilius Syrus asserted in his *Maxims* that women of any age *outshine* men, young and old—*hands-down and* utterly.

Actually, when it comes to scheming, it's not much of a *contest*, guys— the ladies run rings around you. Face it.

See ROMANCE (*noun*)

SCHLOIN — *See* RUSH LIMBAUGH; SCHMUCK

SCHMUCK — *See* RUSH LIMBAUGH; SCHLOIN

"SCHOOL OF HARD KNOCKS" — An informal institution that offers an advanced "degree" which Old Men in particular have come to recognize as all too valid.

Your Auld Author's Sixteenth Street at McGraw origins in the intractably chaotic Zone 8 of central Detroit qualify him as a diplomate of that "school," as do the even harder origins of his father, who was swinging a pick in a coal mine at thirteen and boxing professionally at sixteen.

Most young Americans of today can't even *conceive* of such conditions, which we can only pray will never recur in this country.

SCHOOLS — *Places where in America a <u>shallow</u> and <u>instrumental conformism</u> is now being substituted for what instead <u>should</u> be there: namely, an <u>encouraged preparedness</u> to <u>think imaginatively</u> and to <u>question boldly and critically</u>.*

It is frightening to contemplate that only a precious few <u>Old Men</u> and <u>Old Women</u> educators who are dying out at a geometrically accelerative rate know beyond question or doubt that this definition is true of the great majority of our urban public schools, K-12 (as well as some of those even in staid *suburbia*).

SCIENCE — Reason, logic, and plain old common sense at its *best*—with more than a smattering of curiosity and wonder thrown into the mix.

Simply put, the grandiose-sounding professorial "Scientific Method" is nothing more than the ancient, tried-and-true practices of basic *observation, perception,* and resultant *deduction.*

See **CURIOSITY; WONDER** *(noun)*

SCOTCH *(adjective* and *noun)* — Your Auld Author offers *you* three definitions for Scotch (along with a few *glasses* of it, per *definition* "a"):

a) A drink from the land of my late father's birth that he drank a whole *lot* of, with chasers of beer.
b) A *pejorative* for "Scottish" (Republicans, xyW).
c) A form of tape packaged in a box decorated with a nondescript tartan design, in keeping with the myth that we Scots are *cheap* and keep our worn-out belongings in one piece with *tape* rather than invest in anything *new.*

SCOTS *(noun)* — Fighters and drinkers.

The Irish fight for the fun of it; Scots fight like it's their *calling*—which often it has been. (In ancient Gaelic, the word "Scot" actually and indeed means "*Irishman.*" It might as well mean *drinker,* too.)

Scots, incidentally, are generally very *generous*, albeit *thrifty*—but seldom *stingy* (contrary to the stereotype). Yeer Auld Author's Scottish grandma Maggie and granddad Francis (Frank) would have literally given you the shirts off their backs if you needed to have them.

See **IMBIBERS; IRISHMEN; "LADIES FROM HADES"; "LIKE TO FIGHT"**

SCROTUM, SCROTA *(noun)* — A sensitive and vulnerable small baglike physical appendage whereby the vanishing American middle-class male—black, white, or brown—is being tightly squeezed by corporate moguls and, incidentally, by an emerging matriarchy like the one that has run the Detroit Public Schools into the ground.

Scrotum also happens to be one of this particular Old Man's gleeful and occasional slang words for "Republican."

Plural, *scrota*; as in, "Don't any of those grumpy GOP *scrota* ever intend to stop beating a dead horse? The Health Care Bill *passed*! *Live* with it, already.

(Incidentally, the distaff scatological equivalent of *scrotum* is a three-letter anatomical slang word beginning and ending with "t" that is often referred to in a common colloquialism as getting "caught in a wringer.")

"SECOND SIGHT" — The uncommon gift of being able to see *spirits* (and not while over-imbibing the *liquid* kind) or of being able to see into the *future*, or see *past events* that one didn't personally experience.

See **SEER**

SECRET — Something it is often wise to keep (and even wiser to expect others *not* to).

Many Old Men have learned this the hard way. If you want to get the word out on something while intending that people believe you want it kept quiet, confide the "secret" to the "busiest body" you know. You can rest assure that it will be in the headlines and on Channels 2, 4, and 7 within a fortnight.

The **SECRET OF** *STRENGTH* — *Concentration*.

SECRET SINNERS — Those who are the quickest to sin.

See **CYNIC, CYNICISM; MISANTHROPE**

SECRETS OF THE CENTENARIANS — Here are some key *how-to's* for living beyond a full *century*:

Eat fruits, pickled herring and sardines, food rich with fish oil and flax seed, whole wheat bread, and dark chocolate (in moderation).

Also, don't eat a lot of canned or processed foods.

Stay lean (but not *mean*).

Use *only* vinegar on your salads. Sip sparingly from a molasses bottle once a week. As mentioned elsewhere herein, drink fat-free milk, red wine (in moderation), and an optional weekly bottle of beer. Avoid booze and bar brawls—and don't drink and drive, or text while driving. (Also, always observe the speed limit and drive *defensively*.) Don't smoke—except perhaps an occasional cigar (with an even less frequent snifter of Grand Marnier).

Maintain a happy marriage (if you're married). Have a hobby, and other interests that keep you active. Read often and eclectically, particularly biographies. Don't watch a lot of television—*particularly* not sit-coms. Learn how to speak another language and/or how to play a musical instrument. Have a faithful and interactive pet. <u>Socialize</u>.

Also, if possible, reside (or *vacation*) where the air is clean—in the mountains, perhaps. Go to the movies (in moderation). Befriend a child other than your own. Paint pictures and write poems. Ride a bicycle (but not a motorcycle). Swim. Take daily naps. Think positive thoughts.

Seldom complain, and avoid complainers and negative-thinking people, but at the same time, be tolerant of the foibles of others, and don't "sweat the small stuff"—indeed, if *you* make every fight a fight to the *death*, you're going to *die* a lot of times.

Try to maintain compatible relationships with your grown children, in-laws, parents, and other family members—regardless of whatever neuroses or closeted "skeletons" they may have. (They probably perceive that *you* may have some, too.)

Volunteer, and give of yourself to a noble cause. Celebrate life and stop now and then to smell the roses. (Also, it doesn't hurt to be born female and/or have good genes, and to be a native of Macau, Japan, Singapore, Australia, Canada, France, Sweden, or Italy—and *not* to be a native of Haiti, Angola, Afghanistan, Zimbabwe, Nigeria, South Africa, Democratic Republic of Congo, Yemen, or Pakistan.)

See **DHEA; GIVE, GIVING**

SECURITY — Something that <u>Old Men</u> know must sometimes be boldly abandoned and forgotten in exchange for *opportunity*.

See **OPPORTUNITY**

SEED — Some <u>Old Men</u> find to their sorrow that sons sired of their seed aren't always true and loving sons to them, and find to their joy that sons *not* of their seed, or not *directly* of their seed, can sometimes be *magnificent* sons to them.

See **"SEEDS"**

"SEEDS" — What men old and young are genetically programmed to *sow generically* and *indiscriminately*—some stopping only in very old, old age.

(In their earlier years, those "seeds" they sow are cutely called "wild oats.")

SEER — An <u>Old Man</u> or <u>Old Woman</u> (capitalized). An Aged Sage.

Also, someone with the gift of "second sight."

See **"SECOND SIGHT"; SHAMAN**

SELF-CONFIDENCE — Well-founded faith in oneself and one's abilities.

However, much too *often*—and *less* often, much too *dangerously*— "self-confidence" can also be merely overwhelming faith in a *fool*. (Consider, for example, our 43rd president.)

SELFISHNESS — The Devil's worst curse.

See **EVIL**

SELF-KNOWLEDGE — *Old Men* know that while we frequently note and acknowledge the sins of others, we *in*frequently note or acknowledge our *own*. (This goes for Old *Women*, too.)

SELF-SACRIFICE — A rarity.

See **GIVE, GIVING**

SEMI-**REBEL** — An undecided or lukewarm, partial, sometime, borderline, not-yet-totally-out-of-the-closet, "almost" rebel.

A *semi*-rebel is like a *semi*-erection. He is *sort of* Creative, and *nearly* Insubordinate. With patiently persuasive, stimulative nurturing and coaxing, some *semi*-rebels possess the potential to become *full-fledged*, Creatively *Insubordinate* rebels. Sometimes an unjust deed done by a high-ranking member of the power elite to someone the *semi*-rebel is close to can raise the *S-R* to the full, erect stature of upstanding *rebelhood*.

One of the most intriguing examples of a *semi*-rebel is former President Bill Clinton (although the semi-*erection* analogy doesn't fit too well in his case). Clinton has always seemed to be too nice a guy ever to become a full-fledged, rampant rebel other than in extreme circumstances (except in *amour*—where he was actually more *rogue* than rebel).

See **CREATIVE INSUBORDINATION**

"SENSUS, NON AETAS, INVENIT SAPIENTIAM" ("Good sense, not age, brings wisdom") — The philosopher Syrus again, in his *Maxims*.

From the Aged Sage's perspective, this maxim presents the exception that proves the rule. (Republican congressmen and other *insensate* old wowsers take heed.)

Maybe *you insensate* old <u>Democratic</u> wowsers better take heed, too—particular those of *you* who haven't been supporting your young Democratic president's egalitarian and humanitarian initiatives.

SEPARATION OF CHURCH AND STATE — The only possible political device to ensure that any and all religions maintain their purity, and that religious persecution and bloody sectarian religious strife á la Ireland and sixteenth-century France can never gain a legal foothold in the United States and thus open that Pandora's Box.

SEPTUAGENARIAN — Any robust old rover who, like your 'Umble Auld Author, was born in the Depression decade of the 1930s and thus hath lived and breathed a whole lot *longer* than long enough to be able to write everything that's in this untempered tome—and *more*—from hard, hard, *hard* experience.

Also, what a few of us rickety old rascals who are still lucid and of reasonably unbent posture in our *eighth* (!) *decade* on this planet self-consciously call ourselves to avoid having to reveal our *exact* age. (Yea, Republicans—any battered old badger in his *seventies* hath verily *completed* his seventh decade and *embarked* on his <u>eighth</u>: Get it now? Didn't think so.)

Your Auld Author, naturally, is wont to modestly style himself a "Septuagenarian Sage *Supreme!*" After all, I can call myself anything I *want* to in this dauntless *Dictionary*, since I'm the one who's *writing* it, right?

SEX — Something that Aging Sage William Jefferson Clinton might once have likely called "One of the Nine Reasons for Reincarnation."

(The other *eight* are comparatively *insignificant*—right, Bill?)

<u>Old Men</u> know that sex, if uncontrolled, can *scorch*—but they also know that righteously and prudently channeled, its sublime flame can, through the progeny it produces, *ignite the torch of <u>infinity</u>.*

It was Aged Sage Aristotle who said, "Man has two 'peaks'—thinking and *sex*." That such a legendary thinker would have made such a statement is surprising, because even folks far less Aged and Sagacious than was that ancient and eternally wise Athenian know that these two "peaks" are *antithetical*. (Just ask William Jefferson Clinton, former Detroit mayor Kwame Kilpatrick, and former New York Governor Eliot Spitzer [all Dems], among countless other sadly busted boinkers).

And for the benefit of any lone Republican who may still be trying to decipher this torrid tome, *antithetical* means "directly opposed or contrasted." I guess even wise old Athenian Ari (or *especially* old Ari?) had to stop thinking at least *momentarily* to find time to do a little bit of *boinking* now and then.

To our belated and happy surprise, we <u>Old Men</u> have learned, too, that sex is best (and ultimately most *exciting*) in *mutual monogamy*. Sadly, this is a lesson it has taken some of us self-indulgent old dogs a lifetime to learn. Many of us *never* learn it, to the great sorrow of everyone involved. Also, <u>Old Men</u> who form the upper (or lower) half of the "beast with two backs" with rapturous regularity *live longer* (particularly if they're forming it with their *own* wives and not with someone *else's*).

See **"BEAST WITH TWO BACKS"; BOINK; MONOGAMY**

SEX "REFORMERS" — The kind of folks who in their most extreme incarnation want to put *pants* on chimps and male dogs.

To sex "reformers," *nothing* related to sex is pure. They are therefore the lewdest people of all—and their gospel is their repressed lechery made manifest.

SEXUAL EXPLOITATION — Everything that a certain current U.S. Supreme Court associate justice was indeed alleged to have said to an uninterested Anita Hill about his physical similarity to the celebrated porn star Long Dong Silver exemplifies *sexual exploitation <u>perfectly</u>*.

Sexual exploitation isn't *romantic*—it's <u>*fascistic*</u>.

See **CLARENCE THOMAS; FASCISM**

SHAMAN — A high priest of pantheism; a true Aged Sage—an <u>*oracle*</u>.

SHAMANIC SELF-TRANSFORMATION — An effective holistic tool for many progressive practices which a genuine *shaman* or other seer can teach us.

These include the creation of "sacred space" for the Self and using "spiritual tech" to expand our limited self-concept and make contact with our limit*less* core of potential—thus lessening our "dark edge of *unknowingness* and *negativity*" (and also consistently helping us remember where we put our car keys).

See **SEER; SHAMAN**

SHEEP (*noun, singular* and *plural*) — *Metaphorically*, the plural usage of the word "sheep" is defined here as folks who "form a _herd_ which flocks for protection and blindly follows any demagogue that comes its way."

The late, great Aged Sage Winston Churchill commonly used the word descriptively to denote the timid non-rebel, as in the Churchillian quip "sheep in *sheep's* clothing." (A sheep in *wolves'* clothing is a *pseudo-rebel*.)

"Sheep" is also a word used to describe the sheeplike pseudo-*Democrats* in Congress who followed George Bush II and Richard Cheney into a ruinous war of aggression in 2002.

Alternate definition: The unwilling objects of the affections of Ride 'em Cowboy Clem.

See **DEMAGOGUE; NON-REBEL** (*noun*)**; PSEUDO-REBEL**

SHEEP IN *SHEEP'S* CLOTHING — *See* **SHEEP** (*noun, singular* and *plural*)

SHIT (also pronounced with two syllables, i.e., "SHEE-it", by assorted students Your Auld Author has taught) — As _Old Men_ know too well, *shit happens*.

The Old _Taoists_ know this, too, although they express it with different terminology. So, too, quoth the Aged Sage Confucius (or was that _Confuse Us_?)

And, as a contemporary joke goes, the _Catholics_ say, "_Shit_ happens because you were _bad_"; the _Protestants_ say, "Let that _shit_ happen to _someone else_ "; the _Jews_ say, "Why did this _shit_ happen to _us_?"; the _Hindus_ say, "This same _shit_ happened to me _before_"; and the _Moslems_ say, "If _shit_ happens, it's the will of Allah." (Also the _Hedonists_ say, "Let's _smoke_ this shit!" Yea and verily—but let's _legalize_ it first.)

Alternate definition for _shit_: An acronym for "So Happy I Tried" (usually spoken in bitter frustration at some personal injustice or after having been unfairly _fired_).

SHRIVELED (_participial adjective_) — _See_ **NAPOLEON'S PICKLED PECKER; PENIS; PYGMY** (_adjectival usage_); **REPUBLICAN**

SILENCE — "Is _golden_," as the old saying goes—and it is also something to be fervently longed for when we're surrounded by a bevy of chattering females or within auditory range of booming boomboxes.

Our _own_ silence, however, is something that is extremely _ill-advised_ if we are _luminously_ _wise_—but conversely is extremely _un_wise if we are something considerably _less-than-wise_. The _unwise_ need to sit down, shut up, hark to the _wise_, and earnestly try to become _less_ unwise. They also need to stay off the lecture circuit if their name is George W. Bush, Sarah Palin, or Milky the Clown.

A SILLY (NON)-**SYLLOGISM** — If it's the _tobacco company's_ fault when a four-pack-a-day smoker dies of lung cancer, and it's the _TV set's_ fault if your grandkids become insufferable brats, and it's the _gun manufacturer's_ fault when yet another Detroit kid gets whacked in a drive-by, then if I die while my as-yet-unwrinkled old ass is parked in front of my blinking laptop, my happy heirs should sue _Bill Gates_, right?

(Methinks I must have lived too long to be able to understand this increasingly _wacky_ world.)

SILVER AND GOLD — Mankind's _slaves_—or mankind's _masters_.

These pretty metals would become merely _decorative_ under the en-lightened _resource_-driven and _technology_-driven economic system.

See **RESOURCE-DRIVEN AND _TECHNOLOGY_-DRIVEN ECONOMIC SYSTEM**

SIN (*noun*) — Something frequently *un*acknowledged by the sinner even when confronted with his sin, yet nearly always *magnified* by other "holier-than-thou," finger-pointing <u>similar</u> sinners who haven't been caught sinning—*yet*.

SITUATIONAL ETHICS — What Huckleberry Finn practiced when he hid the slave Jim and helped him escape.

<u>Old Men</u> know that unjust laws are *made to be broken* by those who have sufficient moral courage to break them.

SKIRTS — *See* **CUTIES; KILTS AND TARTANS; "LADIES FROM HADES"**

SKULL — A bony container for the brain—including the sinister brains of Karl Rove and Dick Cheney, which for eight years did double duty as the brains for the AWOL brain of George W. Bush, the former AWOL National Guardsman who had catastrophically become the 43rd president of the dangerously <u>de</u>-*uniting*-United States, which in many areas and arenas have *relapsed* into contentious disunity.

See **BUSH'S BRAIN; DICK'S HEAD; KARL ROVE**

SLAVERY — The "peculiar institution."

See **ABOMINATION; PUBLIC-SCHOOL SEGREGATION; CORPORA-TOCRACY**

SLEEP — <u>Old Men</u> know enough to sleep until they aren't *sleepy* (except maybe in Rio, or in pre-Katrina New Orleans during Mardi Gras).

SLOW LEARNERS — *See* **EDUCATORS WHO HAVEN'T FIGURED OUT YET THAT THE WORST WAY TO TEACH KIDS IS TO *TEST* THEM TO DEATH**

See also **REPUBLICAN**

SLOWING DOWN — If a man ain't able to do a little bit of *slowing down* now and then, he won't ever be able to find the time even to take a good sh--er, I mean, he won't be able to find the time even to have a *healthy bowel movement*.

(Those who have been privileged [or cursed] with the chance to enjoy [or suffer] a long-term closeness to Your Auld Author may note that he would have expressed this observation somewhat differently were his gentle and sainted Danish mama [the inheritress of ungentle and unsaintly Danish Vikings] not sitting up there at the right hand of God monitoring her son from on high: I still recall the day in 1940 or '41 that Dickie Otten and I got our smarty little pre-kindergarten potty mouths washed out with soap—courtesy of that same gentle mama— after she heard us sitting on top of the garage roof telling each other infantile excretory stories about Mr. Poop and Mr. Pee. ["Mr. Poop and Mr. Pee were walking across a bridge, when all of a sudden Mr. Pee fell off the bridge into the river and got all mingled and mixed in with the water and shouted to Mr. Poop, 'Help, Mr. Poop! Help! I'm coming apart! Help! Help, Mr. Poop!'. . .," etc.])

Immediately following our salutary mouthwash, Your Author got a good *walloping* for good measure—and for climbing onto the garage roof. (Your Author considered it very unfair that Dickie didn't get walloped, too.)

See **PEE; POOP** (*verb*)

SMALL-MEMBERED (*hyphenated adjective*) — *See* **PENIS ANXIETY; PENIS UNEASINESS; REPUBLICAN**

SMILE — Something that if you *give* everyone every day will cost you *nothing* but may one day gain you *a million dollars*.

(Having a smile on your face is a cheap and easy way to *look* like a million dollars, too.)

"SO WHAT?" — The universe's most elemental and perennial philosophical question.

This entry comes with the compliments of my old teammate and friend of more than half a century, Jerome J. Catalina—Berkley, Michigan, high school track and football coach *emeritus*.

See **QUESTIONS TO CONSIDER**

SOCIAL ACTIVIST — A Creative Insubordinate. Also, a true *teacher*.

See **C.I.**; **TEACHER**

SOCIALISM — A Utopian political system as envisioned by the idealistic Socialist Sage Karl Marx.

See **HUMANISM**; *RESOURCE*-DRIVEN AND *TECHNOLOGY*-DRIVEN ECONOMIC SYSTEM

SOCIOPATH — A cruel and amoral creature condemned to suffer from an absolute emotional disconnect from all other beings.

(And those "all other beings" are condemned to suffer a whole lot *more* suffering than the *sociopath* is condemned to suffer if they experience the misfortune of becoming entangled in any visceral way with him/her or fall within his/her sphere of power.)

Adolf Hitler was the classic *prototype* of a sociopath—and a considerable number of folks are of the opinion that the unfeeling statements and ruthless acts of America's most recent past vice president (circa 2000–08) placed him on the *borderline*.

See The **DEVIL**; **MONSTERS**; **REMORSE**; **SAVAGERY**

SOCRATES — This timelessly great philosopher's admonition "Know thyself" reaches out to us across the millennia as a referent to what is perhaps the most viscerally vital (and for many, the most *elusive*) knowledge to attain. (Socrates also said, perhaps even more wisely, "All I know is that I know *nothing*.")

As knowledge gradually filled our youthful brains and grew in breadth and complexity throughout our receptive lives, wonder deepened within us and matured like ripe fruit in the masterful minds of us Aged Sages toward the approaching end of our days. It is now that we have the optimum knowledge to share with the young and also to offer to all the world, if for but a painfully brief and precious span of time.

See **A _RIDDLE_ TO PONDER**; **SAGES FOR THE AGES**; **WONDER** (*noun*)

SODA POP — Never ask an <u>Old Man</u> (or an *old man*), "Do you want some soda pop?" He may protest, "Don't call me 'Pop'!" and *pop* you one.

Isn't the English tongue perplexingly complex? Its glorious complexities keep us old teachers of English briskly in business on every continent on earth.

Consider, for example, the pronunciation of these words, according to their usages: "It's time to present the present"; "They were too close to the door to close it"; "A bandage was wound around the wound," etc.

"SOFTNESS OF HEAD" — The only thing worse than "hardness of heart" (per Theodore Roosevelt).

<u>Old Men</u> sincerely doubt that Teddy R. would have *suffered* the contemporary softheaded Americans who are turning against a president who saved the auto industry and passed a jobs stimulus bill, or that Teddy R. would have been happy to see hard-hearted Americans angry that the least fortunate among us are finally getting decent health coverage.

If the GOP really cared about the costs of a watershed health reform like the one instituted in 2010 and its impact on the burgeoning federal deficit, it wouldn't have taken us to war on false premises that have cost *billions*. (Also, where were the *Tea Party* protestors then?)

See The **HEART**; **"TEAPARTYERS"**

SOLITUDE — Individual creativity's *rarest* and *most fertile* ground.

Solitude is the *oftentimes too-rare glory* of being *alone* with one's *thoughts*, in order that one may generate creative concepts.

See **CREATING**

In a darker vein, *see also* **LONELINESS**

SOMETHING THAT HAPPENS TO A BOY DURING PUBERTY — He says goodbye to childhood and enters adultery. (Currently circulating *joke*.)

SOMETHING THAT IS *BORROWED* — Time.

SOMETHING THAT IS *IMMORTAL* — The universe.

SOMETHING THAT IS *INEVITABLE* — Change.

SOMETHING THAT IS *IRRECOVERABLE* — *Time*, after it's gone; *an hour*, after it has passed; often one's *friend* or *spouse*, after we have lied to them or otherwise belittled or betrayed them (or they *think* that we did: *Perception* is *reality*).

SONNET FOR A SAFER SEA (a Sonnet for *Sanity*) —

> This voyage of historic humankind
> Is one whereon we're fated to decide
> If cold creations of the corporate mind
> Shall specify the way we'll live, or die.
> We cruise now with mere *nautical* controls
> Which navigate us up no harbor path:
> We try to steer through anti-social shoals
> With *sextants*, when we need a *sociograph*!
> We automate our elemental selves—
> Computerized, transistorized, yet *blind* . . .
> And thus meander toward unfathomed hells
> Whence it will prove impossible to find
> The sort of *social* innovations we
> Must seek, to sail upon a *safer* sea.

In our current global environment, there are few "safe seas" (and *none* off the coast of Somalia or now—for marine life—in the Gulf of Mexico).

SONS OF THOR — The four mythical sons of the Viking god of thunder, who was represented as wielding a mighty hammer.

The Sons of Thor converted their sire's hammer into the *macro-cosmic* Hammer of Creation. It had four arms bent at right angles referring to the continual motion and revolution of invisible cosmic powers, pointing to the cycles of time within the world's axes and their equatorial belts. The symbol formed the *svastica*—meaning *spirit* and *matter*. The four hooks depicted the motion in the revolving cycles, as a modern cartoonist depicts motion by drawing similar motion lines.

When applied to *man*—the <u>microcosm</u>—it shows him as a link between heaven and earth: The "right hand" being raised at the end of a horizontal arm, the "left" pointing to the earth. Native Americans on our continent's eastern seaboard adopted this symbol, possibly at the time of contact with the Danish Viking Leif Ericson in the eleventh century, and they assigned it similar spiritual meaning.

This peaceful symbol was tragically corrupted forever by the monstrous Nazis in the 1930s.

"SOUL" — Something which is more a *characteristic* trait or *state-of-being* than it is any *tangible* thing—something many African-Americans have and *all* Aged Sages also have.

Sixty-four-dollar question: Can a *Republican* have "soul?" Honest answer: *Yes*, but this publication isn't able to provide an example of one who *has* it (at this juncture). For that matter, there honestly are many *Democrats* who don't have it *either*—nor can they even *begin* to comprehend its *essence*.

If the quotation marks are removed and the word is preceded by an *article*, a *soul* is something all Creative Insubordinates <u>keep</u> and some *uncreative subordinates <u>sell</u>. A Creative Insubordinate's soul isn't for sale.

See **ATMAN; C.I.**

SPARTANS — Citizens of an unenlightened, warlike city-state of Ancient Greece. Surprisingly, Sparta had a precociously *enlightened* <u>resource</u>-driven, <u>non-monetary</u> economic system.

Also, students, staff, alumni, and fans of *Michigan State University*, including my dyed-in-the-green-and-white *Spartan* daughter Katherine Fay Helen Telford Garrett, B.S., MSU, 1996.

See ***RESOURCE*-DRIVEN AND *TECHNOLOGY*-DRIVEN ECONOMIC SYSTEM**

SPRINTERS — *See* **BOXERS**

STATESMAN — A leader who always leads from the *front.*

See **POLITICIAN; POLITICO**

STATUS QUO — Establishment Latin for what is protected by those who say: "Here's the deal—we are the privileged few who've got it all, and we're going to erect ten thousand barriers against *change* in order to *keep* it that way."

See **CHANGE** *(noun),* The **CHANGE**

STEAL — Please don't *steal* this book!

My publisher and I need the money. (Also, please don't read too *much* of it unless you *pay* for it—I've got several charities to support, as well as a sizeable family that includes two ongoingly well-fed animals— not counting your gluttonous Old Author, whose still-sturdy figure has nonetheless expanded considerably from the 165 pounds he carried on a five-foot, eleven-inch frame when he broke 47 seconds in the 1957 NCAA 440-yard dash final, boastfully becoming the first Michigan native to accomplish the feat.)

STEVE AND KATHY SWIGARD — C.I.s (Creative Insubordinates) *Extraordinaire.*

Sometime in the early 1990s, Steve and Kathy Swigard of Nevada were flying their Cessna toward an airport near Lake Tahoe when a sudden loss of hydraulic fluid prevented the landing gear from descending. Practicing instant C.I., this truly Creatively Insubordinate couple *urinated* into the hydraulic system as repeatedly and copiously as they could. Sufficient hydraulic pressure thus presently being restored, the gear came down and they landed safely.

Talk about pissing on your problems! Steve and Kathy get this purple publication's first CIGPM (Creatively Insubordinate Golden Pee Medallion), which will hereafter be called the Steve and Kathy Swigard (SKS) CIGPM in their honor (and with their kind permission).

See **C.I.**

STOCK MARKET — Playing the *stock market* is *gambling*, pure and simple.

Old Men, including *this* one, have agonizedly learned that folks shouldn't invest anything in high- or medium-risk stocks that they aren't prepared to *lose*, and they should be somewhat careful with the "low-risk" ones—even when they've got a *professional* managing them. Your Old Author speaks from *expensive* experience.

The old saw "What goes up will go up *more* after the first of the year" obtains for the ever-rising cost of living but definitely not always for the *stock market*. Consider how the Dow Jones average was affected after 9/11/01, for example, and after the sharp decline in the value of tech stocks that same year, and after the Bush II-generated near-collapse of Wall Street and resultantly of the auto industry, and during the current and ongoing collapse of the housing market, and during the sharp rise of nationwide unemployment (which currently lingers at Depression-level figures in urban areas).

"STRANGELY BELIEVE IT" ("Believe It or Not") — If you'll permit your Amazed Auld Author to digress a moment from the perceptive pearls of wisdom I've been inflicting upon you, I'd like to share with you the *stranger* than strange case of one *Fredrick Federley*, a member of the Swedish Parliament—a case which is enough to bemuse and befuddle the most *Sagacious* of Aged Sages who render judgments in courts of law:

Mr. Federley claimed that he had always campaigned as someone who doesn't take gifts from those he is responsible for regulating. Subsequently, he was called out by the newspaper *Aftonbladet* in February 2010 for having accepted a free travel holiday from an air-line. Denying that *he* accepted the trip, Federley confided to reporters that he happens to be a *cross-dresser*, and that it was his *alter ego* "Ursula" who took the free holiday! "Strangely believe it," indeed! (And to think that this Amazed Auld Author here was naive enough to believe that after 74 *Amazing* years, I'd *seen it all*.)

See **ANIMAL "HUSBANDRY"**

STRING THEORY — A proposition that examines the fundamental compo-nents of the universe and speculates whether a unifying theory exists that can explain all basic physical phenomena.

String theory requires *six extra dimensions* in addition to the three in space and one in time which we traditionally acknowledge. *Hyper-Sagacious* physicists called <u>*string theorists*</u> hypothesize that these six extra dimensions are folded into imperceptibly small shapes called Calabi-Yau manifolds that abound everywhere in space. Your Auld Author isn't making this up to confound gullible Republicans, either (if there are any Repubs who are still trying to read this item). There are an almost infinite number of unique Calabi-Yau manifolds, and there is no known way to discern which, if any, reproduces what *string theorists* such as Dr. Clifford V. Johnson of the University of Southern California and others have depicted in the "standard model."

In physics, the description of our universe is divided into two seemingly irreconcilable realms: the quantum world of the very *small*, and the macroscopic world where *gravity* reigns. *String theory* is the attempt to unify the two domains into a "theory of *everything*." To *paraphrase* again what Socrates lamented 2,400 years ago, "All we know is that we know *very little*." (At least, we know very little about the profoundly puzzling but captivating concept of multiple dimensions—and, accordingly, we know next to nothing about *string theory* and how to "tie the strings together" into a *comprehensible* or even a <u>*contemplatable*</u> package!)

See **INFINITY; TIME**

"STRONGMAN" — A man who makes a *weak* <u>*populace*</u>.

A <u>*strong*</u> populace doesn't need a *"strongman"*—the proverbial "Man on Horseback." It just needs someone to *rally it for <u>justice</u>*.

SUBORDIN<u>ATE</u> (last syllable rhymes with "fate"; *verb transitive*) — To render inferior or submissive.

When warran ted, Creative Insubordinates creatively <u>*subORDinate*</u> the <u>super</u>-ordinate.

SUBORDINATE ("subORDinut"; *noun*) — One who is supervised by a <u>*super*</u>-ordinate. (<u>Old Men</u> know that *superordinates* aren't necessarily always so <u>*super*</u>.)

SUCCESS — To spend all the Carl Sandburgian *"coin* of one's life" doing *what one loves best.*

This definition obtains whether "doing what one loves best" be trading stocks, teaching children, writing books, turtle-hatching, raising and showing purebred dogs, making moonshine, or simply *mooning*!

SUGAR RAY ROBINSON — A man who was born *Walker Smith, Jr.* in Detroit in 1920 and became the greatest prizefighter, pound-for-pound, of all time (and one of Your Auld Author's all-time boyhood and adulthood heroes).

SUICIDE — An unspeakable and final act of self-destruction nonetheless seen by some as the easiest (and often the *only*) way out.

The terminally ill, the elderly, the isolated, the lonely, spurned lovers, abused spouses, convicted and about-to-be-incarcerated (or executed) criminals, and the situationally or clinically depressed are the most likely people to commit this act of no return.

See **ANOMIE; CLINICAL DEPRESSION; LONELINESS**

The **SUN** — A star which is the central body of our solar system.

The sun gives heat and light to the planets that revolve around it, and it gives heat, light and *life* to all the plant and animal inhabitants of Planet Earth, which is 93,000,000 miles away from it, and 1/330,000th its size. Thus, *"this* microcosmic rebel might be seen," as my prize poem goes, "upon *one shining pebble* gleaming green."

Also, the sun is The "Eye of Osiris" (according to the ancient Egyptians).

See The **"EYE OF OSIRIS"**

SUPERORDINATE ("superORDinut"; *noun*) — Someone who supervises a *subordinate*.

Again, one's superordinate isn't necessarily one's *superior*. He/she may be luckier, or *better-connected*. Many Aged Sages have had to brace

themselves (and today _future_ Aged Sages must _likewise_ brace themselves) for the maddening frustration of seeing lazy, unproductive a--
h---s _get jobs_, _keep_ the jobs, or get _promoted_ while the Real Righteous
Rebels among them get _passed over_ for promotion, demoted, or fired—
or never get _hired_.

This is often particularly true of any Aged Sage who just might happen to have a measured IQ of 160 or above. (Here's a _hint_ for you
Republican powers-that-be or female associate superintendents of
schools in Detroit and presidents of some colleges in Southeastern
Michigan who never sought out one renegade, retired, and particularly
radically _seasoned_ crusader to offer him a top central-office job or
an endowed chair, in order that you might be enabled to figure out
how to fill in those _eight blank letters_ in the previous paragraph: they
are e-l-o-s-s _backward_.)

(Of course, some might also suggest that an entire alternate set of
letters could instead be s-o-u-r g-r-a-p-e-s, _frontward_.)

SUPERSTITIONS — Perhaps the mere intuitive foreshadowing of phenomenal
and awful _truths_??

"SWALLOW AND FOLLOW" — When the "swallowing" involves dangerous
doctrines and the "following" occurs behind demagogues, "_swallow
and follow_" is an expression representative of a no-longer-affordable
—and potentially _ultimate_ and _fatal_—weakness as we embark upon
the twenty-first century.

SWEAT (verb) — Something you must _never_ let your _enemies_ see you _do_
(unless you're winning a fist fight or a sprint race).

(Never let them see you _cry_, either.)

T

TACT — "The ability to describe others as they see themselves."

So said Abraham Lincoln, who would thus have undoubtedly applauded the following wish, as expressed in Scots dialect by his chronological precedent, the great Robert Burns: "I would a gift the _Giftie_ gie us, to see _ourselves_ as _others_ see us. . . ." (Burns' "_Giftie_," of course, being our Creator.)

"TAKE THIS JOB AND _SHIP_ IT . . ." — . . . They _did_, overseas.

See **CORPORATOCRACY**

TALENT — For success in sport, music, art, letters, etc.—merely a _starting point_.

TAXES — An onerous but entirely necessary communal burden to pay for police, firemen, public schools, garbage disposal, etc.

People who complain about taxes the _most_ and vote them down every chance they get are the same people who complain bitterly when their houses are burglarized or burned. They are also some of the same people who are quick to cash their government-funded Social Security checks so they can have the monetary means and leisure time to attend Tea Party rallies.

TAXIDERMY — A hobby that a widowed or divorced _Old Man_ re-entering the dating game perhaps shouldn't mention to an unfamiliar lady at first, even if it happens to be his _passion_. . . .

. . . unless in the most *unlikely* possibility that it's also *hers!*

See **PASSION**

TEACH — A divine but excruciatingly difficult act in any of the twenty-plus non-elite public high schools in Detroit—a city which consistently has had the highest per capita murder rate in the nation, and whose schools have the nation's lowest graduation rate and lowest test scores.

Also, the surname of a particularly savage Scottish-born seventeenth-century pirate nicknamed "Blackbeard."

TEACHER — The only professional who can truly *touch eternity.*

I was once approached by an aging mother in a convenience store who to my proud delight told me that her daughter still quoted from an original poem I had taught her many years before.

The one prime characteristic that distinguishes a great teacher from a merely good one is *passion* (for *teaching,* not taxidermy).

(Also, to cite again the oft-cited saying: Thank a teacher today if you can *read* this.)

See **CHRIST; PASSION**

"TEAPARTYERS" (also called "Teabaggers") — Aficionados of that bemusing, sometimes bemused "Tea Party" Movement begun in 2009, very early in the administration of Barack Obama.

Even though the G. W. Bush administration has left America's economy in a shambles, these folks—whose movement is progressively named for the Boston Tea Party of the pre-Revolutionary War era—fail *un*progressively to blame the guilty *Bush* but instead illogically project the blame upon the innocent Barack Obama despite Obama's valiant efforts to undo Bush's mistakes and crimes against these very same people. Go *figure.*

TEENY WEE-WEE — Also referred to as "teeny weener," "teeny-*tiny* weener," "teeny-tiny *wee-wee,*" "teeny-*weeny* wee-wee," "teeny-tiny *pee-pee,*" Oscar Mayer *Economy* Size, and *RPP* (Republican's *Private Part*).

See **PENIS ANXIETY; PENIS UNEASINESS; PYGMY** (*adjectival usage*); **REPUBLICAN, REPUBLICAN,** and *REPUBLICAN*

See also **WEE**

TELEVISION — TV is like junk food—most of it is *insipid*, but we can't get *enough* of it.

See **INSIPID**

TEN TRILLION YEARS — What <u>Old Men</u> sense it may take for the dazzling eternal light on the other side of our <u>*beginning*</u> to rematerialize.

It has been reliably reported that many of us have got a precognitive glimpse of this dazzling light in our dying moments. *Consciously* and credulously, the most reflective of Aged Sages observe that out there far beyond the countless horizons of the infinite ages, ten trillion years *universally* is no different than *ten seconds*.

See The **ETERNAL PRESENCE; GOD**

TENNIS — See **KNEES** (*Owww!*)

TERMAGANT — A *turbulent* woman. (Repubs, xyW.)

<u>Old Men</u> pray that a merciful God may spare us ongoingly therefrom.

See **MEDUSA**

THEOLOGY — An area of study which many old wowsers like to call a *science*, but *by* <u>*definition*</u> really *cannot* <u>*be*</u> one.

THESAURUS — *a*) A book of synonyms that George W. Bush would need <u>*ongoingly*</u> in the unlikely circumstance that he would ever have to write his own speeches; *b*) Something that Bush and Dan Quayle may still believe to be a *dinosaur*.

THESEUS — A legendary hero of Attica in ancient Greece.

Theseus is said to have organized a democratic constitutional government and united the separate city-states of Athens in the fifth century B.C., thus providing an exemplary model for—among *other* nations—our own United States of America twenty-three centuries later. *Let freedom ring!*

THIEVES WHO STEAL FROM PLAIN PRIVATE CITIZENS — Most often, *prisoners* and *convicts*—present and future.

THIEVES WHO STEAL FROM PUBLIC COFFERS — Too often, "pillars of the community" (and hopefully, future *prisoners*).

See **BUREAUCRAT; "PILLAR OF THE COMMUNITY"; POLITICIANS, POLITICOS**

THINGS <u>Old Men</u> HAVE FROM LONG EXPERIENCE LEARNED TO AVOID — Alcohol in excess; hallucinogens; karaoke nights; long waiting-lines at restaurants (unless the *bar* is readily available); motorcycles; open manholes; closing coffins; offers they "can't refuse"; sex with students or subordinates or clients or colleagues (or with colleagues' *wives* or other men's wives); riding in single-engine prop planes; tobacco (except in cigars); traffic jams (except the Detroit restaurant of the same name); nags (except *horses*—if they don't <u>bet</u> on them).

See **ALCOHOL; SEX; TOBACCO**

THINGS <u>Old Men</u> HAVE FROM LONG EXPERIENCE LEARNED TO SEEK OUT — Public libraries; condos on the Detroit River; antique bronzes; rusty old swords; art galleries; country-western bars (some); cider mills; Detroit Symphony Orchestra outdoor concerts at Meadow Brook on the campus of Oakland University in Rochester Hills, Michigan; good fishing; the stark silhouette of a tree against a winter sky; empathic *wives* (hopefully their <u>own</u>); foot rubs; chamber music; opportunities to *nap*; museums; old farmhouses; gypsy violins; folk music; oceans; racehorses (for aesthetic, *non-<u>gaming</u>* purposes); rainbows; sailboats; sunrises; used bookstores; wineries (for *un*-aesthetic <u>drinking</u> purposes); back rubs;

wine-tasting parties (for aesthetic _and_ unaesthetic drinking purposes); padded toilet seats; old copies of _The Ring_ and new ones of _Playboy_ (but not _Hustler_—sorry, Mr. Flynt).

THINKING (_gerund; verbal noun_) — Old Men's and Old Women's (and _all_ men's and _all_ women's) most important work.

The **"THIRD CITY"** — This _Dictionary's Definitive_ appellation for any and all of America's urban ghettos, such as inner Detroit—to be likened to the common term "the Third World," as our planet's most impoverished and underdeveloped nations are commonly called.

THIS OLD MAN'S MANTRA (TOMM) — See _I_

THOUGHT (_noun_) — Something that _has no color._

There are two Old Men still extant on the planet at this writing who simultaneously ideated this cogitative concept and definition in 1966. (Dr. Wayne Dyer happens to be one of those two Old Men.)

Cogitate for a moment on that concept of _thought having no color_ and consider its implications for brotherhood and _sisterhood._

Our _thoughts_ are what we really _are_. We are not our _bodies_. It's eerie to contemplate, but our bodies undergo a total cell turnover every seven years. Our bodies are mere DNA-programmed containers which temporarily house our minds and spirits, wherein our _thoughts_ are _born_. And, as spake Shakespeare's gentle Juliet, "_Love's heralds_ should be _thoughts._" For love not to be _color-blind_ makes no sense. That would be like loving a present's _wrapping_ or the _picture on a package_ instead of the _real thing_ inside.

The mother of a young white man in Grand Rapids, Michigan, who didn't understand this turned her back on him because she refused to accept his bright, college-educated new wife. When asked why she banished him from her life, she replied, "He married a black girl"— in the same flat tone one might say, "He committed murder", or "He died."

· Aged Sages mobilize against the mass psychopathology of racism, knowing that it has created a million similar familial dilemmas, and many horrors even worse.

See **RACISM**

THURGOOD MARSHALL — The United States Supreme Court's late Sage for the Ages, and a *soaring* civil-rights giant.

See **GIANTS** (you younger folks coming up need to know whose shoulders you stand upon)

TIME — "We know exactly what *time* is, until someone asks us to explain the concept." So spake Saint Augustine.

Poet Delmore Schwartz said that *time* is "the fire in which we burn."

Aged Sage Carl Sandburg called *time* "the *coin* of our lives." We must take care to spend those "coins" righteously, productively, and preventatively, and beware lest we invest them with others who spend them *for* us *wrongly* and *un*productively and thus render us bereft of those "coins", or *worse*—use what remains of them to foment some manner of mischief, catastrophe, and chaos.

Also, as Aged Sage Yogi Berra responded metaphysically when asked what time it was, "You mean right *now*?"

A concept incomprehensible to skeptics is a *timeless* theory of one of "The Two Alberts"—*Einstein*—that time *can run backward* as well as *forward*. Potentially and seemingly miraculously, it *can*—and not only in memory and imagination. We're talking about *rewinding* and also *fast-forwarding the reel*! Both space and time become distorted when moving objects approach or attain the speed of light.

Physicists now believe that slender strings of pure energy might have survived in their original state, rather than cooling off with the rest of the universe shortly after the Big Bang. Within this intriguing scenario, it is possible for two light rays from a single star to travel by two different paths of different lengths on each side of one of these strings (depending on the position of the light source) and actually end up at the same place simultaneously even though one of the light rays would take longer to get there, because light always has to travel at the same speed. A spaceship taking the shorter of the two paths at 99.9999% of the speed of light would reach the far side of a string of original cosmic energy at the same moment as a light ray traveling the longer path—and therefore move faster than light, and thus go backward in time!

Your Anonymous Poet once poeticized, "Our end is our beginning's nether twin. / Within this measured stint, *shall be* has been, / And never evermore again can be."

Yet paradoxically, the *shall be* which *has been* perhaps *can be* again. Under the preceding or some other as yet undivined complex but precise set of cosmic conditions, a person could *conceivably* (pun fully intended) go back in time prior to his birth and *kill* his own great- great-grandfather, thus eliminating the possibility of his own conception (and also *sequentially impregnate* his great-to-the-nth-power grandmother and thus f— himself through a perpetually revolving door of existence and non-existence and existence and non-existence, *ad infinitum*.

Here's a piece of Aged Sage Advice from Your Auld Author: Don't contemplate this theory for too long, or you'll go insane—particularly if you're not a non-reflective Republican.

(Anyway, the concept that one of our "grandchildren to the nth power" is coming back from the infinite future to kill us is the least of our worries in a twenty-first century world that is spinning away from rational righteousness and plain *rationality* at warp speed.)

See **ETERNITY; INFINITY; MINUTE** (*noun*)**; SOMETHING THAT IS BORROWED; STRING THEORY; TEN TRILLION YEARS**

TIME *CONQUERED* — *See* **SAGES FOR THE AGES**

TIME *WASTED* — Your time is *never* wasted if you're *wasted* all the time! (Bad joke.)

TIMELESS TALE — There's the *definitively* timeless tale of the Septuagenarian Wayne State University alumnus who was with two smugly arrogant University of Michigan undergraduates—both of the *Pachydermous* political persuasion. When the subject turned to sex, the first U-M student bragged,

"Last night I had sex with my girl *three times*. Then she fell into satisfied slumber—and in the morning she woke up, stretched, yawned, and then assured me that I'm super-duper."

Not to be outdone, the second U-M student boasted, "Last night I had sex with my woman _four_ times, and when she awakened she told me she wants to be with nobody but me forever and ever."

When the old WSU grad didn't react, the second U-M student condescendingly inquired, "And how many times did _you_ have sex with _your_ woman last night, old man?"

"One time."

"Just *one time*? Well, did she say anything at *all* when she woke up in the morning?"

The old WSU grad reflected. "We didn't actually *wake up*, because we never *slept*. And in the morning she just kept panting, "Don't stop, don't stop, don't stop—don't *ever* stop. . . .""

"TO RESTRAIN THE WORST INSTINCTS OF THE PROFIT SECTOR" (*infinitive phrase*) — The reason why the Founding Fathers created a brave new democracy (that hopefully still retains more than a *tattered remnant* of *representative* government today).

It is obvious that those *instincts are* no longer being sufficiently restrained —corporate CEOs are "earning" seventy or eighty million dollars per annum. These are obscene sums which their rank-and-file employees would need about 1,500 *calendar work years* to accumulate. (Try as I might, I can't think of a quip or snappy saying to soften this for *you*, gentle reader—because there's nothing funny about it, except maybe to a *misogynist*, or to a *sadist*. The so-called *"profit sector"* caused the ruinous Wall Street Bailout of late 2008, it caused the Iraq war, and it caused the oil spill in the Gulf of Mexico—as well as also having fomented many other man-made catastrophes that our grandchildren and great-grandchildren will have to pay for.)

Let me again deliver this acceleratingly plaintive exhortation, and deliver it urgently: *Save* us, Barack Obama, if you can; *save* us, Barack Obama, if you can; *save* us, Barack. . . .

"TO SLEEP IS TO DINE" (*infinitive phrase*) — The practical, situational, and _ultra-dietary_ "D'Artagnan Dictum."

When Planchet, the manservant of D'Artagnan—Alexandre Dumas' heroic fourth Musketeer—complained to his master that he was hungry and the soon-to-be celebrated seventeenth century swordsman was still very short on *francs*, he told Planchet to simply take a *nap*, with this helpful advisement.

Indeed, it is a dictum an increasing number of Americans may soon have to adhere to when their unemployment insurance runs out.

TO TEACH (*infinitive*, the word *to* followed by a *verb*) — *To teach is to <u>learn</u>*.

And let me say this once again: To teach is also to *touch <u>infinity</u>*, and thus to become *immortal*. . . .

TOBACCO — <u>Old Men</u> know through sometimes tragic experience that this is an insidiously addictive and noxious weed which in one's youth would have been far better left untouched, except in an occasional *Antony y Cleopatra <u>dark</u>* (a great cigar).

See **CANCER**

TOLERANCE — That which comes with *age*, but unfortunately mostly to Aged <u>Sages</u>—many of whom already had it when they were <u>Young</u> Sages (some such <u>do</u> exist).

See **INTOLERANCE**

TOM BARRY — A Scottish custodian in Plymouth/Canton (MI) Schools, circa 1977, who had fought as a kilted commando in North Africa under Field Marshal Montgomery, and whose soft Scottish burr reminded me of the soft syllables of my Scottish grandparents. When I was an executive director in P/C, a fellow administrator once admonished me for letting Tom call me by my first name. I told him, "Tom Barry was fighting the <u>Nazis</u> when you were in *short pants* and your mommy was chauffeuring you to *Montessori School*. He can call me anything he damn well pleases." The administrator never brought up the subject again. *Guid nicht*, noble Tom—wherreverr ye be.

See **CLASSISM**

TOUPÉE — If an old man must have one, it's advisable that he get a *good* one. *Bad* ones look ridiculous.

TRADITIONAL GRAMMAR — Something every inner-city English teacher in the country needs to teach *again*, in depth.

Also, a daily dose of remedial reading needs to be thrown in—particularly for the *young men*, who increasingly have become major grist for the prisons. The hip-hop patois and mentality have taken over the ghetto, overwhelmingly. Black kids *must* master the language of the market place in order to survive in the twenty-first century, because as I have emphasized, the limits of their language will *circumscribe* the limits of their world. (No, Repubs—I'm not talking here about removing *foreskins* —I speak of removing the barriers that *circumscribe* minds.)

TRAGEDY — Ironically and too often, one's resultant *attainment* of what was once one's *fondest* wish.

A TRAGIC TRUTH(?) — "*Two* women are worse than *one*." So lamented the Aged Sage and ancient Greek playwright *Plautus* (certainly *not* the less Aged and less *ancient* Sage *Telford*!).

TRANQUILITY — *See* **PEACE**

TRIFLES — (No Repubs, these aren't little sweet chocolates. Those are *truffles*.) Trifles are comparatively *tiny* concerns that one should none-theless take time and pains to deal with, because little irritations left untended can expand into *big problems*.

In 1912, a comparatively *tiny* iceberg sank a ship that was absolutely *titanic*—which, indeed, was that mammoth ship's imposing *name*.

TRUTH — "The pure and simple truth is rarely 'pure' and never 'simple'."

Oscar Wilde said this.

TRYING NOT TO THINK ABOUT IT (*gerund phrase*) — a) A mental method for remaining excruciatingly *celibate*—used by a moderate number of male _un_creative _sub_ordinates and a _less_ moderate number of young Republicans; b) The main method of most *uncreative subordinates* and too *many* Republicans for coping with *injustice*.

See **INJUSTICE; *UNCREATIVE SUBORDINATE***

TWENTY THOUSAND TEENAGERS — The approximate number of high-school-age kids in Detroit who aren't in any public school, charter school or suburban school on the city's periphery, are totally beyond the control of their mothers or grandmothers, and are playing permanent hooky.

The Detroit Public School District needs to hire truant officers, round those kids up, and get them back in school before they do some things that will be very expensive for the police, the courts, and the greater Detroit metropolitan community to deal with.

(And this level of truancy isn't just a *Detroit* phenomenon—it's happening in urban centers throughout the country.)

See **FIVE THOUSAND TEENAGERS**

The **TWILIGHT OF THE AGED SAGE** — In the twilight of Old Men's days within this "mortal coil," a bright flame yet blazes forth from these Sages until the end, to light the way for *you* brave young soon-to-be Keepers of the Flame who must take up the flagging Torch of Reason and Righteousness, and raise it *ever higher*.

Then you must run with it like an animal that runs all night every night of its life, as *this* Aged Sage has demonstrably and dutifully done for half a century and more (please google www.ALifeontheRUN.com).

TWO TALES OUT OF (SUNDAY) SCHOOL — A Sunday School teacher told her students, "We've been learning about powerful Biblical kings and queens, but there's a Higher Power. Can anybody tell me what it is?" One eager little fellow piped up, "*Yes*—it's _aces_!"

Another Sunday School teacher who was teaching the parable of the Good Samaritan asked, "If you saw a man lying by the roadside all torn up and bloody, what would you do?" A little girl answered, "I'd *throw up.*"

(Paraphrased from Porcupine Press Publications of Munising, Michigan.)

TYRANNY — Wherever *tyranny* reigns, _revolution_ is on the horizon.

U

UFO — A familiar acronym for "Unidentified Flying Object."

Sages of the Ages have observed what now are commonly called UFO's for veritable *millennia*, and no one has been able to prove that perhaps some of them truly *aren't* of this earth.

Alternative definition: Acronym for "Ultimate Flying Orgasm"—and *that* is <u>definitely</u> "of this earth"—in fact, it maketh the earth to <u>move</u>!

See **GRAND-DADDY** (alternate definition)

See also **INFINITY**

"UGLY" *(adjective)* — Something, as the colloquially ungrammatical saying goes, that "God <u>don't like</u>." (Thus, in *Romans 12:19, it is written*, "'Vengeance is *mine; I* will repay,' saith the Lord.")

(But there's nothing wrong with lending the Lord a mean mortal hand sometimes, right?)

There's also nothing one bit unholy about *celebrating* when the punishment *has been meted out* by the Lord, *whether or not* it was exacted via the *hand of <u>man</u>. (Proverbs 11:10*: "When it goeth well with the righteous, the city rejoiceth. And when the wicked perish, there is *shouting*.")

In the great scheme of things, "ugly" <u>is</u> as "ugly" <u>does</u>. Better an "ugly" face than an "ugly" deed. On a similar but less serious note, this brings to mind a decades-old *New Yorker* magazine cartoon in which a lace-clad little girl sits next to an equally belaced elderly lady at a large, munificent dining table. The little girl is reaching to take a piece of meat from a tray on the table with her bare hand, and the elderly lady is preventing her from doing this by *sticking her _fork_ in the little girl's _hand_*. The caption reads, "Handsome _is_ as handsome _does_, Melissa." This was an effectively corrective and God-fearing little old lady indeed.

UGLY FAT — The quickest way for a heavily-weighed-down woman to take off 150 pounds of *ugly fat* is simply to *tell the old geezer to _get off_*. (Old joke.)

UNCONSCIOUSNESS — My Uncle Alfie's usual state after consuming a pint of Jack Daniel's.

"UNCONTROLLABLE" *(adjective)* — What Your Auld Author has been frequently (and accurately) called, once by a female Southfield, Michigan, Board of Education member who told a friend of Your Auld Author that I'd never get her vote to be that school district's superintendent— for this *curious* and *unsettling* reason.

See **"UNREASONABLE" MEN**

*UN*CREATIVE *SUBORDINATE* — A non-rebel.

An *uncreative Sub*ordinate is someone who leads a safe, boring, essentially *un_reflective_* life (also called "The *Un_examined_* Life").

See **CREATIVE INSUBORDINATION; REPUBLICAN**

UNDERSTANDING *(noun)* — A two-way street.

Understanding is affected through *dialogue* and *communication*, which in turn are rooted in genuine *listening*, which in turn effects true *hearing*, which in turn can engender *true empathizing*, which in turn can finally make for the *_full_* and *_mutual_* understanding which my activist friend Yusef Shakur creatively terms "*_over_standing*."

See **EMPATHY**

UNIONS — The organizations that once were the backbone of America.

"All for *one*; one for *all*" – the pertinent slogan of Athos, Porthos, Aramis, and the Gascon hero D'Artagnan in Alexandre Dumas' *Three Musketeers* —is one of Your Auld Author's all-time favorite quotes, and one that he and his cousins Carl and Dick adopted in our boyhood and main- tained into adulthood. It is also a slogan that some unionized workers in this country have forgotten and need again to remember, *pronto*.

A UNIQUELY HUMAN ENIGMA — To struggle to stay spiritually *young*, when *old*.

This is a struggle which wrestles with the *uniquely human enigma* of why we Aged Sages are obliged to remain frustratingly grounded in our failing flesh while our soaring minds reach higher and higher around the world and beyond the stratosphere. As the great Celt W. B. Yeats poignantly poeticized, "Consume my heart away—sick with desire and fastened to a dying animal."

Aged Sages have solved this conundrum by expanding *exponentially* to begin the liberating metaphysical process of merging with the time- less universe and its Creator—the Eternal Presence of story and song. (For, as one goldfish in the bowl metaphysically inquired of a less con- templative fellow fishy, "If there's no *God*, who changes the _water_?")

See (On) **DYING**

The **UNITED STATES OF AMERICA** — Still *one* democracy, still *one* constitution, still *one* destiny.

God bless America, land that *this* old All-American will love until the day I draw breath no longer.

The **UNITED STATES SENATE** — An august body that an *I.Q. test* (obviously and regretfully) isn't a requirement for _election_ to, by the admission of one of its own (Republican) members.

The **UNIVERSE** — One vast, perpetual generation and re-generation of worlds by the Eternal Presence, without beginning and without end.

The infinite universe is at once _simply_ and also _profoundly_ an _awakened_ and _collectively conscious creation_ and also a _sign_ of the sacred Godhead that "passeth all [_human_] understanding."

See The **COSMOS**

The **UNIVERSE OF IDEAS** — The benign ideational realm where dwell the benevolent _Souls_ of all _inventive_ and _mentoring_ Earthly Aged Sages— past, present, and future.

From those nurturing Souls—that collective, cumulative, projected _presence_ which is one with the _Eternal_ Presence—there emanates an ethereal light and a low _murmuring_ initially indecipherable to all young not-yet-Sages. The light from these Sagacious Souls becomes discernible and their murmurings gradually decipherable to a _rare_ and _select few Sages-in-waiting_ over an indeterminate number of increasingly _enlightening_ years. The fragile _intellectual_ heritage of that shallow spiritual strain of _humane_ and _enlightened_ humankind thus remains preciously preserved, in order that it may continue its ongoing endeavors to save untold numbers of its _much-harder-to-enlighten_ fellow human Souls from _themselves_. (_Pray_ for its preservation.)

See **Young Men; Young Women**

UNIVERSITIES — Ideally, places of light, liberty, and liberality.

Contrary to this ideal, too many colleges have devolved into _implosive places_ of political back-scratching, pointless research, nepotism, dogmatism, mutually masturbatory professorial _faux_-poeticizing, pointless theorizing, and _esoterically surreal_ fantasizing in the face of a _real_ world that is about to _explode_.

UNJUST — Out of synchronicity with what is fair.

For example, ethnic discrimination of any kind is _unjust_.

See **INJUSTICE; JUSTICE**

"UNREASONABLE MEN" — Men <u>Old</u> and Men <u>Young</u> who move the *immovable*, transform the *non-transformable*, and reform the *unreformable* and the *deformed*—against *daunting* odds.

See **FANATIC; PASSION; RADICAL** *(noun)*; **REBEL** *(noun)*; *RENEGADO*

UNSUNG POETS — Those many great and deserving poets who while alive will *remain* unsung so long as only *dead* poets and *pseudo*-poets are praised.

URANUS — Oh, yeah? Well, up *Uranus*, too—and stick a plug in *urethra* as well!

Actually, Uranus is perhaps the *planet* whence G. W. Bush possibly *came*. (He has to have evolved (devolved?) from *somewhere* out of *this* world, right?)

See **ANIMAL "HUSBANDRY"; ANUS** *(descriptive noun)*; **GEORGE W. BUSH; "STRANGELY BELIEVE IT"**

URETHRA — A body part that seems to *narrow* peskily in old men—and, unhappily, in <u>Old Men</u>, as well.

See **URINE**

URINE — A pale yellow liquid that can get dark and putrid when it backs up in an old boy's bladder.

When this backup happens, it can cause infections and kidney stones. (Your long-suffering Auld Author has had them—*no fun*—particularly when a smirking nurse sticks a catheter in you that feels like a telephone pole.)

See **KIDNEY STONES; URETHRA**

UTOPIA — An idealistic, visionary system of social, political, and economic perfection.

The word "utopia" derives from the socially, politically, and economically idyllic (and sadly, _imaginary_) island as described in Sir Thomas More's 1516 treatise of the same name.

See **RESOURCE-DRIVEN AND _TECHNOLOGY_-DRIVEN ECONOMIC SYSTEM**

V

"VALLEY GIRLS" — *See* **INSIPID**

The **VAMPIRE'S FAVORITE SOUP** — Cream of *tomato* (corny joke).

VANITY — A rarely *fatal* folly.

According to the sagacious eighteenth-century French philosopher Jean-Jacques Rousseau, *vanity* remains the sole addiction of which universal man has *vainly* (no pun intended) *endeavored* to rid himself. Two great World War II generals, Douglas MacArthur and George S. Patton, were notably and *insufferably* vain in the *extreme*. Given their equally extreme services to their country, posterity can *suffer* them that inconsequential folly.

Doubtless other overly vain folks like Your Auld Author who are far less entitled to be vain than were those two superb soldiers also are less entitled to be *suffered* in that regard.

Still, for most of us, our pathetic little vanities remain, thank God, a relatively harmless conceit.

VARICOSE — Close by. (Definition reserved for Republicans.)

VARIETY — The "spice of life."

This old saw can be ascribed *myriad* meanings, so ascribe some for yourself—and be imaginative.

The **VEDA** (*sometimes a plural noun*) — The entire sacred scriptures of Hinduism.

See The **"ANCIENT WISDOMS"**; The **"EYE OF OSIRIS"**

VENUS — The Roman *goddess* of love and beauty.

In exoteric Brahmanism, the *planet* that was named for Venus is regarded as the most occult and mysterious of all the celestial bodies that revolve around the sun.

In *astronomy*, that planet reigns as the most brilliant of the *solar planets*. Its orbit is next inside the Earth's and second from the sun.

In *earth science*, Venus is a planet whose temperatures Earth will one day approach, and it will approach them much *sooner* if humankind doesn't sharply reduce its consumption of and dependence upon fossil fuels—and do it <u>soon</u>.

See **AL GORE**

VI-<u>AGG</u>-RA!! — The little blue pill that is delighting a whole lot of old (and young) women.

<u>Old Men</u> know that for Viagra to work best, one should have a *partner*— preferably an attractive, interactive, and *sober* one. <u>Old Men</u> also know not to eat or drink too much before taking it.

<u>Vee</u>-va Vi-<u>agg</u>-ra!!

(*Note to Cowboys Clem and Earl*: Cowboys Clem and Earl, we're talking about a <u>woman</u> partner here—not some pretty little heifer with long eyelashes, or that struggling, screeching <u>owl</u> Earl's got ahold of.)

See **OWL**

VICE — "There will be *vice* as long as there are *men*." – the ancient Roman Aged Sage Tacitus.

(Hey, Tacitus, don't be so *taciturn*—you didn't mention <u>women</u>!)

VIETNAM WAR — *See* **IRAQ WAR**

VIGILANCE — It was the Aged Sage and Founding Father *Thomas Jefferson* who presciently wrote, "Eternal *vigilance* is the price of liberty."

Amen. It's high time for us lovers of freedom and liberty to become more *vigilant*—or else very soon we're going to need a *multitude* of *vigilantes*.

See **VIGILANTISM**

VIGILANTISM — Your Auld Author's *father's* frequent *avocation*.

Also Your Auld Author's father's *son's* frequent *temptation*, as revealed in this verse, titled "The Mad Vigilante from the Java Café":

> I'm the *Mad Vigilante from the Java Café*,
> And I just wrote this *poem*—I just wrote it today.
> Now *vigilantism's* part of my creed.
> *Vigilantes* have become what we *need*.
> So proffer me a *smoothie* and an *Uzi*, my good fellow.
> The smoothie's for my belly, and the Uzi's for the yellow
> *Four-syllable curse word* who beat the old man.
> He beat the old man.
> He beat the old man!
> He BEAT
> The old man.
> *Yes*, I just wrote this poem—I just wrote it today.
> I'm the *Mad Vigilante* from the Java Café.

After young thugs beat a ninety-year-old man in the parking lot of a Detroit convenience store in 2007 and stole his car, your Outraged Old Author penned this base bit of doggerel, printed it in his *Telford's Telescope* column in the *Michigan Chronicle*, and recited it at a gathering of poets at the Java Café at 440 Burroughs in Detroit. Incidents like that one which inspired this verse are proliferating all over the country in this Bush-generated economic collapse, and *vigilantism* may (God forbid) become *indispensable indeed* in the midst of the coming *chaos*.

See **CHAOS**

The **VIOLIN** — An absolute *queen* of instruments, divinely designed in the less-than-divine (but unquestionably *sublime*) tradition of the High Renaissance.

Call her a violin or call her a *fiddle*—by either name, her sound and symmetry transcend the toll of time. The arthritic left hand of Your Auld Author sometimes still feels truly <u>transformed</u> once again as—now sadly *infrequently*—my aching fingers arch and twist to form the chords that my lovingly stroking right hand on the bow can still transmute to the lilting tunes of my Celtic forebears.

See **OLD VIOLINS**

VISIONARY (*noun*) — A leader—and often, of necessity, a Creative Insubordinate.

("Where there is no *vision*, the people perish." – *Proverbs, 29:18*)

Detroit Federation of Teachers president Keith Johnson called my memoir, *A Life on the RUN—Seeking and Safeguarding Social Justice* (Harmonie Park Press, 2010), "the sensational saga of a visionary human-rights crusader." He also called me a "great man"—humbling me perhaps just a *teeny bit* for one of the few times in my life.

A social *visionary* this Old Author here may be or may have been, but now his *physical vision* is no longer sufficient for him to be able to read *street signs* without his glasses—and sometimes he can't even <u>find</u> his glasses without a *metal detector*. That's why I've written *What <u>Old Men</u> Know*, while I can still see to write (and <u>survive</u> to write). It's this old ex-dashman's way of *passing you young folks the baton*—and I'm also passing it symbolically to our young *president*, who is proving to be a *real, <u>true</u>* visionary, for whose health and ongoing triumphs I pray every night and every day, as I hope *you* will.

See **OBAMA**

VOODOO — A variant conglomerate of mysterious rites of African origin.

These rites are of the nature of sorcery and conjuration, which remain prevalent in some areas of the West Indies and the southern United States.

Some practitioners of *Voodoo* claim to have actually effected Muhammad Ali's historic upset victory over the far younger, harder-punching, and until-then unbeaten heavyweight boxing champion George Foreman in Zaire, Africa. The fearsome Foreman had knocked out all but three of his forty vanquished foes.

See **"BLACK" WITCHCRAFT; PARAPSYCHOLOGY; "WHITE" WITCHCRAFT**

The **VOTING RIGHTS ACT** — Signed into law by President Lyndon Baines Johnson, the Voting Rights Act paved the way for black Americans to become full participants in our democratic process.

Sadly, today many of them don't avail themselves of this basic right that their forebears were brutally denied—and a right *unexercised* is *indeed* a right *endangered*.

A memorable and pertinently *heartfelt* Lyndon Johnson paraphrase: "We are all fellow passengers on a dot called 'Earth.' Each of us, in our span of time, has really only a moment among our companions." President Johnson made the most of his moment on the "dot called Earth" with that one superb signatory act.

W

WAITING FOR THE DEER — Something Your Auld Author has done on many a very early morning sitting alone in his family room looking out the big window at his large retreat on his little lake.

One early March morning in 2010 just before sunrise in the third month of my seventy-fifth year, I was rewarded with the delectable vision of two delicate deer stepping tentatively to the barely melting edge of the still-frozen lake and bending to sip the icy inch of surface water that presaged the coming of spring.

In a certain allegorically *cosmic* sense, aren't all of us just wistfully *waiting for the deer?*

WAITRESSES — Women whom <u>Old Men</u> intentionally *over-tip*.

This over-tipping occurs particularly when it involves *overworked* waitresses with sweat-wet armpits and running mascara in dingy little chicken shacks on Detroit's decaying east side or in little roadside diners in Silver City, Mississippi; Bucksnort, Tennessee; Menominee, Michigan; Barberton, Ohio; Sandoval, Illinois, Tecumseh, Ontario. . . .

WAKING UP GRUMPY — Something <u>Old Men</u> *never* do.

(<u>Old Men</u> know that it's far <u>wiser</u> to let her sleep!)

WAR — An enterprise for which men old and young are uniquely *wired* for *psychologically* and equipped for *neurologically*.

Indeed, we are absolute geniuses at finding new and improved ways to kill each other in geometrically multiplying numbers. In this expanding nuclear world of the dawning twenty-first century, *war* should have become a political and societal *anachronism* by now, but national governments and their generals haven't got the message yet, and it's uncertain whether even a world-wide domino-effect *holocaust* would convince any of them of the validity of that message (that is, any of them who might be left <u>*alive*</u> after it).

War is the Devil's most dangerously grotesque creation, the art and science of human destruction. It is pure hell, *horrific* and *absolute*— no matter who starts it or the "reason" it's fought. All men who have seen battle know this, and those who haven't can't *begin* to imagine what it's like to see a comrade blinded and rendered deaf, or to see his limbs or jaw or genitals blown away, or to see his head explode into bits.

Aged Sages are viscerally aware that war is the *final proof of the infantilism of man;* yet they know, too, that it still remains an eventuality as inevitable as the sunrise so long as there are significant numbers of men old and young who aren't dedicated above all to rejecting corporate greed or "religious" fanaticism and who need to become inclined instead toward developing and nurturing a moral nature not only within themselves, but *communally* within all of humankind.

The tragedy of war is that it uses man's best to do man's <u>worst</u>. The valiant soldiers win the battles, and the generals far behind the lines get the credit—if "credit" is the right word for killing. If yet we must wage war, let us not wage war to win <u>*war*</u>, but rather to win <u>*peace*</u>. World War I was confidently called the war to end all wars. It didn't. The great general Dwight D. Eisenhower, the supreme commander of the Allied forces in the European theater during World War II, said afterward that people who speak of a preventive war should be told to go and fight it themselves if they're so keen about it, because after his long experience with it, he was <u>*through*</u> with it. That wonderful warrior (a <u>*Republican*</u>!) had come to *hate* war.

See **ABOMINATION; CAPITALISM; FASCISM; HELL; HORROR; INSANITY; LUNACY; PEACE WITH** *JUSTICE*; **RESOURCE-**DRIVEN AND *TECHNOLOGY-*DRIVEN ECONOMIC SYSTEM;** <u>*REX REBORN*</u>; THE <u>*RIDDLE*</u>

"WAR OF WHORES" — An unprincipled tug-of-war between multinational corporations to possess and control the world's wealth.

WARLOCK — A male witch or consort of a female witch.

Also, a <u>Man</u>—<u>Old</u> or Young—with the gift of "second sight."

See **"SECOND SIGHT"**

The **"WARRIOR WITHIN"** — <u>Old Men</u> know that there remains a *latent warrior* inside most of us.

The introspective ritual of rekindling the *fires* within us to re-awaken the lost *warriors* within us can give our lives new purpose at any age. It can *rededicate* our inner warrior to a path of honor and strength. Warriors and revolutionary *warriorship* are not just who and what we *are*, but how we <u>live</u>—except now we must try to *live* to fight to <u>preserve</u> lives rather than to <u>take</u> them.

See **CREATIVE INSUBORDINATION; REBEL** *(noun)*

"WASTED" AFFECTION — Something that doesn't exist.

Affection never is wasted.

WASTELAND — Much of Baghdad—and most of the Detroit Public Schools.

In 2009, Your Auld Author stirred up a considerable furor by repeatedly (and correctly) pronouncing most of the Detroit Public Schools a vast "wasteland" on radio, television, and the print media—and urging refugees therefrom to come to the nearby Madison District Public Schools, where I was their bearded old pony-tailed superintendent. *Hundreds* came, to the consternation of many ethnocentric Madison residents, who successfully demanded my *firing* for it. In this instance and regarding this incident, the word "ethnocentric" is an understated *euphemism*—Republicans, xyW. (*See* **RACIST**)

Note: Unlike what many of my angry fellow Detroiters surmised, I wasn't calling the *students, teachers,* or *principals* a "wasteland." I was referring to the inept DPS board and central administration.

WATERBOARDING — A particularly insidious form of torture used on illegally detained prisoners at Guantanamo during George W. Bush's administration.

Article Five of the Universal Declaration of Human Rights states: "No one shall be subjected to torture or to cruel, inhuman, or degrading treatment or punishment." *Eighty-one nations* practice torture—probably including (between 2002 and 2008) the nation where you're reading this publication.

See **DICK CHENEY**

WAYNE STATE UNIVERSITY — Your Auld Author's triple Alma Mater.

WSU is a highly regarded urban center of learning right smack in the middle of dynamic Detroit, sitting in a veritable *hotbed* of swift high school sprinters. WSU needs to restore its vaunted and historic men's track and field program, *pronto*. It eliminated it in 1987—the first year in the twentieth century that it didn't field a track team. (I hope the University's as-yet-unchosen new president is *reading* this.)

WEALTH — Among mankind in general, the god most revered.

"WEAPONS OF MASS DESTRUCTION" — They were never *there*, Mr. Bush— they were never *there*! May God forgive you, because *I* can't—and our *country shouldn't*.

WEE — A Gaelic adjective indicative of the size of the dram of Drambuie a Yank should sip, unless he happens to be a first-generation *Scottish* Yank.

"Wee" is also a word quaintly used to describe the allegedly puny peckers of many Republicans.

See **DRAMBUIE; REPUBLICAN; TEENY WEE-WEE**

WEE-WEE (*verb*) — When preceded by the word *go*, infantile Euro-American slang for what Septuagenarians like Your Auld Author do upwards of five times a night.

The hyphenated nouns *wee-wee* and *pee-pee* are equally infantile slang for *penis*, as in the admonition my cousin Diane once gave her three-year-old son in the mid-1950s when he walked around continually clutching himself: "If you don't stop holding your wee-wee, it's going to turn black and fall off." (It didn't, even though her helpful words caused him to clutch it even tighter.)

See **GOING WEE-WEE; PEE** (Doesn't anyone ever use the word "urinate" anymore?)

See also **PEE-PEE**

"WELL-ROUNDED" — A treacly term which means "possessing an admirably *eclectic* background." (Repubs, xyW.)

This here authoritative *source* what you be breathlessly poring over prefers to define "well-rounded" as a term descriptive of a *hypocritical yes-man who will roll in any direction you push him*. *Alternative example*: The *ample physionomy* of Dolly Parton.

WET WIPES — *Tissues* which, after the age of say, *sixty-five*, any prototypical old diarrheic dodderer should keep on hand in *plentiful* supply.

WHACK (Ebonic and gangland slang) — *Assassinate*.

WHAT HAPPENS WHEN AN <u>Old Man</u> DIES — An entire world of memories and infinitely unique and incidental knowledge dies *with* him and for the most part is forever lost.

See <u>Old Men's</u> **CHILDHOODS AND YESTERYEARS OF YOUTH**

WHAT HAPPENS WHEN AN <u>Old Man</u> TRIES TO PLAY FULL-COURT BASKETBALL — See **ATHLETICS; HEART ATTACK; KNEES**

WHAT <u>Old Men</u> DON'T KNOW — That would fill a much more *voluminous* publication than the one which you, gentle reader, are now ingesting— in fact, it would fill an *infinite number* of them.

As stated elsewhere in this sometimes deeply philosophic tome, one of the *Sagest* of philosophers by the name of *Socrates* said, "All I know is that I know *nothing*." Even the oldest and wisest of <u>Old Men</u> have thus far been unable to calibrate the boundless capabilities of the human mind, quantify the immeasurable capacities of the human heart, or penetrate the mysteries that lie beyond the limitless "limits" of the remotest galaxies.

What <u>Old Men</u> *don't* know anything about and fail utterly to even *begin* to fathom is the *foreverness* of the untold universe and of the enigmatic Eternal Presence permeating it. Nor, as mortals, shall any merely *old* men or even Sagacious <u>Old Men</u> ever be able to ascertain the locus of the Eternal Presence's most mysterious of dwelling places out in the still-forbidden vastnesses of undiscovered worlds, or indeed right here on our little pebble we call *Earth* (not to mention our being unable to ascertain emperically even that Presence's *Infinite* <u>*Existence*</u>).

Of less cosmically ponderous portent: It's no wonder that even the most Sagacious of <u>Old Men</u> don't have a clue regarding, say, the whereabouts of Judge Crater and Jimmy Hoffa, because most of us don't even know how to find our *reading glasses* or our *hearing aids* without our better half's help (if we still *have* a better half). And I'm not even going to <u>*mention*</u> our car keys or coats.

(An *aside*: Many <u>Old Men</u> don't consider themselves *old*—they just regard themselves as *rare antiques*, or *vintage wine*. While Your Auld Author regards himself as neither a rare antique [yet] nor vintage wine [yet], he still wouldn't mind <u>*sipping*</u> some vintage wine with some frequency. *Senior citizen discounts* ain't hard to take, either.)

See **AIN'T; INFINITY**

WHAT <u>Old Men</u> KNOW — Although this is the *title* of this too-terrestrial *tome*, maybe (because of its brevity, compared to *Webster's*) it should have been entitled *Just **Some** of What* <u>*Old Men*</u> *Know*, or <u>*Only a **Little Bit** of*</u> *What* <u>*Old Men*</u> *Really Know **for Sure**.*

Also, a few disgruntled Republicans or other *sectarians* (Republicans, xyW) may say it should have been entitled *What Just **One** Dotty, Doddering Old Democrat **Thinks** He Knows.*

Or maybe instead it should have been entitled *What Old Men Should Know*, or *What Some Old Men Know*, or *What A Precious Few Men Occasionally Learn in Later Years if They Have Just a Teeny-Tiny Smattering of Brains and a Whole Lot of Luck*.

Sad to say, many of us old *hombres* (and *young* ones, too) are painfully slow learners. Even *more* of us never *ever* learn what old men, Old Men, and young men alike viscerally need to know in order to offer succor to our fellow men—as well as to our *women* (woe-men?)— in this all-too-briefly-visited world of woe, where we worldwide wanderers only *infrequently* find fleeting, precious, too-brief little bits of the true happiness we seek, throughout the seemingly interminable years.

WHAT ONLY Old Men KNOW—AND HAVE LEARNED TO THEIR INFINITE SORROW — *See* **"ENCORE ANXIETY"**

WHEEZY GEEZER — *See* **CODGER; COOT**

"WHITE" WITCHCRAFT — A comparatively benign form of *witchcraft* practiced to the benefit of those who are benevolent and good.

"White" witches have also been known to practice Black Magic upon the *un*-benevolent and evil—being obliged then to dabble dangerously with entropic forces and grim entities, and even to modify *healing* techniques to inflict *harm* instead. This is dangerous and unfamiliar territory for *this* particular Aged Sage, so we'll take it no farther here.

"WHO" — *Absent* the quotation marks, a *relative pronoun* that rhymes with *screw*.

In this tacit tome, however, "who" is a *noun*, rather than a *pronoun*. In the *nominative* sense, "who" is an acronym for "White, Honest and Old" —what Your Old Author's volatile young African-Irish-Native American wife Gina once pronounced him in 2007, with the *implicative emphasis* on "*honest*" (read, *outspoken* and *blunt*).

Alternative definition: The repeated call of a *hoot* owl. (Also spelled *hoo*).

See **OWL; "WHOM"**

"WHOM" — *Absent* the quotation marks, a *relative pronoun* that rhymes with *boom, doom*, and Khartoum.

However, specifically exclusive to *this* publication, "whom" is a *noun*, rather than a *pronoun*.

"Whom" is an acronym which, in addition to calling him a "who", Your Old Author's volatile young African-Irish-Native American wife *also* called him—a "White, Honest, Old *Male*." The fourth characteristic in this appellation (*maleness*) rendered it even less possible for Your Auld Author to prevail in his copiously publicized battles with the matriarchy that was mismanaging the Detroit Public Schools, circa the second half of the first decade of the twenty-first century, had he simply been a *problematically* honest "*who*."

See **"WHO"**

See also **KHARTOUM**

WHOP (*verb transitive:* variation of *whip*—or, as Muhammad Ali would say, *whup*) — To administer an old-fashioned Sixteenth Street Detroit Zone 8 ass-whipping.

Also, *bash,* as in, "This *book* is a *basher* of *Bush*."

WHORES — Governmental or corporate bureaucrats who sell their goods and skills to the highest bidder regardless of principle.

Aged Sages characterize *whores* as any individuals—male or female— whose only motivation is monetary gain and whose only instinct beyond it is to survive.

"WHUMPERER" (*noun*), **"WHUMPING"** (*participial adjective*) — A kind of Jabberwockian/Lewis Carrollian, non-defined, pair of not-yet-*words*.

Your Auld Author hasn't decided exactly what "whumperer" and "whumping" (or "whump") should *mean* yet, but I love the way they look on a page and the way they sound when you say them. Please feel free to use them any way you choose. Maybe *you* can give them a definition. (I have *used* them in here *twice* already.)

See, for example, A (*NON*)-**POETIC PARODY**

WICCA — A loosely defined and essentially benign ceremonial sisterhood and brotherhood of *witches, warlocks, seers,* and *soothsayers*—ancient and contemporary.

See **"BLACK" WITCHCRAFT; PAGANDOM; "WHITE" WITCHCRAFT**

"WILL YOU STILL LOVE ME IN THE MORNING?" — The question a woman asks a man when she fears she may have made a terrible mistake.

(Ladies, trust me—it's better not to *ask* him if he'll still love you *in the morning*, because he may be gone *before* morning if you *ask* him that.)

A "WINGED RACE OF MEN" — Something the Aged Sage Plato described in his *Phaedrus* in the third century B.C.

In the twenty-first century A.D., humankind has become truly that "winged race," *figuratively* and *actually*—and we even *now* have the technological potential to soar ultimately far beyond the confines of our fragile planet and its one dead moon.

See **RESOURCE-DRIVEN AND TECHNOLOGY-DRIVEN ECONOMIC SYSTEM**

WINSTON CHURCHILL — The wartime prime minister who rallied the British (and the Americans) to save the world from fearsome fascist powers.

Never a man to pass often on a drink, when admonished one evening by a patrician hostess, "Mr. Churchill, you are *drunk*," the great man retorted, "True, madam—and *you* are *ugly*. But *I* will be *sober* in the morning."

See **GIANTS**

WISDOM TEETH — If *you* haven't cut them or had them knocked out or pulled by the age of *sixty*, leave them *in*—you're absolutely no less wise *with* them than *without*.

WISE OLD WOMEN (W.O.W.) — *See* **GRACE LEE BOGGS; MINISTER MARY EDWARDS; Old Women**

WITCH — A person (usually female) who professes or is believed to practice the "Black Arts" and/or more *benign* magic.

Also, a pseudo-teacher Your Auld Author had in the third grade.

See **"BLACK" WITCHCRAFT; WARLOCK; "WHITE" WITCHCRAFT**

WIZIANS — You'll need to delve further into this item for the *definition*.

All Old Men (according to this book's *definition* of "Old Men") have come to recognize that people of all ethnic origins and all races— black, white, brown, and every shade in between—are *equal in the sight of* God. And yes, Matilda, this *does* include ethnic Wizians, even though many Americans regard most of them—particularly the *males*— with considerable suspicion. (And this is entirely understandable, because it's a verifiable fact that all ethnic Wizians have on occasion been called *clannish, unclean, quarrelsome*, basically *unlettered, promiscuous*, and *inherently dishonest*—even by the most *unbiased* observers.)

This may *surprise you*—but radical, hopelessly ultra-liberal Democrat though Your Auld Author professes to be, I'm sincerely sorry to have to say that I must agree with much of this. For instance, no truly learned academician can conscientiously deny that Wizians *do* happen to be *quarrelsome* and *clannish*. And you can take it from me as a most reliable source: I'm definitely here to tell you that almost *any* hot-blooded male Wizian wouldn't hesitate to *boink your wife in a Minnesota minute*, given the opportunity. Anthropologists have noted with studied interest that a few of those sexy rascals even have *vestigial tails*. And finally, while I hesitate to have to be the one to tell you this, on the night of April 1, 2010, I actually *saw* your *wife* going into the E-Z Rest Motel on Telegraph Road in Southfield, Michigan, with a particularly *big, greasy* one. . . .

Okay, admit it—that sneaky old Telford fellow had you going for just a brief, teeny-weeny minute, there, didn't he? Actually, "Wizians" are an invention of the National Science Foundation, which did a study testing Americans' *prejudice level*. These seldom-seen, rascally dogs definitely came out on the short end. On a scaled rating, most respondents, regardless of race or ethnicity, declared those feisty *Wizian* folk—who happen not to even *exist*—to be "least desirable" in almost every category!

There's a visceral lesson to be learned here—and much of the world still hasn't learned it. In one of his best-selling-self-help books, the great Wayne Dyer, who wrote the *Introduction* to this entrancing tome, *uncommonly* reversed the words in a common phrase, thus: "You'll *see* it when you *believe* it." Sadly, some people are ready to *believe* it when "it" doesn't even exist.

(Now, on the other hand, if I had described the sexy _female_ Wizians . . .! Also, if Heather Locklear can say that a good man is one who "lies down, shuts up, and stays *hard*," shouldn't *this* poor, long-suffering <u>Old Man</u> be similarly permitted to *envision*. . . . Oh, _never_ mind.)

WONDER (*noun*) — The <u>seed</u> of science.

See **SCIENCE**

WOODY — Ebonic slang for penile *tumescence*. (Repubs, xyW.)

See **ERECTION**

WORMS AND MAGGOTS — *See* **CEMETERY; THE CAPITOL BUILDING IN WASHINGTON, D.C.; LOBBYIST; PARASITES**

WOUNDS — Something Aged Sages convert to wisdom.

"Turn your *wounds* into *wisdom*." So spake Oprah Winfrey.

"WRATH OF GOD" — A Biblically-prophesized and well-deserved come-uppance that may come tardily, but it *will* come.

As the cleverly reversed saying goes, "Time *wounds* all *heels*."

"WRINKLED WHITE ASS" — An actually as-yet-*unwrinkled* body part of Your Auld Author's that the then-chief instructional officer of the Detroit Public Schools in 2001 told an assembled group of her sycophants that she was going to *fire* from an instructional (post-retirement) executive directorship for whistle-blowing—and she *did*.

A year later, DPS CEO Kenneth Burnley released her and brought me back to head up his Division of Community Affairs, but my angry old ass—still *unwrinkled*—got fired again the year after that when Burnley's young chief of staff wrote a gag memo to my fourteen parent and community liaison officers forbidding them to communicate with community leaders without clearing it with her, and I blew my top. I then went to teach at Detroit Finney High for my old protégé Alvin Ward, becoming the only retired superintendent in America—black or white, urban or suburban—to return again to teach in an inner-city high school (and, as mentioned elsewhere, I was still doing it in my *seventies*). At this writing, Mr. Ward has just been promoted to head up the district's Health, Physical Education & Athletics division, and we all expect great things from him.

WRITERS — Wordsmiths who can sometimes become a tad too enamored of their own verbosity.

Your Auld Author once arrogantly inquired of his sometimes less-than-worshipful young wife, "Do you have any *idea* how few *truly great* writers there are?" She replied insightfully, "Yes—probably *one less than you think*."

See **ARROGANCE** (*noun*); **VANITY**

X

XERXES (pronounced ZERKseez) — An ancient Persian potentate.

Old graybeard monarchs like *Xerxes* have found that if they get to thinking they're some kind of superior personage, all they need do is try to *command a cat*—or even someone else's *dog*—to get a quick lesson in humility. (Significantly, Hitler hated cats, as did Napoleon.)

And the great autocrat Xerxes himself discovered the utter impossibility of getting lions, cheetahs, jaguars, ocelots, or any other kind of feline, large or small, male or female—to pull his chariot. Dogs, yes; oxen, yes; camels, sometimes; elephants, if he wanted to use them (and *feed* them); horses, indeed yes—but *cats*, decidedly and emphatically no, *non, nyet*! Cats hadn't the slightest interest in pulling the great sovereign's chariot. This is why in Alaska, they use *dogs* to pull sleds. (Also, dogs are generally larger than cats and in this circumstance at least, seemingly far less intelligent.)

See **HUMILITY**

"xyW" — "Check your *Webster's*" (the *longer Dictionary*!).

"xyz" — "Check your *zipper*."

(The "x" represents "check," the "y" stands for "your," and the "z" is short for "zipper")

Forgetfully befuddled old fellows—and careless *young* ones—get that coded admonishment whispered to them a *lot*. (Right, Gina?) Or, as Ron Hunter, one of my old athletes, whispered to me in the cafeteria at Southeastern High School in 1962, pointing discreetly to my carelessly unzipped zipper, "Coach, you're going to *lose* something."

See **ZIPPER**

Y

"YES-MAN" — *See* **JACKAL; LAPDOG**

YOU — The young (or old) mischief-maker that your shadow doggedly *dogs* every day.

He—or she—is the biggest agitator *you* or *any* mortal man or woman have/has ever had to deal with. "See my shadow cross the wall, climb the stairs, and walk the hall. Everywhere he follows me, and he keeps me company. . . ." You may, if you like, write to Your Auld Author and tell him more about the "*I*" and the "*me*" that is <u>*you*</u>.

And always remember:

> *You* are the power in everyone;
> *You* are the dance of the moon and sun;
> *You* are the force that never died—
> <u>*You*</u> are the turning of the tide!

(In 2008, Your Auld Author made his students at Detroit Finney High memorize and constantly recite in unison this slightly altered David Icke poem that appears in his book *And the Truth Shall Set You Free*, except that I changed the pronoun from "you" to "I.")

See **I; ME; A <u>RIDDLE</u> TO PONDER**

"YOU'LL *SEE* IT WHEN YOU *BELIEVE* IT" — *See* **WIZIANS**

Young Men — Those rare, chosen, precocious few who demonstrably possess the potential to become <u>Old Men</u> and Aged Sages.

young men (not capitalized) — Absolute "babes in the wood."

These are gamboling louts whose mothers shouldn't even let most of them out of the *house* into the hard world without an "Instruction Manual" in hand (except for the fact that most of them are too immature to *comprehend* one yet).

While many young men and Young Men alike are often prepared to *die heroically* for a noble cause, many *Young Men* (capitalized) also prefer to *live humanely* for one. Our young men are the first *victims* of war, and they are the first *fruits* of peace. It takes twenty years of peace to produce a young man, but it takes less than two seconds of war to destroy him. Think about it.

See **IMMATURITY; PEACE; WAR; Young Men**

Young Women — Those rare and chosen few who have shown that they possess the potential to become Old Women and Aged Sages.

See **AGED SAGES; Old Women**

young women (not capitalized) — Sleek, lissome lasses who often can make old men (and Old Men) feel mighty happy.

Some of the brighter young ladies among them can also become Old Women if they live long enough, and *wisely* enough.

See **AGED SAGES; Old Women**

YOUR AULD, *AULD* AUTHOR — The poetic old geezer who penned this extraordinary exigesis for you (see cover pic—taken at age seventy-four). A bewhiskered, pony-tailed, (formerly) devastatingly handsome old husband, lover, father, stepfather, father-in-law, grandfather, godfather, brother-in-law, cousin, proud son of a Scotland-born coal miner/prize-fighter/defender-of-the-underdog father who sired a defender-of-the-underdog son in his spittin' image; a faithful friend and implacable foe; an oxymoronically optimistic pessimist; a schizoid, cigar-puffing artist; an occasional violinist; a high school and college track coach and athlete; conqueror of Olympic champions; an intractable braggart; and now, incredibly (at least, *incredibly* to him)—a *Semi*-Settled Septuagenarian

Sage Supreme! (See www.AlifeontheRUN.com and scroll to the Press Room section and read some of the reviews—particularly in the *Detroit Free Press*, the *Michigan Chronicle,* and *Dome Magazine*.)

YOUR AULD AUTHOR'S GRANDMA'S COOKIE RECIPE — Cream together one cup of lard and one cup of butter. Add two cups of sugar, two eggs, three tablespoons of milk, one-quarter teaspoon of salt, and one *scant* teaspoon of baking soda. Beat into hardening dough with an eggbeater. Roll the dough into "sausages." Put them in the ice box and slice them thin when hard. Beat an egg and brush it on each cookie. _Delectably_ delicious!

YOUR DESTINY — Something that is determined by _choice_, not *chance*.

YOUR WIFE'S BIRTHDAY — A *dark* day(?)

"*Dark* be this day that demandeth a *present*. *Dark* indeed it do *be!*" We're paraphrasing Ovid here, but his Latin was doubtless more contemporary (for his time).

And darker *yet* will this day be, should *you*, Sir Hapless Husband, haplessly happen to *forget* this day—and forget to pre-_zent_ the *present*!

Z

ZACK ROBINSON — Jackie's older brother.

Precious few folks know or remember that Zack finished second to the great Jesse Owens in the 1936 Olympic 200-meter dash.

See **JACKIE ROBINSON**

ZIPPER — Like a young (or old) man's lip, his zipper is something that he sometimes neglects to *zip* when he should zip it.

When one *particular* absent-minded old Septuagenarian Son of a Celt carelessly leaves his house with his zipper unzipped, his young honey hisseth at him urgently, "Xyz, you semi-senile, old peckerwood—and *keep* it zipped!" (Actually, she [usually] doesn't really say it that way.)

"Xyz" be street code for "Dude, check yo'self down dere!" Your Auld Author forgets what "peckerwood" means, but in 1940s African-American street vernacular down home in Zone 8 on Sixteenth Street and McGraw in Detroit, it used to mean something *really bad*—as in *nasty*—a *fightin'* word.

Whether you're young, old, or *Old* with a capital "O," when you're out and about *literally* and *figuratively* in life's fortuitous but unforgiving streets, it's often good to keep your lip *buttoned*, even better to keep your eyes *open*, and always *best* to keep your zipper *zipped*.

See **FLY** (*noun*); **"xyz"**

ZOOS — Places where no *animals* (but a whole *lot* of *people*) belong. When leaving a zoo, it's a neat idea to start running toward the exit yelling "Run for your lives—they're *loose*!!" (Because we *are*.)

"ZZZ ... ZZZ ... ZZZ ..." — A depiction of the *snoring sound* many blissfully unaware Americans make while they *cop some Z's* as our democracy shivers and shakes around us.

Many Americans are *asleep at the wheel* as we hear more news from the Feds regarding what your Cautionary Auld Author warningly calls an "Economic '*Wake Up*!' Package." (Actually, the Feds less urgently but also less *accurately* and more *euphemistically* refer to it as an "Economic '*Stimulus*' Package.") Your Alert Auld Author first learned via a fascinating message circulated to me on the ubiquitous Internet that later this year (2010) we Americans are to receive another *economic* "*stimulus*" *payment*. Indeed, this would appear economically to be an exciting "*stimulating*" prospect which might best be explained by a sample Question/Answer format the government could helpfully sponsor, and thus further enlighten us regarding it, *to wit*:

Taxpayers (*Tea-Partyers*?): What exactly *is* an "*economic 'stimulus' payment*"?
The Feds: It is *money* that we will send to you.
TPs: Where will you get this money?
Feds: From *you*.
TPs: You mean you're giving me back *my own money*?
Feds: Only a *teeny-tiny* portion of it—and *taxes* are *due* from you on that *gift* from us.
TPs: Then what is the *purpose* of this so-called "gift" to us?
Feds: The plan is for you to buy a new 3-D high-definition TV set, thus *stimulating* the economy.
TPs: But isn't that stimulating the economy of *China*?
Feds: *Don't ask us any more questions.*

Oh, *my*! Now, anyone who has perused (*endured*?) the entire 300-plus pages of this *taxing* tome can have little doubt that Your Auld, faithfully *taxpaying* Author will forever be a *dyed-in-the-donkey-mane Democrat*. Nonetheless, given the "answers" in the preceding suppositional "Q's and A's," *this* time the *taxpayer* part of me actually tends to lean toward (yet still not *vote* with) a significant segment of the Tea-partyers!

Here, therefore, follows some helpful advice for boosting our country's economy by spending your pie-in-the-sky "*stimulus*" check more wisely than on a 3-D high-definition TV set:

First, you need to be aware that if you spend your "*stimulus*" money at specific conglomerate convenience stores, e.g., *Walmart*, it will go to nations on the other side of the Pacific Ocean. If you spend the money on a computer, it will go to the Hindustanis. If you spend it paying your credit cards off, it will go to managerial bonuses, and they will hide it in offshore accounts. If you spend it on gas and oil, the money will go to the Arab nations. If you buy fruit and vegetables, much of the money it will go to countries south of the border.

Instead, as this referenced Internet message actually suggested, you should keep your "*stimulus*" money entirely in America by spending it at *yard sales* or going to *ball games* or giving it to *hookers* or spending it on *booze* or *tattoos*. (These are some of the few businesses still operating with full success in the U.S. at this writing.)

Conclusion: You should spend your day and your "*stimulus*" dollars at a ball game with a tattooed hooker that you met at a yard sale, booze it up in a bar during the evening, and then at night, _sleep_ with her (ZZZ . . . ZZZ . . . ZZZ . . .).

Or *else*, my esteemed fellow Americans, _face it_: Rather than ZZZ . . . ZZZ . . . ZZZ away our democratic heritage on hookers, bars, booze, tattoos, 3-D high-definition TV sets, etc., it is time now for you to _wake up_ and give *harkening _heed_* to (*most* of) this "ZZZ" Item.

Also, you of *necessity* need to heed (almost) *all* of the many other edifying Items preceding this one in the illuminatingly ingenious *exegesis* (Repubs, xyW) that your still *devotedly Democratic* Auld Author has ingenuously entitled (*drum roll*, please). . . .

What OLD MEN Know!!!

THE LIVING END

Acknowledgments

For all that _this_ OLD MAN Knows and has benefited from in my three-quarters-of-a-century sojourn on this mystical blue/brown sphere that lends life to all of us earthly beings, there are _many_ such earthly beings I must thank, to wit:

Karen Simmons of Harmonie Park Press did a magnificent job of editing, itemizing, and proofreading these pyrogenic pages, with the able back-up of Darlene Brown, Darlene Jankowski, and Colleen McRorie. Vice president David Gorzelski gave this publication, along with my 2010 autobiography, _A Life on the RUN—Seeking and Safeguarding Social Justice_, the rare and privileged chance to amuse, electrify, educate, and edify the world, as we forthrightly trust that it ultimately will.

My gorgeous and tempestuous young Irish/African-American wife Gina was (usually) wonderfully forgiving of the _psychical_ time I spent away from her (and yet physically _with_ her) while I composed the last part of this exegesis in our spacious family room overlooking a little lake at our retreat in Shelby Township, Michigan. It was from there and from my primary residence in the River House in my troubled hometown Detroit that my antediluvian mind climbed far into the timeless cosmos and then back to _terra firma_ in wild Motown and also imagined myself in our nation's capitol ("Send _out_ the clowns!")—as my arthritic Old fingers roamed restlessly across my laptop keyboard to produce this, my breathlessly anticipated _Magnum Opus_, which you seekers and keepers of the light have sampled and pored over now to become duly edified (or horrified).

I'd also be sorely remiss if I didn't tip my hat to my hard-working son Steven Telford, my dauntless daughter Katherine, my ex-Marine son-in-law Rich Garrett, my beautiful grandchildren RJ and Tori, my stepson Michael, and my intrepid godson Rick Boudro and goddaughter Joy Hatcher Chambers—the offspring of my late, lightning-fast track teammate and lifelong friend Cliff Hatcher. My contemporary cousins Dick Boudro (a multi-decorated Vietnam veteran) and his late brother Carl (father of Rick) provided me with loyal longtime friendship few men are fortunate enough ever to experience.

I'd be remiss, too, if I didn't grudgingly acknowledge—in another and darker vein—the hundreds of reactionary racists and other assorted bigots and bullies whom I battled in various jobs and venues. The richly ironic fact remains that *all* of them helped to ignite not only the reformative and educative authoring of some of the fieriest chapters of my memoir *A Life on the RUN*, but *also* lent inspiration to the palpitating pages the reader now holds.

A few still-practicing politicians and school executives who were offered the opportunity to write testimonials for this publication (and a year earlier for my memoirs) took a rain check *twice*, demurring that parts of both books—and *I* personally—remain "too *controversial*" for them to comment on comfortably for the record. Such reticence renders me all the more grateful to those many forthright and courageous souls who *did* go on record with their lavish testaments at the beginning of both books. That *reticence* also serves as mute testimony supporting one of the many reasons why the books so badly needed to be written and so badly need to be read—and read *widely*.

In a happier vein, I wish to cite some individuals who merit my *particular* acknowledgement. The wise (if not always heeded) counsel of my late, sainted mother Helen Telford (1907–98) sustains me yet today. The ancient familial code of my late Scottish grandfather Frank Telford—that weathered old Sean Connery lookalike—has also charted my journey. His late, lovely school teacher daughter Letty Telford and his late film and TV producer/director son Frank Telford the younger—whom my father put through college with his boxing earnings—jump-started my incipient social views in many a spirited conversation in the long-gone family house on Twelfth Street at McGraw in Detroit. Now years later, the younger Frank's sixty-six-year-old son Jeff Telford and I maintain that old Celtic Telford tradition of spirited social discourse over cigars and Drambuie (enhanced by half, of course, with good Scotch).

My Detroit Public School teachers and my Wayne State University professors, my valiant and long-suffering colleagues in school districts and social agencies, my countless high-school and university students old and new, many other faithful old and new friends, including Jerry Catalina, Al and Gloria Tellis, Reggie and Cynthia Bradford, Alvin Ward, Hiram and Judy Badia, Pete and Kelly Conway, Pete and Lois Petross,

Dr. John and Dolores Schultz, Janina Jacobs, Dr. Bill Keane, R. E. Wollack, Joe Hudson, and Shawon Respress, my intellectual avatar Geraldine Barclay, and my first wife Lynn—whose faithful companionship was mostly undeserved—all helped to solidify the social and political philosophies set forth in this book.

Dr. Wayne W. Dyer, the world-renowned author who has lent his illustrious name to the authorship of the Introduction to this work, has been first a protégé, then a trusted friend, and finally a guide and inspiration in my life. The late Taras Hubicki—a Ukrainian immigrant who was a violist in the Detroit Symphony Orchestra—gave me free violin lessons and enlisted me in his citywide youth orchestra (The Detroit Fiddlers' Band) when I was eleven and had proudly mastered the *third position*. He also schooled me gratis in the sometimes maddeningly difficult musical theory that subtly facilitated my later logical thought-processing.

My high school athletic coaches—Jack Rice and Ralph Green, and my boxing trainer, Tom Briscoe—steered me in a righteous direction at two pivotal points in my teen years when I had veered briefly but dangerously into a wrongful path.

Finally, I would like to thank my late, great Wayne State University track coach David L. Holmes (1888–1960) for teaching me to hate mediocrity and love the underdog. He also taught me *tenacity* and *audacity*—and thus how to find a way to win against all comers, whether these antagonists were athletic, academic, political, and personal.

Above all, Old Coach Holmes taught me to have an inquiring mind and express it freely in the face of frequently fearsome opposition—and to allow nothing and no one to keep me from my righteous crusades.

That was perhaps the lesson I learned the best.

JOHN TELFORD
Doctor of Education

July 4, 2010

Index of Names

About the Author

Dr. John Telford has been called a human-rights legend and a lightning rod for controversy. A first-generation Scottish-American, he retired in 1991 as the Deputy Superintendent of Schools in ninety-seven percent white Rochester, Michigan, where skinheads shot bullets into his home at midnight for hiring black administrators. He was fired from two Detroit Public School executive directorships for blowing the whistle on corrupt and inept top officials, and he was fired from a superintendency in another majority-white Detroit suburb for recruiting and enrolling hundreds of black students. He is also an award-winning poet.

Undefeated at 400 meters in Europe as an NCAA All-American quarter-miler and U.S. Team member, Dr. Telford coached champion high school and college runners and wrote a book on the quarter-mile—*The Longest Dash*. It was published by *Track & Field News* Press in 1965 and 1971. In 1978, he was inducted into the Wayne State University Athletic Hall of Fame. He has written more than a thousand newspaper columns and directed or served on boards of several human-rights agencies. In the early 1970s, he directed the 3,400-student Division of Basic Education at Macomb Community College, where he was suspended for insubordination when he brought in the Black Panthers to speak to the students. More recently, he taught at Wayne State and Oakland universities.

Wayne State University named Dr. Telford its Distinguished Alumnus of the Year for civil-rights activism in 2001, when he addressed thousands of graduates in Detroit's huge Cobo Hall and urged them to become *educators*. In 2003, the Detroit Finney High School track was named the John Telford Track. In 2010, the 267-member Detroit Track Old-Timers organization gave him its Lifetime Achievement Award. Throughout the past five decades, his university students and his Detroit high school students have consistently pronounced him a great teacher. Of all his many accolades, those from his students and colleagues are the ones that mean the most to the seventy-five-year-old educator.

To learn more about Dr. John Telford and his remarkable memoir, *A Life on the RUN—Seeking and Safeguarding Social Justice*, google his website, www.AlifeontheRUN.com—and scroll to the Press Room section to read the reviews. You can get that book at your local Barnes & Noble store or directly from our website, www.harmonieparkpress.com.

QUICK ORDER FORM

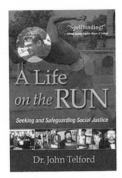

A Life *on the* RUN:
Seeking and Safeguarding Social Justice
by Dr. John Telford

Dr. Telford pulls no punches telling his often scandalous, sometimes humorous, yet poignant and inspiring life story—which former Detroit Mayor Dennis Archer calls *"Spellbinding!"*, Michigan state Senator Hansen Clarke calls *"Unadelterated dynamite!"*, and a former ACLU national legal director calls *"A triumphant tale of teaching fighting, racing, rebellion, and raw courage."* In this blockbuster autobiography, an electrifying educator, athlete, lover, and poet bares his soul. Once you start reading it, you won't be able to stop!

ISBN: 0-89990-149-2 / Hardcover / 435 pages / 2010
$24.99 USA / $31.99 Canada
No. of Copies _____

What OLD MEN Know:
A *Definitive Dictionary and Almanac of Advice*
by Dr. John Telford

An innovatively *different* kind of reference book. Written by a seventy-five-year-old activist educator and former world-class athlete whom his professorial colleagues call a "genius" and his activist compadres call a "legend," its 300-plus breathtaking pages of savagely hilarious political satire are seasoned and tempered with timeless philosophy.

ISBN: 0-89990-154-9 / Softcover / 317 pages / 2011
$16.95 USA / $23.95 Canada
No. of Copies _____

Name _____

Address _____

City / State / Zip _____

Daytime Phone _____

Please add 6% sales tax for books shipped to a Michigan address

Make checks payable to:
Harmonie Park Press
Liberty Professional Center
35675 Mound Road
Sterling Heights, MI 48310

To order online:
www.harmonieparkpress.com